NOBODY SEES THIS CREATION

THE ORIGIN OF THE DEVIL AND HIS REPLACEMENTS

PAUL RENFROE

PARADIGM LIGHTHOUSE
Destin, Florida, United States of America

© 2023 Paul Renfroe

Published by Paradigm Lighthouse, PO Box 48, Freeport FL 32439 www.ParadigmLighthouse.com.

Nobody Sees This Creation: The Origin of the Devil and His Replacements
by Paul Renfroe

ISBN 979-8-9853944-4-3 paperback; 979-8-9853944-5-0 hardcover

LCCN 2023905412

BISAC: REL099000, RELIGION / Christian Living / Spiritual Warfare

REL067010, RELIGION / Christian Theology / Angelology & Demonology

REL006140, RELIGION / Biblical Studies / Prophecy

Cover Design by Hannah Linder

Editing by B. Kay Coulter

Interior Design by Faithe Thomas, Master Design Marketing, LLC

Publication Consulting by Susan Neal

Except where indicated, Scripture quotations are from the New King James Version®. Copyright © 1982 by Thomas Nelson. Used by permission. All rights reserved.

Greek words and phrases are from the Aland/Black et al 3rd edition of the Greek New Testament, published in USA by American Bible Society, New York NY, 1975.

Printed in the United States of America
First Edition

I am so happy that I somehow connected with you and your books. I feel how I imagine Helen Keller may have felt when she finally understood what Annie Sullivan was trying to communicate to her.

I have read the Bible using the one-year method, and different commentaries on passages where I was confused, but I still missed so much! I was a complacent and lazy reader but your books presented a challenge to me and I am so grateful to you!

Lisa Fulkerson, educator, Columbia Station, OH

A stunning exposè on the devil's origin, travels, tricks, and trades. Paul Renfroe's work in Book 3 delivers searing insights and empowering knowledge for all spiritual warfare warriors "lest satan takes advantage of us" (2 Corinthians 2:11). You may never view IOUs or the story of creation the same again!

Chris Manion, multi-award-winning author *of God's Patient Pursuit of My Soul, The Light We Cannot See*, Destin, FL

I am very impressed with the amount of research and analysis that has gone into this book. Paul supports every proposed scenario with scripture. He teaches the importance of words God used in giving us His story of creation. The Bible will have new meaning for me my next time through it. And I can't wait to read Book Four in the *Unseen* Series!

Jerry Mullis, retired manufacturer and plant manager, church leader, Freeport, FL

I thank you for including me as a test reader for your book and cannot put into words the impact it has had for me. There is so much to take in and process as my thinking is adapting to the truths you articulate so beautifully. The biggest impact on my walk as a believer has been your book's revelation of the commitment and integrity that God has in all His communication. As someone with a history of trust issues, this was huge for me.

After every chapter I feel well fed. I can take it in and walk it out. And I look forward so much to the next chapter. I am eager for the entire series to be published, to see what other truths you have mined out and prepared for us. The spiritual warfare over this project has been fierce, I am sure, because it will do massive damage to the demonic realm. You and your wife will continually be in my prayers. Thank you for offering me the honor and privilege of a test reader in your amazing series. Thank you!

Janice Fortune, nurse (retired), Vale, SD

This book takes you in depth into a subject that has been a mystery to many for centuries: the origin and fate of kingdom of darkness. You will learn answers to questions that you have always wondered, but have never pieced together. It is so interesting to learn how God's creation process is interwoven into the downfall of satan and his followers (the fallen angels). This book will give you more knowledge about the nature of the kingdom of darkness so that you may be equipped to stand firm against them. Great job on the book!

Rebecca Porter, educator and military wife, El Paso, TX

I asked God many times to give me understanding of Revelation (and similar books). Not receiving His interpretation, I quit reading Revelation and other books I did not understand. This book is an answer to my prayers. Paul takes us through Scripture in a way that allows Scripture to explain itself.

Lundy Carpenter, lawyer and nurse, Germantown, TN

Paul Renfroe is an author who combines the health and wisdom of solid evangelical Bible understanding with the gifts of prophecy given by our Good Father through His Spirit. I love how he bridges gaps to a greater life in Jesus.

Paul Hughes, founder of Forerunner Ministries, a proven global influencer and former InterVarsity staff, Birmingham, AL

OTHER BOOKS BY THE AUTHOR:

Christian, What Are You? Removing the Blindfolds
Inadequacy
The Pains of the Christian: Desire, Glory, Joy
available through ParadigmLighthouse.com

CONTENTS

FOREWORD

When I was a young believer, the supernatural realm fascinated me. Now, after forty-five years of walking with Christ, I have discovered much about it.

Yet I have never read a more thorough description of its origins than Paul Renfroe's *Nobody Sees This Creation: The Origin of the Devil and His Replacements*.

Before I was a believer, a dark spirit appeared in bodily form late one night, in my bedroom. I wasn't merely afraid. The experience put intimidated fear in me for many years.

Therefore, I didn't need convincing. I knew from direct experience there was an unseen realm all around me. Of course I knew the devil was bad and angels were good. But I needed to be educated about them, because I had very little theology or Bible understanding. Where did these beings came from? How did they operate? The limits on their powers weren't clear to me, and I was afraid.

As a teenager, my newfound faith in my Savior Jesus Christ made me a new creation, with lots to explore and learn. I have been a student of the Bible and the Spirit ever since. During that process, from Scripture, God revealed to me the solution for fear: that He lived inside of me, and that He sent angels from His angelic host to protect me. Now when I perceive those unseen beings, just out of my natural view but very real, fear doesn't dominate me.

At first, I didn't realize the importance of understanding the unseen realm, or how greatly it matters to our entire Christian faith. The impact of the world we cannot see—both on our spirit-led life and on the visible world—is profound. It is imperative that every student of the Word be equipped for our constant interaction with the unseen beings. Only with understanding can we fulfill what God created us to be. When we understand our unseen enemies, we can activate the authority of Christ within us.

This book gives you a clear understanding of God's divine plan for His enemies. After throwing satan and his cohorts down to the earth, God chose this very planet to birth the human race. In each day of His creation process, God systematically destroys the dominion that satan had claimed over earth. God brings forth a thriving planet and creates a new race to dominate it: beings created in His image.

Decades of walking with Christ, ministering to people, and learning have given me a solid understanding of that cosmic battle. After you read this book you too will understand—without fear. God is building blocks of truth into the foundation of your faith, which cannot be shaken.

Nobody Sees This Creation brings you fascinating new perspective for the entire Word of God. His strategic plan, from eternity past to eternity future, is summarized in these pages. The devil's responses are exposed, such as using science and evolutionary theory to discredit the biblical account of creation. Such understanding will transform your life and those you influence.

The *Unseen* Series, and this installment, *Nobody Sees This Creation: The Origin of the Devil and His Replacements*, won't simply inform your walk with Christ. These truths will also empower you to fulfill God's dominion mandate in your life.

Dr. Jane Hamon
Apostle: Vision Church @ Christian International
Author: *Dreams and Visions, The Deborah Company, The Cyrus Decree, Discernment, Declarations for Breakthrough*

PREFACE

Many fields and authors attempt to explain the influences on people: philosophy, comparative religion, astrophysics, economics, history, ancient writings, and Christian literature. The explanatory power of the nine-book *Unseen* series unveils the unseen influencers and spirit entities, both today and throughout history.

The series purpose is to equip you, the reader, for righteous and effective function among unseen spirits. At the end of this book, *About the Unseen Series* summarizes the initiating protocol for that.

The test readers have asked me about my audience. It's you: curious, growing, unsatisfied, inquisitive, or charged to help such people. Like you, many now sense the unseen realm. The nine-book *Unseen* Series explores the Bible in depth to offer explanations for what you perceive. Your own process of testing will reveal if these explanations are satisfying to you.

You are holding Book Three of the series: *Nobody Sees This Creation: The Origin of the Devil and His Replacements.*

Almost all conversation about origins involves the Bible's six-day account in Genesis 1. But this Book Three is a deep dive into different Scriptures which describe additional creating actions by God. Building on your past understanding, this book reveals the biblical origins of satan. We discover that dominance over Earth defines the war between God's unseen kingdom and the unseen kingdom of darkness. After completing this book, you'll be more capable to identify the influences of the kingdom of darkness.

God has culled His Church from humankind for a purpose: to replace the devil and his partners as the rulers of Earth. Yes, you and I are the replacements that God put here to dislocate satan and the kingdom of darkness. But how?

Book One, *Nobody Sees This You*, equips you to live as a spirit in the unseen realm. Its subtitle is *How to Live as a Spirit in the Unseen Realm.*

We call it unseen because we can't visit it, deduce it, figure it out, or experiment scientifically on it. Our only source of information about the unseen is someone in it—a spirit.

Spirits have always communicated with people; each must be tested. Because no opportunity for scientific study is available, not all spirits can be trusted. Each book of the *Unseen* series includes additional wisdom for that testing.

> Beloved, do not believe every spirit, but test the spirits, whether they are of God; because many false prophets have gone out into the world. By this you know the Spirit of God: Every spirit that confesses that Jesus Christ has come in the flesh is of God, and every spirit that does not confess that Jesus Christ has come in the flesh is not of God. (1 John 4:1–3)

Only One is trustworthy. He created the unseen world, followed by the visible world. Jesus as God in flesh revealed it. First, His power validated His revelation; next, His predicted resurrection from death made His qualifications indisputable. People filled with His Holy Spirit have supplied a global validation ever since.

Book Two is titled *Nobody Sees This Unseen Realm: How to Unlock Bible Mysteries*. There, I equip you to find the unifying explanation of reality in the Bible. That reality is the unseen one, which God hid for us in His Word.

Our God has revealed everything He wants us to know, but some is hidden in the Bible. Maturity is required to know the unseen; otherwise, we twist His revelation into our immature understanding. God wants us to live in both His seen and unseen realms as His partners.

CHRISTIAN OR NOT, OR ON THE WAY

You may not think of yourself as a Christian; that isn't necessary to get some benefit from this book. On the other hand, you may be a lifelong Christian. In between are many stages of spiritual hunger and maturity.

I write to help you mature as a living human spirit, as Jesus intended. People can easily settle for what we already have, afraid to risk it by aiming higher. We all know someone who isn't receptive when offered help to mature. Thinking all is well, resisting change, many people simply don't desire to mature. This is true of Christians as well as the general population.

The Bible consists of words on a page; so does this book. You can read either one without agreeing or accepting what you read. Many people know the Bible but content themselves with the satisfaction they have; you have that freedom with this Book Three of the *Unseen* Series as well.

To know God is a life of trading the lesser for the greater. We die to what partially satisfies, in order to live with the One who fully satisfies. I want everyone to be a Christian for their own benefit, but few people choose to follow Jesus Christ. Change and maturity is a necessary element of doing so. When we resist that, we can know *about* God, without *knowing* God as our Father, Judge, and Friend.

But in what follows, I presume that you are different. Far from settling or resting on your laurels, you desire instead to mature spiritually. Otherwise, why would you buy this book? For brief guidance on maturing as a living human spirit, see *About the Unseen* Series in the appendix.

ABOUT CAPITALIZATION

To disarm religious awkwardness, and to identify personal participants in the unseen world, each book in the *Unseen* series follows these guidelines.

We often refer to God or a person of the Trinity, and capitalize the first letter of those pronouns. Current style guidelines regard this as archaic; I regard it as respectful. It also helps us keep the characters straight as we talk about the many spirits in the unseen world.

Because capitalization suggests honor, I've chosen not to use an uppercase first letter for the devil and the kingdom of darkness, even though it may irritate your traditional expectations. The word *satan* means accuser in the Bible; that is a functional description and therefore not capitalized. Created as a cherub, his name appears to be Lucifer (Isaiah 14). As a name, it has a first letter cap as his given name prior to falling.

You'll learn that the Bible reveals active but unseeable personal entities—but the revelation of them is shaded, not direct. When I refer to them, it is with an uppercase first letter. Examples are Creation, Sin, and Earth. When lowercase first letter, those words indicate the acts of creating and sinning, or refer to land, dirt, or acreage.

TESTING

I cite the Scriptures discussed right in these pages, using the New King James translation of 1982. My accountability is to write with the greatest care for truthful, effective communication.

You, reader, are accountable for testing it, holding onto what is true, and forgiving me for the balance. With a digital or printed Bible of your own, you can test these study results and revelations for yourself.

Private reading and testing should precede defaulting to the explanations of others. Listen to God and ask Him about any passage or truth that intrigues you, or doesn't sit well with you. Listen to your own common sense about people and situations first. Form your own opinion first.

After that, ask others' opinions: Bible students, commentators, church leaders, or pastors. They may be very sincere Christians with powerful ministry, but they can still be wrong—just like you or me. The Church remains inexperienced in matters of the unseen after many centuries.

To dig deep is its own reward; you can find friendship with God. There are many books offering spiritual benefit; the Bible is the only book to deliver the ultimate prize.

PRODUCTION NOTES

In the following pages, some phrases and words of the New Testament appear in the Greek alphabet—the language and alphabet of the New Testament authors. The purpose is to enable you to test my interpretation. If these Greek words and phrases do not interest you, proceed without hesitation; those words will also be transliterated into the English alphabet.

Volunteer test readers help sharpen each book of the *Unseen* Series. They represent many age groups and walks of life. Unknown to you, each reviewed this Book Three in manuscript form. Such "beta" readers earned all our gratitude; they catch many potential misunderstandings and add much clarity to my writing. If you would like to volunteer as a beta reader for future installments of the *Unseen* Series, please join the Paradigm Lighthouse forum (described below).

HELP OTHERS

Churches often have study groups for books like this one that help us know and apply the Bible. Please help me publicize this *Unseen* Series for the benefit of many; the appendix of each book includes Reader Engagement Resources. These include discussion questions and reflection starters.

I have a private forum for the *Unseen* Series, so we can discuss and test our Bible discoveries about life as spirits. Each reader can request log-in credentials at ParadigmLighthouse.com.

INTRODUCTION

A foundational question for you, reader, is whether you can receive revelation from the Bible that is new—or even upsetting—to you. Many disdain the Bible today as a book of antiquity at best, and a tool of oppression at worst. You may be on that scale; you are welcome without judgment. On the other hand, you may be an avid Christian, church member, or Bible reader. You also are welcome.

All pre-conceived notions must yield to God and His Word. The discoveries in the following pages challenged me and manhandled my conclusions. After forty-eight years of Bible study, I thought I knew about Creation. New revelation humbled me—the same Bible discoveries awaiting you in these pages.

> Nor do they put new wine into old wineskins, or else the wineskins break, the wine is spilled, and the wineskins are ruined. But they put new wine into new wineskins, and both are preserved. (Matthew 9:17)

THE BIBLE: LOVE OR HATE, LIFE OR DEATH

> "Safe?" said Mr. Beaver.... "Who said anything about safe? 'Course he isn't safe. But he's good. He's the King, I tell you." (*The Lion, The Witch and The Wardrobe*, C. S. Lewis, New York: HarperCollins, 1950; page 86)

The Bible is not an ordinary book. Our safety depends upon our response to Him in this Book of His making.

Jesus' most hostile adversaries were not the militaristic, violent Roman occupiers, but the most Bible-loving people of His place and time: His fellow Jews. The Jewish leadership were Bible pros. Jesus magnetized these antagonists, who couldn't resist sparring with Him. Their hopes were

Bible-based, the many prophecies in our Old Testament. Jesus fulfilled their hopes better than they could imagine. In fact, He fulfilled them better than they could *accept*, and they rigidly rejected Him for it.

In Jerusalem, just three days before they crucified Him, Jesus gave them one last warning in Matthew 23. He pronounced eight woes upon these leaders for abusing the Bible. Finally, in front of the Roman governor who wanted to release Jesus, these Bible-lovers had one last opportunity to retract their hostility. Instead, they yelled, *"His blood be on us and upon our children"* (Matthew 27:25).

Receptivity to new understanding of Scripture is critical to your spiritual health. Failure is fatal. All books of the *Unseen* Series place strong emphasis upon meekness. Love for the God who gave us His Word always creates a thirst for Him in it. The Bible becomes dangerous when we settle for what we already find in it; it confirms our choice. We become those who say, "Don't confuse me with the facts."

The unseen world engages living human spirits, and we are thoroughly inadequate for that. That's one reason so many people blindly tolerate their oppression by God's enemies; we are easy for unseen enemies to trick and deceive. A proper estimation of our poverty of spirit is protective. Only One can engage these unseen powers who hate us humans: the Holy Spirit. That's one reason He lives in us when we follow Jesus wholeheartedly.

To understand God's revelation, we have to make some inferences, to read between the lines, so to speak. Remember: *"it is the glory of God to conceal a matter, and the glory of kings to search it out"* (Proverbs 25:2). In the Bible, God has laid a trail of breadcrumbs for all of us. Can we follow it? Or do we refuse? Do we love what we think the Bible says, or do we love the God who reveals Himself in it? Follow the trail with me. Fear not: it leads to a sumptuous feast, the best I have ever enjoyed.

> Ho! Everyone who thirsts,
> Come to the waters;
> And you who have no money,
> Come, buy and eat.
> Yes, come, buy wine and milk
> Without money and without price.
> Why do you spend money for what is not bread,
> And your wages for what does not satisfy?
> Listen carefully to Me, and eat what is good,
> And let your soul delight itself in abundance.

Incline your ear, and come to Me.
Hear, and your soul shall live. (Isaiah 55:1–3)

THE BIRTH OF THE UNSEEN SERIES

For nearly five decades, I both sought and imparted Inductive Bible Study training. With my wife Diane, I have trained hundreds to read the Bible. These decades have proven to me: God's Word always yields fresh revelation from familiar passages—if we will but listen.

This book is your invitation to revisit what God has revealed. Thus, we named our ministry Paradigm Lighthouse. A paradigm is a new way of seeing things, a new grid for interpreting God's revelations. When we have that, we become a lighthouse, guiding others safely to understand and prosper in the war of two unseen kingdoms.

In July 2017, I finished a study of Esther with a church small group in my home. As usual, I asked the Holy Spirit what to study next. Imagine my surprise when He assigned the middle chapters of Ezekiel to me. Who starts in the middle? When I got there, the topic was judgment on ancient nations, most of which no longer even exist.

I kept asking the Holy Spirit about the many puzzles I found there. One enigma dominated: "how is this relevant?" I could not see any relevance at all. I had read these chapters when I used a one-year reading plan—and once was enough, right? Everything in me wanted to leave Ezekiel's middle chapters. I felt something sweeter or more applicable to us today would be a better use of my time—or at least be less boring. But study them?

Yet I didn't want to abandon the discipline God imposed. Finally, I relaxed and accepted the assignment without complaint. After simple observation, the facts began to intrigue me; curiosities piled up within me.

I served as a leader in evangelical ministries for five decades. My Bible understanding gave me a grid for interpreting life. Although mysteries persisted, that grid's explanations were comfortable.

But suddenly, Ezekiel's middle chapters rendered that template of interpretation outdated. The former answers were inadequate. The Bible manhandled my grid. To continue with my previous understanding would be stubborn sin, requiring me to ignore God's actual word choices in the Bible.

I yielded, read slowly, and tested each conclusion by other Scriptures. Over a process of months, the revealing Spirit shocked me. It felt as if He had flipped a "paradigm light switch" within me. The kingdom of darkness suddenly leapt off the page into my understanding. The structure of the devil's kingdom began unfolding in every Bible cross-reference I reviewed. Passion inflamed me that the Church lost these scriptural truths. They were so relevant, I asked God if I could write and publish them. The *Unseen* series was born when He replied within me, "Please do."

SYNOPSIS OF BOOK THREE

What can you expect to read in coming chapters of this Book Three of the nine-book *Unseen* Series? Throughout the book, we use the Inductive Study principles explained in Book Two—to build your ability to understand the Bible's mysteries.

This installment reintroduces you to the origins of people and fills gaps about the origin of evil spirits. For the creation of people, the primary passage is Genesis 1–3, three chapters. The Bible also has three chapters that reveal the creation of the devil: Ezekiel 28, Isaiah 14, and Revelation 12. In them, God reveals the origin and policies of the kingdom of darkness.

Book Three is organized around three catastrophic changes by God. Part One is *The Calamity of Heaven*, where we study those three origin passages. We will uncover hidden surprises in the creation of people and satan.

Originally the highest created being in the unseen heavenly realms, Lucifer was second only to the Triune God. None but God excelled his nature, his body, his position, or his privilege. We will see why God took those from him, and how he became satan.

With his angelic allies, satan attempted to replace God. We will learn why. The rebellion had many consequences for this once-great archangel. Insatiable craving for power is now satan's nature. Hoarding power, satan prefers as few partners as necessary. We will see how he accumulates power from people.

God punished these power-hungry angels in several ways, which we will discover in the above passages. He withdrew His nourishing favor from them. He instilled fire into their very beings, and then He exiled them to Earth. These would-be usurpers remain angelic, even though cast down to Earth. They continue to exist because God wills it, but exiled from His presence, genuine life eludes them.

Many Scriptures affirm another surprise: the fallen angels of darkness crave moisture. The fire which God placed within them permits no rest without moisture; Jesus affirmed this in Luke 11:24. This single fact explains many Bible passages; Ezekiel 24–32 is one example we'll review in the coming chapters.

Part Two is *The Calamity of Earth*. God created all physical reality in Genesis 1:1, and His work was complete. The rebellion of Lucifer occurred after that. Beginning in Genesis 1:2, the events of six days are revealed. There is a long period of time between the two verses, as we will see clearly in upcoming chapters.

Much debate revolves around the six days as if they tell the creation of everything. Without doubt, the six days dramatically transform all physical reality—but are not Creation itself. That event occurred long before in Genesis 1:1. How God did it is not specified.

After satan and his partners were cast down to Earth for their punishment, they reshaped it to satisfy their need for moisture. The result of that deforming by darkness is described in Genesis 1:2.

The earth was without form, and void; and darkness was on the face of the deep. And the Spirit of God was hovering over the face of the waters.

The Holy Spirit found nothing but water, and why? Because the kingdom of darkness had turned Earth into a great, watery deep. Earth was formless, empty, dark, landless, and completely unresponsive to God's Holy Spirit. But God reversed Earth's condition. Beginning with light in Genesis 1:3, He turned the table on the kingdom of darkness in only six twenty-four-hour days.

In one short week, God disrupted satan's cozy, cooling deep, and reclaimed dominion of Earth. I describe His reclamation project in Part Three, *The Calamity of Darkness*. The sequence concluded with our creation as land creatures, charged to dominate Earth on His behalf.

God's six-day project to reclaim Earth followed its ruination by the devil, between 1:1 and 1:2. In the debates about evolution and creation, a recurrent phrase is "the primordial soup." The phrase manifests the half-truth tactic of darkness. Yes, life came out of the primordial soup, but not us or our ancestors. It was the serpent.

Discussion and reflection questions for the Preface and Introduction can be found in the Reader Engagement Resources.

CHAPTER ONE

OUR ENEMIES INTRODUCED

Apostle Paul described our enemies—plural—in Ephesians 6:12.

> For we do not wrestle against flesh and blood, but against principalities, against powers, against the rulers of the darkness of this age, against spiritual hosts of wickedness in the heavenly places.

The kingdom of darkness originates in the unseen realm, which the Bible often calls *the heavenly places*. In popular understanding, heaven is for good people after they die. In fact, the unseen realm is the heaven Scripture refers to. Time there is not linear, sequential, or directional. In the heavenly realms, spirit rules the physical.

Our opponents there are not human, but unseen spirits organized in hierarchical ranks, with governing powers. Although fallen, they are still angelic in their nature. Paul knew it from wrestling them, as the book of Acts records. Like him, we are enemies to them all—and they to us.

THE RESPECT OF THE ANGELIC

Scripture reveals glimpses of the nature that fallen angels still have. Despite the poor choices of these angelic rebels, they still have the nature of angels that God created them with. Because they remain His creation, we respect their nature. The original position He gave them is worth honor, even though they rejected it. They are morally culpable for their fall, precisely because God created them to choose His service.

God judged Jerusalem with total destruction because of His people's persistent disobedience. Yet God still expected His original choice of Jerusalem to be honored afterward.

The same applies with the rebel angels. His original anointing upon them still justifies our respect, even though they are fallen and evil now. Both Peter and Jude emphasize not speaking disrespectfully about them as we will soon see.

Scripture tells us that angels can behold the face of God. Gabriel said that he stands in the presence of God (Luke 1:19). The angels rejoicing at Jesus' birth (Luke 2:13) could see God's favor on men. To rebel from these privileges, as Lucifer and his angels did, is damnable.

THIS IS FOR US

While we are content with the limits set by Scripture on what we can know, we are not content with the limits placed by tradition on what we can ask about.

A choice to rebel against God is an eternal choice for such exalted beings. The accountability for this rejection of God's preeminence is eternal and final. Their fall is severe and irreversible.

The angels' lofty nature makes it even more so—they should have known better. Nowhere does Scripture indicate that an angelic being can repent.

The Bible doesn't describe the fallen angels plainly; asking about them gives rise to our beginning puzzles. Who are the fallen angels? How about the demons? How many are there? What can they do? How do they interact with people? Yes, we wrestle them, but how does it happen? Can we identify a fallen angel or its activity? A quick Bible review of the holy angels provides a baseline for comparison with the fallen angels.

THE ANGEL OF THE LORD

The Old Testament mentions angels rarely. Far exceeding them are its many references to "the Angel of the LORD," compounding the mystery. The one angel mentioned overwhelmingly in the Old Testament is the Angel of the LORD. He is Jesus in His resurrection body, outside our timeline.

The authors of the Old Testament called Him THE Angel of the LORD. He acts and speaks in ways that imply both a physical body and a divine nature. People who saw Him knew they had seen God face to face.

2

The bodily resurrected Jesus could walk through walls and disappear. Likewise, time was no barrier to Him. Outside of our timeline, He appeared to Old Testament people. The triune nature of God was not yet revealed, so they called Him the Angel of the LORD.

Further confirmation: the New Testament has no reference to that title. The Angel of the LORD was Jesus; the term was no longer needed. He may even have told the disciples about it. Jesus certainly affirmed His preexistence when He rebutted the Jewish leaders by saying, "Before Abraham was, I AM" (John 8:58).

Restricting God's actions to our timeline is impossible and unwise. In the unseen realm of spirit, it is always now. The risen Jesus in His resurrection glory can jump into our time wherever He wishes. After all, He was part of creating time, and it would vanish instantly if He didn't keep time in operation. Of course He isn't bound by it.

All things were made through Him, and without Him nothing was made that was made. (John 1:3)

… Upholding all things by the word of His power … (Hebrews 1:3)

For by Him all things were created that are in heaven and that are on earth, visible and invisible, whether thrones or dominions or principalities or powers. All things were created through Him and for Him. And He is before all things, and in Him all things consist. (Colossians 1:16–17)

OLD TESTAMENT ANGELS

The dominant angel in the Old Testament is the Angel of the LORD—Jesus—but some regular angels receive mention as well.

Angels first appear in Genesis 18, about 2200–2000 BC. Three men visited Abraham and Sarah, who welcomed the strangers with a meal—from scratch. Meal preparation began with killing the calf for meat and included grinding grains to make bread. During the entire time until serving and eating, the three guests remained on the premises, not a short while (18:3–7). The three also ate the calf meat and cakes with the aged couple (18:8).

The passage quickly reveals that one of the three men is God Himself. If Abraham had New Testament revelation, he would have recognized the Second Person of the Trinity, with a body able to walk, eat, and talk with men.

Jesus tells Abraham that He has come specifically to evaluate Sodom and Gomorrah. The other two "men" travel on. We learn they are angels upon their entry to Sodom (19:1); they resemble men so greatly that everyone calls them men (19:12).

The LORD stays to confer with Abraham and afterwards, He is no longer active in the event. The other two perform all subsequent actions. They walk to Sodom; Lot, Abraham's nephew, greets them at the city entrance. At his insistence, they eat a meal he prepares; they accept his invitation to stay the night at his home.

These two angels appear intent upon starting their evaluation of Sodom after their night's rest with Lot (19:1–3). But they hasten the judgment after the citizens' assault on Lot's home. The two angels strike people blind and protect Lot's family.

These events reveal much about the holy angels. Lot's response indicates that they appeared to be worthy men. Everything about the two angels seemed like physical bodies. The angels ate Lot's food and had beds to sleep in. The wicked men desired homosexual relations as if they were regular men. Using physical hands, the two angels pulled Lot inside from the besieging Sodomites and shut the door. When Lot lingered leaving the city, the two angels pulled his family by their hands.

Two generations afterward in 1900—1800 BC, Jacob dreamed the many angels going up and down on their ladder; it stretched from heaven to Earth (Genesis 28:12). His dream revealed that angelic citizens of heaven were active on the Earth. Much later in 800–750 BC, Elisha saw God's angelic army and asked for his servant to see them as well (2 Kings 6:17). After another long period, Daniel in 550 BC spoke with archangel Gabriel, who also told him about archangel Michael.

Considering the two-millennia time span, angels are few and far between before Jesus came.

NEW TESTAMENT ANGELS

The New Testament is far different, recording far more about angels and their activity. The four gospels alone mention angels fifty-two times. Angels are very active in the events surrounding the young Jesus. With joyous gusto, they praised God in unison to the shepherds the night of

Jesus' birth (Luke 2:13). They warned the magi and Joseph in dreams so the Baby remained safe.

The book of Acts alone refers to angels twenty-one times; they are very active for the newborn church. The letter to the Hebrews addressed angels repeatedly; its recipients had fallen prey to a misplaced admiration for angels at the expense of their attention to Jesus. This distressed the author of Hebrews: that Christians would exalt angels' privileges over our own. After all, we are the ones Jesus died for—not angels.

> For He has not put the world to come, of which we speak, in subjection to angels … . For indeed He does not give aid to angels, but He does give aid to the seed of Abraham. (Hebrews 2:5, 16)

The New Testament affirmed what the Old revealed: the angels can speak with men, touch men, and appear in our dreams. Angels can feed us and can strike us dumb. They can roll back stones, reveal their glory at will, and send people into unconscious paralysis. Jesus said the angels experience joy every time someone is saved (Luke 15:10).

A WARNING FOR US

People try to avoid direct engagement with God Himself, by focusing on spiritual things they like. Thus we can paper over our frightening poverty of spirit and become angel-chasers.

Angels are popular for this reason, and many give far more attention to the modest angels than to the God right before them. This is just like Lucifer who forsook God's presence for his widespread trading.

The angels' engagement with mankind includes a special relationship with children, based on Jesus' statement in Matthew 18:10. He warned His disciples against prohibiting children from worship because *"in heaven their angels always see the face of My Father."*

Jesus spoke plainly and repeatedly about their engagement with His final appearing, for example in Matthew chapters 13, 16, and 24–25. They are witnesses to the rightness of God's judgments on us at the end of time (Luke 12:8–9).

ANGELS IN REVELATION

By far, the book of Revelation reveals the most angels, three times more than any other book. Many distinct individual angels perform actions in Revelation, a greater number than all the other angels of the Bible. What do we find there about them? The usual popular characteristics are there: their flight, their impressive glory, their might, and power to intervene on the earth.

But not so popular is their unerring, unwavering obedience to do what they are told. Each individual angel has a preassigned part, just like one of our dramas: each has a line. Each separate angel has a task in advancing the drama. Every angel seen in Revelation responds to a cue—both for when to enter John's attention, and when to recede from it.

Just as our dramas have stars with many supporting players, Revelation clearly shows that God Almighty, Three-in-One, is the star—who was, who is, and who is to come (4:8). We would categorize the angels as supporting cast members—no Oscars, no attention, not named on the marquee, but quietly playing their unique assigned part in advancing the drama.

Ezekiel 28 reveals that discontent, pride, and widespread trading culminated in Lucifer's downfall; we review that widespread trading in depth shortly. These qualities are completely absent in the holy angels. The corruption infected only the fallen angels.

When you combine the iniquities of the fallen to angelic nature in general, what do you see? In the Introduction, we listed several such puzzles about them and their demons. Understanding angelic nature and capabilities will enable us to make inferences about demons and fallen angels, and solve those puzzles biblically.

THEIR LEADER

We normally talk about the devil being our enemy. But when he describes the unseen powers who wrestle us, Apostle Paul doesn't even mention satan (Ephesians 6:12). He teaches us about the entire leadership corps of darkness. One angelic enemy may intimidate us enough, but an entire hierarchy of them?

Paul was not hesitant to identify satan's direct activity (2 Corinthians 12:7). Apostle Peter also warned about satan's direct actions, in 1 Peter 5:8.

Be sober, be vigilant; because your adversary the devil walks about like a roaring lion, seeking whom he may devour.

Peter would know because God's destiny for Peter put him in satan's crosshairs. Peter had at least three experiences with satan and temptation that are recorded. When Peter corrected Jesus' prophecy about crucifixion, Jesus rebuked him as someone speaking for satan (Matthew 16:23). The second was during the Last Supper, when Jesus told Peter, "*Satan has asked for you, that he may sift you as wheat*" (Luke 22:31). Evidently, God gave satan permission to sift Peter if Peter's denial of Christ is the result (Matthew 26:34–35).

Yet one more incident reveals Peter's knowledge of the devil's deceit. Even after being filled by the Holy Spirit of God, Peter could be led astray—a cautionary lesson to each of us. He had three visions from God to accept Gentiles in Acts 10. But when critical Jewish Christians came to inspect the first majority-Gentile church, Peter segregated from non-Jewish Christians. Apostle Paul was present and witnessed Apostle Peter's failure. Paul challenged Peter face-to-face in front of the entire church of Antioch, recorded in Galatians 2:11–14.

We know Peter repented, as he did with Jesus in John 21. When Peter warns us about the devil, he is drawing upon his own uncommonly extensive experience. Apostle Peter exhorts us to resist the devil vigilantly and implies that his worldwide hierarchy wrestles against every Christian worldwide.

Resist him, steadfast in the faith, knowing that the same sufferings are experienced by your brotherhood in the world. (1 Peter 5:9)

Resisting the devil is one thing to say, and another to do. The nine-book *Unseen* Series trains readers in identifying and disarming the strategies of darkness.

THE COLLECTIVE RULERSHIP OF DARKNESS

The chapter opened with the hierarchy of darkness in Ephesians 6:12. Paul's statement zooms out like a camera lens from Peter's exhortation about the devil. Through both, the Holy Spirit reveals our enemies: the kingdom of darkness has a collective rulership.

For we do not wrestle against flesh and blood, but against principalities, against powers, against the rulers of the darkness of this age, against spiritual hosts of wickedness in the heavenly places.

Apostle Paul uses four words and phrases which are very similar—so much so that English translations often interchange them. Paul says they are mighty, they rule, they are unseen, and they are evil. *Principalities* is the first word he uses. We transliterate the Greek word "tas archas." The same Greek root word is translated "beginning" in John 1:1, "*In the beginning was the Word.*" Jesus, the Word of God, was the founder of the kingdom of God. Likewise, these principalities are the founders of darkness—those on whom its kingdom is built. They are principals in the unseen realm, just as our businesses and schools have principals.

The second Greek word used in Ephesians 6:12 is *powers* (transliterated "tas exousias"). We might think of movie-like superpowers, but these beings have the power to dictate affairs. These *powers* are like tyrants and dictators. With no care about people or spirits, they impose their power over all others.

Paul's third Greek word for the leaders of darkness is *rulers*, transliterated "kosmocratoras." Paul says what they rule: the darkness of this age. Like our words *autocrat* and *bureaucrat*, these "cosmo-crats" make decisions for everyone in the kingdom of darkness, both seen (people) and unseen (evil spirits). Note, their decision authority is time-limited, to our current age only; their rule will come to an end when our age ends. The root word is *kosmou*; Jesus used *kosmou* to designate everything in the visible realm (more in chapter eight).

The last phrase of Ephesians 6:12 identifies one more layer of leadership in darkness: "*spiritual hosts of wickedness in the heavenly places.*" Transliterated, it reads, "ta pneumatika tes ponerias en tois epouraniois." The word *hosts* reveals that there are many of them. They are wicked, and they dwell in the unseen realm, *a.k.a.* the heavenly places.

Movies describe organized crime as a family. Paul reveals that the corps of unseen evil rulers is organized also, like a crime family.

Our legal systems investigate crime organizations; these crime families are known by pride. They are unconcerned about others and devoted to their own personal gain. Criminal organizations achieve this by intimidating and oppressing others. Their pattern comes from the kingdom of darkness.

RELEASE

In TV shows and movies, crime families have victims who cower under their threats. These oppressed ones just try to hang on and scrape by, avoiding the unwelcome attention of oppressors. They feel trapped. This fictional portrayal mirrors the condition of every unsaved person; thugs of darkness pretend to be protectors, but actually create an oppression like Jesus described in John 10:10.

The thief does not come except to steal, and to kill, and to destroy.

Many Christians and churches are willfully ignorant of deliverance ministry. Christian leaders often don't want their members to mature past the leaders' level or receive ministry from others.

But when Christians receive deliverance ministry, we can perceive the oppression for the first time. When a Christian becomes free of these tormentors, it's much easier to forsake the inclinations of iniquity. Everyone who receives deliverance ministry treasures it, as Jesus said in John 10:10b.

I have come that they may have life, and that they may have it more abundantly.

My wife and I benefited from the deliverance ministry of Restoring the Foundations (https://www.restoringthefoundations.org). We expelled the oppressing spirits in our lives and relationships, and have been vigilant against them ever since. My new freedom was pronounced—even after being a Christian thirty-five years. Jesus warned in Luke 11:24 that evil spirits try to regain entry, and we learned how to identify and repel them at every opportunity.

But when I urged my longtime Christian friends to receive deliverance ministry, I quickly learned not every Christian desires release. May God bless them with the desire to be completely free.

Jesus described His ministry after His forty days of direct temptation by the devil. He entered the place of worship and cited Isaiah 61:1–2. He chose a prophecy that He would release people from captivity and oppression.

The Spirit of the Lord is upon Me,
Because He has anointed Me
To preach the gospel to the poor;

He has sent Me to heal the brokenhearted,
To proclaim liberty to the captives
And recovery of sight to the blind,
To set at liberty those who are oppressed;
To proclaim the acceptable year of the Lord. (Luke 4:18–19)

Jesus, the Son of God, was incarnated as a human being. He offers full release from every sorrow, oppression, and imprisonment by darkness. But Jesus does not force us to receive this liberty. After all, He even permits people to reject His salvation.

God permits us to cower, just as the victims of crime syndicates try to scrape by without undue attention from their oppressors. He will judge all such cowardice on Judgment Day.

That is the day when He will confirm the eternal destiny of our choices. Jesus repeatedly uses a distinct phrase for one quality shared by everyone He welcomes. Eight times in Revelation alone, Jesus' description for saved people is "*he who overcomes*." In contrast are those do not overcome, for reasons such as cowardice.

> He who overcomes shall inherit all things, and I will be his God and he shall be My son. But the cowardly … shall have their part in the lake which burns with fire and brimstone, which is the second death. (Revelation 21:8)

Jesus came to release us from the oppression of these evil leaders of darkness. To pursue the release Jesus earned so dearly for us requires us to stand up to our oppressors. Will we wholeheartedly choose that complete liberty He came to give us? Or will we cower, fearing to upset our oppressors—and even claim faith in Jesus while yielding to their authority?

We can yield like cowards to the *kosmocrats*, with their rule of this age. We can also courageously dare to defy them in Jesus' name.

MEEK, MOURNING, POVERTY OF SPIRIT

The unseen enemies are powerful with skills practiced for centuries. Constantly, they attempt to insinuate their oppression into our lives. Jesus said after we expel these enemies they try to return (Luke 11:24).

This is why Jesus commands us to be overcomers. Simple belief without maturing as a spirit leaves the Christian a baby. Such babies are vulnerable to *powers* and *hosts of wickedness*. But if we mature, we overcome more all the time and receive His welcome into heaven.

Humanity has two extreme responses to darkness. On one hand, most people ignore it. On the other, some seek to use and manipulate it. But we Christians can make a third choice: meekness that admits our poverty of spirit. We let Jesus release us from the oppressive spirits. In Him, we have liberty and authority. The meek person alone receives His resources. That is how we overcome; we simultaneously admit inadequacy and walk in His liberating love.

In Books One and Two of the *Unseen* Series, we thoroughly explored the importance of meekness, and the vigilant reader will take full advantage of those considerations. Simply stated, we are not competent to wrestle against the leadership that Paul describes in Ephesians 6:12. They are spirits, and we are poor in spirit.

Yet this very condition of poverty, Jesus calls blessed in Matthew 5:3. He tells why: because ours is the kingdom of heaven, a possessive term. We are therefore engaged in heaven's war. In our own poverty of spirit, we are wrestling ancient spirit enemies—very intensely. In the Beatitudes, Jesus revealed how to resolve this tension: meekly confessing and mourning our spiritual bankruptcy. We lower our self-assessment and we trust: because God exalts us, we don't have to.

The Bible plainly describes the tremendous contrast between what we deserve and what we actually receive. Faith in what God says resolves this contrast.

Blessed are the meek, for they shall inherit the earth. (Matthew 5:5)

I bestow upon you a kingdom, just as My Father bestowed one upon Me. (Luke 22:29)

If anyone loves Me, he will keep My word; and My Father will love him, and We will come to him and make Our home with him. (John 14:23)

But God ... made us alive together with Christ (by grace you have been saved), and raised us up together, and made us sit together in the heavenly places in Christ Jesus. (Ephesians 2:4–6)

Set your mind on things above, not on things on the earth. For you died, and your life is hidden with Christ in God. Colossians 3:2–3)

Behold what manner of love the Father has bestowed on us, that we should be called children of God! (1 John 3:1)

You are of God, little children, and have overcome them, because He who is in you is greater than he who is in the world. (1 John 4:4)

EXALTED

Our enemies are ancient spirits. With their spiritual abilities, they actually entertained the idea of replacing God Himself, as we shall see in chapter three. One might wonder why He placed humanity on the same Earth where He exiled these indescribably powerful and evil spirits. Why would He put us in such a helpless, precarious, and exposed situation?

We can't escape asking this question when we have the code key for the Bible: meekness. How could God make this plan? How can we mortals contest a crime family of eternal evil spirits? Meekness, by definition, means it's hard to consider ourselves exalted.

This is why faith is God's way for us. We exercise His authority by faith in what the Holy Spirit reveals: God exalts us into heavenly authority. It can't be weighed or tested with reason or scientific experiments because it is unseen. Jesus commended faith in the centurion (Matthew 8:10). His faith recognized: the spirits of the unseen world had to submit to Jesus' limits and comply with His authority. The same is true about us born-again spirits. They have to yield to us—not vice versa. Jesus put it this way to the disciples.

And I will give you the keys of the kingdom of heaven, and whatever you bind on earth will be bound in heaven, and whatever you loose on earth will be loosed in heaven. (Matthew 16:19)

This promotion is undeserved, certainly—completely by the grace of God. But it is real and authoritative, nonetheless. People can shrink back with excuses. "I'm not worthy; you don't know what I've done; my faith isn't strong enough; I have problem xyz." These all signal cowardice to God, our unwillingness to defy the spiritual oppressors He came to liberate us from. If I repeat that in my life, it shows that I am not an overcomer.

The solution is not to look in the mirror and puff ourselves up. Instead, we yield to and believe what He says. He makes existence the way He wants it, crafting moment after moment to affirm our obedient faith. Our work is to believe what Jesus says.

12

Then they said to Him, "What shall we do, that we may work the works of God?" Jesus answered and said to them, "This is the work of God, that you believe in Him whom He sent." (John 6:28–29)

We work by believing. By faith, we yield to what He says we are—despite any natural evidence to the contrary.

Paul described our meek weakness as the opportunity for God's power. He relates a conversation with God in 2 Corinthians 12:7–10. What *the thorn* was is not specified, except it was a messenger of satan. Possibly it was his poor eyesight (Galatians 6:11). There would be many candidates frankly, for a man with the physical torments he listed in 2 Corinthians 11. Paul didn't identify the thorn; his emphasis is living with the impairment. Watch how our exaltation manifests through our weakness, not our pride.

A thorn in the flesh was given to me, a messenger of Satan to buffet me, lest I be exalted above measure. Concerning this thing I pleaded with the Lord three times that it might depart from me. And He said to me, "My grace is sufficient for you, for My strength is made perfect in weakness." Therefore most gladly I will rather boast in my infirmities, that the power of Christ may rest upon me. Therefore I take pleasure in infirmities, in reproaches, in needs, in persecutions, in distresses, for Christ's sake. For when I am weak, then I am strong.

WITNESSES

But God ... made us sit together in the heavenly places in Christ Jesus ... that in the ages to come He might show the exceeding riches of His grace in His kindness toward us in Christ Jesus. (Ephesians 2:4–7)

Paul says God is showing His rich grace, but to whom? To every being who exists in the unseen realm, both holy and unholy. We become living human spirits when we follow Jesus, and our salvation proves that God is kind to all inhabitants of the unseen realms.

The holy angels see His favor upon us. At Jesus' birth, they witnessed God's favor upon mankind and exulted in it. The angels grouped together and sang in unison to the shepherds in Luke 2:13–14.

And suddenly there was with the angel a multitude of the heavenly host praising God and saying:

"Glory to God in the highest,
And on earth peace, goodwill toward men!"

But the holy angels are not the only witnesses in the heavenly places. Other witnesses are angelic, but not holy: the principalities, powers, rulers, and hosts of wickedness.

Imagine the furor of the devil and his partners when they see God exalting us mortals to His throne—where they had hoped to be. Imagine their vexation seeing us in their seats, next to a living, bodily human—the resurrected Jesus. These principalities think they deserve those places.

God's punishment for these evil rebels includes this furor and vexation. God's weakest creature, He would raise to the authority they once held but forfeited. This was always the plan of God, which Paul wrote in Ephesians 1:4. "*He chose us in Him before the foundation of the world.*"

Does that mean He chose us even before He created Lucifer? Where does satan's creation occur on the timeline? And how? We turn now to the first of three origin Scriptures about satan—Ezekiel chapters 26 through 28.

---

*Discussion and reflection questions for Chapter One can
be found in the Reader Engagement Resources.*

PART ONE

THE CALAMITY
OF HEAVEN

CHAPTER TWO

TYRE, SYMBOL FOR LUCIFER

Three chapters of Ezekiel reveal the origin of the devil. Chapters 26–28 use the city-state of Tyre as a symbolic stand-in for Lucifer. God tells us the beginning of the kingdom of darkness, long before human beings existed. He first created the unseen beings of heaven, including the archangel Lucifer. Only afterward were people created. Genesis chapter one does not say the two creations happened at the same time.

We are interested in Lucifer's creation for two reasons. First, God wants us to understand it; that's why He revealed it. Second, Lucifer's transformation into satan reveals his patterns and tricks. This knowledge is practical, so we can identify and resist his works. A failure in this skill prevents Christians and churches from fulfilling Matthew 16:18 and obeying 1 Peter 5:8–9.

> On this rock I will build My church, and the gates of Hades will not overcome it.

> Be sober, be vigilant; because your adversary the devil walks about like a roaring lion, seeking whom he may devour. Resist him, steadfast in the faith....

God discloses the devil's origin in the prophecies about Tyre and its king. We begin with the historical context—a basic Inductive Bible Study habit described in Book Two of the *Unseen* Series.

EZEKIEL'S JOURNAL

The prophet Ezekiel kept a journal, as I do and perhaps as you have. Ezekiel's journal is now the portion of your Old Testament labeled *Ezekiel*. He began each entry with a date, just like you and I do. His dating system began with his exile from Judah to Babylon (1:2). He only recorded God's expressions and revelations to him—a journal, in contrast to a diary where a person records unrelated thoughts and experiences.

Ezekiel recorded two ways God communicated to him. One type was visual. In fact, Ezekiel was first inducted into the prophet's ministry by seeing heavenly beings and events. The other type he described with the introductory phrase *The word of the LORD came to me*. That type was more frequent in Ezekiel's journal—forty-nine times. For comparison, the next most frequent user was Jeremiah with twelve times. Christians today also experience God communicating with them in those two ways, and many more.

THE ACCOUNTABILITY OF ISRAEL'S ENEMIES

Ezekiel tells us that chapters 25–32 came from the word of the Lord. These prophecies are only for the neighboring nations around Judah and Jerusalem (interchangeable names for God's people). He judges each nation because they did not show the proper respect for God's chosen people.

That theme appears often in the Old Testament. Zechariah 1:15 is an example:

I am exceedingly angry with the nations at ease;
For I was a little angry,
And they helped—but with evil intent.

Jerusalem went into exile when the Lord judged His people's infidelity, but it did not diminish the respect for those whom He had chosen. The failure of God's people did not excuse the surrounding nations.

HONORING GOD'S ANOINTED

Consider King David's example. When he was on the run from Saul, he emphatically respected Saul as the Lord's anointed. Even when Saul was at his worst, David honored him as a king established by the Lord. In the same way, Jerusalem was due a similar respect as the Lord's chosen city, even at its worst.

Ezekiel chapters 25–32 show that the Lord expects honor for Himself and for His choice of a city, of a people, of a kingdom. He then blesses or judges others based on their response to His choice.

In the Bible, God rewards many outsiders in keeping to their response to His chosen ones. Laban, Jacob's uncle and father-in-law, said it directly: "*I have learned by experience that the Lord has blessed me for your sake*" (Genesis 30:27). Another example is the wealth of Solomon's kingdom. His rule had benefits for all the neighboring kingdoms, and they became rich as well. The pattern repeats when the City of God receives the nations' wealth (Zechariah 14:14, Revelation 21:24–26).

The nations were accountable to mourn the fall of Jerusalem. The neighboring peoples gloated instead and only saw opportunity. God reveals to Ezekiel their judgment.

THIS IS FOR US

The principle is that God expects unbelievers to honor His choice of place and people—but that's not the only principle. Our self-understanding as Christians requires us to believe that respecting God's choice means honoring us, whom He has chosen. Those who do not honor us, do not honor God who chose us. Jesus says this Himself, in John 5:23-24, 8:54, and 12:26.

CAUTION

God created Lucifer and placed him in a prominent position, which the coming chapters explore. After rebelling, he became satan. Respect for God's original choosing also mandates our respectful honor even toward satan and the angels who fell with him. Their sin does not nullify the honor God originally gave them. It is their loss which God laments; shall we dismiss what He mourns losing?

Lucifer no longer holds his exalted position in the heavens. Yet even the other archangels exhibit respect for satan because he was originally God's exalted angel. His nature is still angelic—albeit deformed.

The Bible strongly warns against impugning him. Disrespect for the devil reveals an inflated view of ourselves and dishonors God's original choice to create him.

> Likewise also these dreamers defile the flesh, reject authority, and speak evil of dignitaries. Yet Michael the archangel, in contending with the devil, when he disputed about the body of Moses, dared not bring against him a reviling accusation, but said, "The Lord rebuke you!" (Jude 8–10)

> They are presumptuous, self-willed. They are not afraid to speak evil of dignitaries, whereas angels, who are greater in power and might, do not bring a reviling accusation against them before the Lord. (2 Peter 2:10–11)

When Ezekiel prophesied, Jerusalem stood for the nation of Israel. After centuries of disobedience, their territory was shrunken. Their population was exhausted, and their wealth siphoned by other nations. Only the one capital city remained. Yet, for all their flaws, they were still the Lord's people.

Apostle Paul had been a colleague of Jerusalem's leaders who engineered Jesus' crucifixion. He had taken part in their persecution of Christians before God confronted him. Yet, after all that, Paul wrote that God's choice is the basis of honor for Israel.

> Concerning the gospel they are enemies for your sake, but concerning the election they are beloved for the sake of the fathers. For the gifts and the calling of God are irrevocable. For as you were once disobedient to God, yet have now obtained mercy through their disobedience, even so these also have now been disobedient, that through the mercy shown you they also may obtain mercy. For God has committed them all to disobedience, that He might have mercy on all. (Romans 11:28–32)

Recipients of God's gifts and calling are responsible for what they do with them. Yet even when those recipients are failures, it does not excuse observers from honoring God's choice.

FAIR JUDGMENT

Is God right to judge nations based on their response to Israel? Judgment discerns what is not fair and takes action to rebalance so that justice prevails. What is the standard of fairness?

Today we might dismiss the nearby countries' behavior as competitiveness, or basic human self-interest. Our broadcasters and print news would disallow judgment of any kind. In our day, we might judge the nearby nations on their merit and demerits. The standards of judgment we use are the humanity, ideal, need, or merit. But these are not the standard of God's judging.

The standard is honor for God and His choice. "*He who touches you touches the apple of His eye*" (Zechariah 2:8). God chose Israel to be His people. Jerusalem was the city where He caused His name to dwell (Deuteronomy 12:15), and Judah was its territory of influence. His judgment of Israel's gloating neighbors restores the justice that His choosing deserves. We honor His kingdom because we honor Him, not because of its merits or needs. The importance of this truth will become more clear in Book Five of the *Unseen* Series, *Nobody Sees This Israel: God's Vanguard Against Darkness.*

TYPES FOR DARKNESS

At face value, the prophecies against Israel's neighbors are no longer relevant, because those nations no longer exist. A reader naturally asks, "why are they in the Bible that the Holy Spirit has compiled for us?" The reason is their value as symbolic stand-ins, in which He reveals the unseen world.

In Book Two of the *Unseen* Series, we discussed typology and symbolism in the Bible. A type can be an incident, a person, a nation, or a relationship. God reveals through these types the oft-repeated patterns of the unseen world. The New Testament authors heartily affirmed this understanding of Scripture. Its authors found types throughout their Bible, our Old Testament.

As we study His words to Ezekiel about Israel's neighbors, we will find that God reveals the origin of satan and the kingdom of darkness by using such a type, or pattern.

THE HISTORICAL SYMBOL OF SATAN: TYRE

Tyre, the subject of Ezekiel 26–28, was a neighbor nation to Israel. Four centuries before, its king Hiram was close to Israel's kings David and Solomon. First Kings chapters 5–10 record the significant commerce between Tyre and Israel.

The city-state occupied an entire island; Ezekiel describes Tyre as a nation *in the midst of the seas.* It stood almost a mile off the Mediterranean Coast in present-day southwest Lebanon and had daughter villages on the coast itself, such as Sidon.

Tyre was the Phoenicians' trading capital. The seafaring nation dominated the sea trade throughout the Mediterranean Sea. They also created trading outposts such as Carthage in Northern Africa (later defeated by Rome in the Punic Wars).

THEIR END COMETH

Tyre, the trading powerhouse for centuries, no longer exists. In the same way, the powerhouse of darkness will one day no longer exist.

Ezekiel's journal dating places chapter 26 in the year 593 BC. In it, God promises to send Nebuchadnezzar, king of Babylon, against Tyre. A mere twenty years later, Nebuchadnezzar conquered Tyre in 573 BC and fulfilled 26:7–11. A period of empire shuffling ensued after Cyrus overtook Babylon, and Tyre regained its status as a trading powerhouse during that time.

Finally, Alexander the Great conquered and demolished Tyre entirely in 332 BC, 261 years after Ezekiel's prophecy—the second stage of fulfillment. His army spread the stones of its ramparts into the sea to form a causeway where Tyre once stood.

TYRE AND PRIDE

Zechariah recorded God's assessment of Tyre as a symbol of pride. His prophecy also promises the city-state's death in water, a judgment completed by the army of Alexander.

For Tyre built herself a tower,
Heaped up silver like the dust,
And gold like the mire of the streets.

Behold, the Lord will cast her out;
He will destroy her power in the sea,
And she will be devoured by fire. (Zechariah 9:3–4)

In Ezekiel's journal, the LORD first reveals His judgment on Tyre for its jealousy of Jerusalem (chapter 26). Next, God responds to the trading prowess of Tyre (chapter 27). Finally, in Ezekiel 28:1–10 below, God directly addresses the prince of Tyre. Witness his overweening pride and claim to be divine—definitely not meek. In the parentheses, God accurately describes Tyre's wealth and position, but definitely not as an affirmation.

The word of the Lord came to me again, saying, "Son of man, say to the prince of Tyre, 'Thus says the Lord GOD:
"Because your heart is lifted up,
And you say, 'I am a god,
I sit in the seat of gods,
In the midst of the seas,'
Yet you are a man, and not a god,
Though you set your heart as the heart of a god.
(Behold, you are wiser than Daniel!
There is no secret that can be hidden from you!
With your wisdom and your understanding
You have gained riches for yourself,
And gathered gold and silver into your treasuries;
By your great wisdom in trade you have increased your riches,
And your heart is lifted up because of your riches),"
'Therefore thus says the Lord GOD:
"Because you have set your heart as the heart of a god,
Behold, therefore, I will bring strangers against you,
The most terrible of the nations;
And they shall draw their swords against the beauty of your wisdom,
And defile your splendor.
They shall throw you down into the Pit,
And you shall die the death of the slain
In the midst of the seas.
Will you still say before him who slays you,
'I am a god'?
But you shall be a man, and not a god,
In the hand of him who slays you.
You shall die the death of the uncircumcised

By the hand of aliens;
For I have spoken," says the Lord GOD.'"

Five times God singles out the Tyrian leader's claim, *I am a god.* The same pride of invincibility was God's tool for their disaster when Alexander approached Tyre. He requested to worship in its temple, but the Tyrians didn't simply decline. They killed Alexander's emissaries and dumped their bodies over the city's 150-foot wall into the sea. Tyre's "divine rulers" exhibited a blinded arrogance, disdaining Alexander's soldiers less than a mile away on shore—tens of thousands. Soon Tyre was no more.

Ezekiel's prophetic declaration of Tyre's pride fits with the previous two chapters about them. God pronounces a severe judgment for the island nation, and He gives the reasons. The claim to divine stature made Tyre's leaders a good symbol for the fallen Lucifer.

GOD LAMENTS TYRE'S FALL

Chapters 26–28 record four laments about Tyre—prophetically, as if the destroying judgment was past. The first tells about the wailing of other rulers. Another is the bitter mourning of its trading partners. Two of the four laments are God's own.

AS SEEN TODAY

God instructs Ezekiel to lament for Tyre as if it had already been destroyed—preceding the actual event by 261 years. Such a prophetic "as if already done" voice is frequent in Scripture because the events of heaven are always NOW. The prophetic perspective can appear very fluid in its time references, using the time trombone.

Songs of lament express deep personal sorrow. A permanent loss gives rise to lamentations. People lament both death that interrupts intimacy and regret over avoidable tragedies. Laments are mournful songs full of grief.

God's lament about Tyre's destruction reveals how acutely He grieves the loss of Lucifer, whom Tyre represents in Ezekiel 28. His grief is focused on Tyre the island nation because it was a symbol for Lucifer. The exalted creation and role of Lucifer had been dear to God Almighty, and when the "cherub who covered" rebelled, God felt loss. He laments Tyre as a symbol; His sorrow is the tragedy of Lucifer's corruption.

Why does God lament the loss of Tyre? And why two times? While Tyre doesn't seem very lamentable, it is a type of the loss of Lucifer. With all its offensiveness, the pride, and the jealous animosity that Tyre showed to Jerusalem at its fall, Tyre was a good choice to represent Lucifer to Ezekiel. In fact, God's first lament actually begins with their pride: *"O Tyre, you have said, 'I am perfect in beauty.'"* (Ezekiel 27:3)

THE TRADING OF TYRE

There are at least five reasons God laments Tyre's destruction; the fifth comprises the next chapter.

Tyre's trading was the first loss God lamented. The island nation was a commercial powerhouse. They traded with every nation throughout the Mediterranean. Tyre's capitalistic prowess made many cities and rulers rich. Productive activities employed many people as a result of Tyre's shipping network.

Jerusalem was their competitor. It sat as prominently on land trade routes as Tyre did for sea trade. After Nebuchadnezzar leveled Jerusalem in 587 BC, the Tyrians rejoiced that the former trade through Jerusalem would now depend on them. God's lament quoted their rejoicing.

Aha! She [Jerusalem] is broken who was the gateway of the peoples; now she is turned over to me; I shall be filled; she is laid waste. (Ezekiel 26:2)

God told Ezekiel that after He judged Tyre, the city would be a terror. The destroyed Tyre would bear a clear and terrifying message throughout the known world: no city, no wall, no impregnable fortress was ever safe again (26:15–21). This terrible reality caused the lament by the rulers of Tyre's trading partners.

This ripple effect of Tyre's destruction also captures the heavenly consequences of Lucifer's rebellion. He, like Tyre, becomes a terror throughout the unseen realm. If such an exalted spirit can be so corrupted, then no spirit can relax in vigilant honor for God.

Ezekiel 27 records God's first lament. There He named forty distinct places and peoples, each touched by the trading of Tyre. God knew the trade network intimately and named their products: fifty distinct commodities. The prophecy also revealed a detailed knowledge of Tyre's trading contracts.

God laments not only the loss of the commercial economy centered in Tyre. In Ezekiel 27, He also laments the loss of the skills and individual ethnic prowess of each trading group. He also prophesies the laments of businessmen.

The trading network represents commerce in the heavenly realms as well. The continuing prophecy in Ezekiel 28 shows that the misuse of trading by Lucifer was the source of his iniquity. Yet God likes good trading and laments its loss.

The Lord's judgment makes Tyre vanish: "*You shall be no more; though you are sought for, you will never be found again*" (26:21). Imagine you have shipped three loads of expensive purple cloth, you have a bill of lading, and you are expecting a six-figure last payment. Imagine your disbelief and horror upon the word of Tyre's destruction by Alexander. Feel the dismay, holding contracts to deliver to and take delivery from Tyrian ships—all your life and your employees' lives built around those contracts.

THIS IS FOR US

Tyre gives meek people some valuable practical guidance for our business lives. God's listing of all the contracts, trading partners, and commodities shows God understands business and pays careful attention to it. He likes business and trading—it's the pride and arrogance He doesn't like. God styles this as a lament, in part because all these trading relationships will be lost to the world for a period after Tyre's destruction.

Part of our creation mandate to dominate the earth is to engage in business activity, trade earth's resources with

continues on next page

What action would you take? Immediately, you would try to contact your Tyrian trading counterparty. Without cell phones and email, you would board a ship and go there. Imagine your first sighting of the empty spot where stood the once-mighty capital of trade. The sight would never leave your memory. You find mighty Tyre completely leveled, so complete its destruction—and you left holding the worthless bill for which no one will pay, your expensive export lost and unaccounted for, your plans demolished just like Tyre. God prophesies the laments of such business-people in Ezekiel 27:25–36.

Patterns of trade distinguish the kingdom of darkness from the kingdom of light. In Ezekiel 28:16, God's second lament describes how Lucifer's corrupt trade contributed to his fall. Trading also figures prominently in Revelation 17–18, in the destruction of Babylon and all its trade.

Ezekiel's prophecies about Tyre are symbols God uses to reveal how Lucifer's self-exalting trading patterns can corrupt us. To avoid a similar outcome requires discernment about our own commerce. By understanding the biblical patterns, we can conduct our business today for the kingdom of God. Knowing the devil's trading scheme protects us from falling into its patterns. The nine-book *Unseen* Series illuminates this useful discernment.

one another, add value through the chain of production, and create wealth for each contributor to the process. When our failure of attitude causes His judgment against our excellence in business or our economies, God laments it.

GOD INVITES REPENTANCE OR JUDGMENT

A second reason God revealed to Ezekiel His lament over Tyre: He hoped they might repent. It's possible that Ezekiel forwarded this prophecy to the Tyrians. You would and I would, don't you think? That matches up with what God did for Nineveh through the reluctant Jonah. Apostle Peter stated, "*The Lord … is not willing that any should perish*" (2 Peter 3:9).

Certainly the detailed listing of chapter 27 would have persuasive power: trading contracts, suppliers, customers, and commodities. A reader in Tyre would be in disbelief that a Jewish priest on the other side of the desert knew these things.

If a citizen of Tyre had a heart to repent, this prophecy would give them opportunity. God shows His love, actually lamenting the fall of His Jerusalem's trading rival. The destruction occurred as prophesied, however. If some individuals repented, it wasn't the island nation or its rulers.

A third reason Ezekiel received this prophetic lament was his physical location in Babylon. Daniel was one of several Jews with standing in the royal court; it would be easy for this prophecy to come before Nebuchadnezzar. Perhaps it even sparked Nebuchadnezzar's decision to "pay a visit" to Tyre. After all, Daniel's dream interpretation sparked him to set up an idol of gold (Daniel 2–3).

The time trombone explains the fourth reason God lamented Tyre. The great trading city was a type for the parallel passage in Revelation 17–18. There, Apostle John beholds a great trading capital, the symbolic Babylon. He sees how her trading made her the mother of abominations. The two chapters in Revelation closely mirror Ezekiel's prophecies about Tyre.

God showed Ezekiel about Tyre. For the prophet, it was like having his music stand on the sliding portion of the time trombone, not the stationary part. The sheet music close to Ezekiel's time described Tyre specifically, and the sheet music far out from his time described God's ultimate judgment on the trading system of godless mankind.

The fifth reason: Tyre was a symbol for Lucifer and his lamentable fall.

Discussion and reflection questions for Chapter Two can
be found in the Reader Engagement Resources

CHAPTER THREE

LAMENTING LUCIFER

The fifth reason is that God lamented the fall of Lucifer. He used Tyre as a type for the once-exalted cherub. God's laments for Tyre reveal the origin of the devil in Ezekiel 27–28. Isaiah 14 reveals Lucifer's attempted usurpation of God's rulership. Revelation 12 reveals that Lucifer incited an entire war in heaven, trying to unseat God Almighty.

All these passages presume that heaven is a real place with physical attributes. Though unseeable by us, its inhabitants have bodies. Heaven's physical qualities include distance, sequence, and communication. If your concept of heaven is spiritualized, the following may take extra effort. God revealed this because He wanted you to know, so that effort is worth it.

Ezekiel 28:11–19 is to the kingdom of darkness as Genesis 1 is to us: the beginning.

Moreover the word of the LORD came to me, saying,

"Son of man, take up a lamentation for the king of Tyre, and say to him, 'Thus says the Lord God:

"You were the seal of perfection,
Full of wisdom and perfect in beauty.
You were in Eden, the garden of God;
Every precious stone was your covering:
The sardius, topaz, and diamond,
Beryl, onyx, and jasper,
Sapphire, turquoise, and emerald with gold.
The workmanship of your timbrels and pipes
Was prepared for you on the day you were created.

You were the anointed cherub who covers;
I established you;
You were on the holy mountain of God;
You walked back and forth in the midst of fiery stones.
You were perfect in your ways from the day you were created,
Till iniquity was found in you.

By the abundance of your trading
You became filled with violence within,
And you sinned;
Therefore I cast you as a profane thing
Out of the mountain of God;
And I destroyed you, O covering cherub,
From the midst of the fiery stones.

Your heart was lifted up because of your beauty;
You corrupted your wisdom for the sake of your splendor;
I cast you to the ground,
I laid you before kings,
That they might gaze at you.

You defiled your sanctuaries
By the multitude of your iniquities,
By the iniquity of your trading;
Therefore I brought fire from your midst;
It devoured you,
And I turned you to ashes upon the earth
In the sight of all who saw you.
All who knew you among the peoples are astonished at you;
You have become a horror,
And shall be no more forever."""

The king of Tyre is the type of Lucifer. The kings and peoples under him are a type of Lucifer's rebel partners, the topic of chapter five.

This is a person trombone, like the time trombone. A person on the seen, linear timeline symbolizes a person in the unseen, always-NOW of heaven. Three times in chapters 26–28, the Lord describes Tyre's punishment as going down to the Pit. That same Pit is Satan's punishment in Isaiah 14 and Revelation 20—further confirming this typological interpretation of Ezekiel 28.

THE EXALTED LUCIFER

The measure of Lucifer's iniquity is his exalted creation. God formed Lucifer with an assigned task. All the splendor, wisdom, and beauty needed, he had. He had a one-of-a-kind privilege—an exclusive relationship with God.

This, Lucifer willingly forfeited. The exile of Lucifer for this forfeiture was sorrowful for God, and He laments, proclaiming His grief about Lucifer.

LUCIFER THE SEAL

In 28:12 cited above, God—Himself perfect—describes Lucifer as "*the seal of perfection*." Seals in ancient times were images impressed into hot wax. Such seals signified official boundary-setting.

To enter an area past the seal on it required a special authorization. Without that, the transgressor of the boundary risked a penalty. Walk in the woods to see a seal of ownership: NO TRESPASSING. Most stores have one door with a seal of privacy, EMPLOYEES ONLY.

These publicly announce a prohibition, just like the ancient hot wax.

The seal warns everyone not to cross the boundary. To do so without authorization brings a penalty. Pilate's seal on the tomb of Jesus is one example; the seven-sealed scroll in Revelation 5 is another. Apostle John saw those seals as impenetrable.

> So I wept much, because no one was found worthy to open and read the scroll, or to look at it. (Revelation 5:4)

Lucifer, in his exalted existence, was a seal. This exalted archangel was not perfection himself, but a very public sign of perfection—God's. Lucifer was the exclamation point on God's glory. He was the boundary on the "*mount of God*," authorization was required to pass him and approach God's throne.

LUCIFER IN THE PERFECT EDEN

God says that Lucifer as the seal of perfection was in "*Eden, the garden of God*." We know the Eden from Genesis 2, where God put Adam and Eve. But when we first find the serpent there, in Genesis 3, he is anything

31

but perfect. One word describes him—crafty. In the Eden of Genesis 2 is not a perfect Lucifer but one deformed into satan, who leads the mortal human race into sin.

Eden as a word meant a pleasure garden, a paradise. Ezekiel 28:13 describes Lucifer's presence in just such a paradise—*the garden of God.* This Eden where Lucifer was perfect predated the Eden in which God put our first parents. The Eden of Genesis 2 had just been created during the six days.

One possibility: the earthly Eden was a replica of *the garden of God* where Lucifer had been the seal on God's perfection. A heavenly garden in the unseen, unbound realm would be the original Eden. Jewish tradition has long held this interpretation.

LUCIFER'S BODY

Lucifer's body was not your standard-issue angelic body, either. God reveals vivid detail in Ezekiel 28. Speaking to Lucifer, He recalls *"the day you were created."* His body's skin was sparkling gemstones, and God lists nine such stones, plus gold. Imagine having a body like this: the sparkle of the diamonds, against the shadowless black of the onyx stones. Anyone looking at you would see blue, green, turquoise, red glints from the semiprecious gemstones—all set in gold filigree.

God says He prepared Lucifer's body to produce sounds, and not just talking. There were built-in pipes, like woodwinds, or the pipes of a pipe organ. Timbrels on its surface were like our tambourines—percussion on the flat and bells on the edges.

Because of this musical body, preachers sometimes describe Lucifer as a worship leader. His duties (next in our inquiry) reinforce this interpretation. God equipped his body uniquely for musical expression and heart-stirring audible expression.

God made Lucifer to be like no other. He and his body were unique in the heavenly realms: beautiful to behold, making beautiful sounds, expressing God's perfection and wisdom. Nowhere else in the Bible is a

STILL TRUE TODAY

How poignant and intimate a description He gives of Lucifer! It's clear that God is not a distant, disengaged judge, but One who Himself suffers the judgment He must inflict. That's why God's statements about Lucifer are a lamentation in 28:11.

body described in such detail. God reveals what Lucifer looked like—but not Jesus or the Angel of the Lord.

God Almighty laments the fall of this wonderful creature who had been the seal of perfection. It's understandable why He told Ezekiel to *take up a lamentatio*n (28:12).

THE EXALTED ROLE OF LUCIFER

Not only was his body unique, but also his responsibility. Lucifer was the anointed cherub *who covers* (28:14). God says, *"I established you;"* He specifically anointed Lucifer for a one-of-a-kind task.

Anointed means God singled Lucifer out and set him in place for an exclusive role. What does *covers* mean in 28:14–15? He covered the ground around the throne, *"on the holy mountain of God, where he walked back and forth in the midst of fiery stones."* (Soon, we'll see these same stones are now infused into satan.)

This unique anointing to cover suggests that he controlled access to God. In our language we might call Lucifer the gatekeeper to the Throne. But why would God need a gatekeeper? If that is true, then access to God was an item of scarcity, with restricted supply.

THIS IS FOR US

In our culture, *cherub* means the creature on a Valentine's Day card, and his name is Cupid. But as Scripture uses it, a cherub is a heavenly being anointed for God's direct, continual presence. The cherub is therefore ferocious, fearsome, and intimidating—the opposite of our popular image.

As strange as it seems to speak of an omnipresent God in these terms, I believe it is the best way to explain what He reveals about Lucifer's role. The physical attributes of heaven would have a throne, an exalted setting, and a limited space around it. The explanatory power of this interpretation is affirmed in the many other Scriptures we will review.

We are told that Lucifer had *sanctuaries* (plural) (28:18). What form would that take for Lucifer, and why? Translators consistently choose the English word sanctuaries, from the Latin *sanctus*, meaning holy. Ezekiel wrote in Hebrew using the word *qōdeš*, from their word for holy. Lucifer had multiple places where angels honored his unique anointing and function.

The invisible realm is physical, even if unseeable by us. Lucifer was not omnipresent; he had a physical body. He could not be in more than one place at a time; that's why God says that he *walked back and forth*. Lucifer conducted an *abundance* of trade in multiple locations using sanctuaries. We are not told where these locations were; the realm is not visible to us.

We'll review the range of his trading shortly. Clearly, Lucifer's business did not restrain him to one place. Wherever he went, sanctuaries that he controlled were involved.

It's plausible that his anointed gatekeeping commanded outposts for the meetings and business required. Wherever he went, other angels would honor his elevated position and trust him. In Lucifer's sanctuaries, he would be lord.

Imagine the effect upon you: being lord everywhere you go, respected as perfect. A person could get a false idea about himself. In His lament, God singles out Lucifer's abundance of trading as the seedbed for his violence.

Perhaps this is where he got the idea he could replace God. In his sanctuaries, other angels were acting as if he was. Everywhere Lucifer went, he was lord in his sanctuaries. Our idea of trade uses words like outposts, stores, trading posts, conference centers, trade shows, or exhibits. God chose the word sanctuaries rather than those because Lucifer let the honor go to his head.

After we test these interpretations, we will find great explanatory power for many Scriptures and Christian experiences.

THE TRADING OF LUCIFER

God listed to Ezekiel all of Tyre's trading contracts and relationships in Ezekiel 27. Tyre's trading is a type of Lucifer's trading. Ezekiel is told in God's lament that Lucifer's trading was a cause of his fall.

The favored archangel suffered from his trades in three ways that God names. It led him to violence. He became enrapt with his own splendor. He conducted trades iniquitously (28:16–18).

By the abundance of your trading, you became filled with violence within. (28:16)

Your heart was lifted up because of your beauty;
You corrupted your wisdom for the sake of your splendor. (28:17)

You defiled your sanctuaries
By the multitude of your iniquities,
By the iniquity of your trading. (28:18)

LUCIFER'S DISDAIN

Imagine yourself anointed to guard God's throne, see Him face to face, and lead His worship. Imagine that your authorization was required before anyone could relate to God.

What message would you broadcast if you regularly departed His sanctuary and went trading in your own sanctuaries? Wouldn't it appear that you disdained your exclusive privilege?

Archangel Gabriel supplied a stark contrast when he rebuked Zacharias for disbelief. The old priest doubted what the archangel said, but Gabriel didn't claim validity based on himself, his nature, or his status. One basis alone validated his trustworthiness: *"I am Gabriel, who stands in the presence of God, and was sent to speak to you"* (Luke 1:19). Gabriel left God's direct presence only because God sent him—in contrast to Lucifer, whose trading travels were elective.

> **COMING FEATURES**
>
> In Book Nine, *Nobody Sees This Victory Yet: The Destruction of Darkness*, we'll see much more of God's attitude about trading: He loves it. Lucifer's problem was not trading, but the sin in him which arose through his misuse of trading.

God permitted Lucifer's trading and travel. Ezekiel 27 about Tyre showed His intimate familiarity with trade. He named contracts, commodities, and delivery systems. God didn't take it personally because it wasn't Lucifer's trading that was a sin.

But imagine what all the angels would see. What would you think of such a uniquely privileged person? Would you wonder why Lucifer preferred his own sanctuaries rather than *the mountain of God*?

Put yourself in the archangel's shoes. If trade with anyone, anywhere enticed you away from God's direct presence, what would you have to feel about God? about your position? What would be your motive for having multiple sanctuaries for yourself?

Jesus experienced this. Martha was busy in the household, while Mary sat at Jesus' feet to be with Him. Martha's hospitality efforts were not bad. Jesus said nothing until Martha bitterly asked Jesus to make Mary work. He then admonished Martha's distraction, but commended Mary for her choice to focus on Him.

> Now it happened as they went that He entered a certain village; and a certain woman named Martha welcomed Him into her house. And she had a sister called Mary, who also sat at Jesus' feet and heard His word. But Martha was distracted with much serving, and she approached Him and said, "Lord, do You not care that my sister has left me to serve alone? Therefore tell her to help me."
> And Jesus answered and said to her, "Martha, Martha, you are worried and troubled about many things. But one thing is needed, and Mary has chosen that good part, which will not be taken away from her." (Luke 10:38–42)

Luke's gospel didn't record how Martha responded. But when Jesus says that to the Martha in us, I hope we would drop everything and sit with Mary.

Did God have such a conversation with Lucifer? Ezekiel 28 doesn't answer, but I believe it is unlikely. As an angel, the most privileged angel, Lucifer would receive no warning, performance reviews, or chance to improve. The moment God found sin in him, Lucifer was punished (28:15–16).

LUCIFER, TRADING PARTNERS, AND IOUs

Who did Lucifer trade with? To decipher this mystery, we can reverse engineer from what Scripture reveals plainly.

His trading partners were not people, because this prophecy in Ezekiel 28:11–19 describes Lucifer prior to the creation of Adam and Eve. We mortal humans were not yet created and the only other interactive, personal creatures revealed are angels. Lucifer's trading had to be with angels because they were the only candidates.

What could Lucifer offer in any trade? He monetized his gatekeeping responsibility; he could scrutinize angelic requests. Angels needed the permission of this anointed covering cherub to interact with God. Any supplicant angel had to satisfy Lucifer first; only then could that angel engage with God directly.

What would the trade be? Lucifer was in the catbird seat, as the saying goes. He could designate the price and exact obligations from any angel, in exchange for direct access to the LORD God. The supplicant angel would have to agree to Lucifer's price.

If this is how the trade worked, what happened next? Lucifer would vouch for the angel to approach God's throne. This pattern is common in the throne rooms of the biblical kingdoms; Nehemiah had such a responsibility for the Persian king Artaxerxes (Nehemiah 1:11).

But what could any angel offer Lucifer? He was the seal on God's perfection, and beheld God directly with no such gatekeeping.

To trade with someone, you must have something they value which they want from you. Lucifer had something valuable to offer, using his position on the mount of God and his control over access to God. An angel could get access to God by offering something desirable to the gatekeeper of the throne.

But what could they offer to Lucifer? Or what could he receive in exchange? His creation was the most exalted; he needed no one's permission to be face-to-face with God. What could Lucifer want from them? The evidence shows what he asked: "what promise or IOU can you give me?"

Hebrews 1:14 says angels are ministering spirits, revealing that God made them to be satisfied when they can serve and fulfill obligations. When someone is in power, they can accumulate obligations from others. We call this an IOU, "I owe you." Even if

SAME WAY TODAY

Trading is another word for exchange. Goods, rights, properties, information—all these have a value to a buyer. But can the buyer provide a good, right, property, or information that the seller considers to be of equivalent value to the seller? Usually not.

That's the origin of money, which serves as a stand-in for the buyer to pay the seller in something other than the goods, rights, properties, or info that the seller really wants. Money is a means of facilitating exchange.

But if a buyer has neither the things the seller would like in exchange, nor the money that the seller specifies, what happens then?

The seller can walk away and say, "no deal." But what if the seller tells the buyer, "take it, good friend. We'll figure out later how you can pay me"— what happens then?

Voilé—an IOU.

these trading partners could give nothing he lacked, he could ask them for an IOU.

It's a system we understand, and an age-old element of trading. Lucifer could do a favor for an angel and grant a moment of access to God. But that favor would have to be repaid somehow, sometime. Lucifer would let them know, and it would be solely at his discretion.

The explanatory power of this understanding opens many Bible revelations and illuminates our own experience with satan and his followers.

AGREEMENTS WITH THE DEVIL = FINE PRINT

People's universal experience with the devil is trading. To get what he wants, satan still conducts trades. This trading becomes increasingly significant in the Bible's revelation about darkness and human sinfulness.

The devil's trading is an IOU system of indebtedness for something to be specified at a future date. To accumulate power, satan collects IOUs from other beings. It's how he enlisted angelic partners in his rebellion against God. In contrast, God's trading system does not rely on IOUs or indebtedness. Both systems feature prominently in other books of the *Unseen* Series.

Now it's people who are the victims of these powerful deceptive fallen angels. The enemies offer us trades which allure us with real spiritual power. We desire what they offer and we unknowingly agree. But their IOUs always have fine print, some unwelcome and unforeseen requirement. These unseen enemies can call in the IOU when and how they wish.

From our infancy, the twisted evil rulers trick each person into unwitting agreements with satan. We are poor in spirit, defenseless against them, so we all grow up agreeing with the kingdom of darkness. The evil ones rejoice because our entire life is an argument with God, impairing His favor upon us. They demand payment of our

AS SEEN TODAY

These devilish IOUs explain why there's so much fiction about agreements and contracts with the devil. It's a central theme in a wide variety: from Goethe's *Faustus,* to Tommy the guitarist in *O Brother Where Art Thou,* to Nicolas Cage in *Ghost Rider.*

These IOUs can never be satisfied, like money from a loan shark. He and his partners will let you have what you want—in exchange for an eternal debt.

IOU under circumstances we didn't expect. And we can never satisfy their demands. People are damned like them, and they still won't be satisfied.

The nine-book *Unseen* Series arms readers to maximize our meekness and open doors for God's power to free us. Only that way can we resist and expose our IOUs with satan. Awareness of satan's tricks is very useful.

Lest Satan should take advantage of us; for we are not ignorant of his devices. (2 Corinthians 2:11)

And have no fellowship with the unfruitful works of darkness, but rather expose them. (Ephesians 5:11)

When we seek and discover our hidden contracts with darkness, we can break them. Confession is healing because it exposes the works of darkness to trick us.

Genuine Christians have a superseding contract with Jesus Christ and it has zero fine print. He alone liberates us from the house of satan's prisoners. In maturing, we integrate our lives with Him. Our agreement with God gradually replaces the agreements with darkness if we are diligent.

THE EGOTISM OF LUCIFER

God established Lucifer in authority. He created him beautiful and gave him unique privileges. Lucifer had the nature of a cherub and a body producing the most exquisite music and sounds.

But Lucifer thought he *was* what he only *did* and *had*. Lucifer's egotism mistakenly considered these qualities and privileges his possession to keep. He thought it was his permanent identity. So he rebelled against God, believing he would be unaffected.

He was confident: after ascending God's throne, he would keep his beautiful gemstone covering in gold filigree. Lucifer believed his authority and control would

JUST AS FOR US

God said to the fallen Lucifer, *I established you.* Psalm 100:3 applies it to us: *It is He who has made us, and not we ourselves.* In His lament, God reminds Lucifer, "you didn't establish yourself—I did."

What you are is what God has made you. What you can be is what God has said you can be. Whether you become that, He has left to your choice. You co-operate with Him or argue with Him.

continues on next page

Each of us can resist agreement with who He made us. We can idealize ourselves using satanic ideas filtered through our culture and education. God responds by blocking our progress to fulfillment and potential.

We can yield to Him and cooperate with His idea of who we are. This actualizes God's intent for you. To prevent this, the kingdom of darkness manipulates us, and we tolerate it in exchange for what they offer.

continue unchanged. He was confident—but he was wrong.

In fact, Lucifer's anointing was solely because God established him. Just as Jerusalem and the Jews had to learn: an anointing from God is not a permanent possession, not even for the Temple itself (Jeremiah 7:14).

His angelic qualities were not his own possession. Just as he undervalued the privilege of God's direct presence, Lucifer also disdained God's establishment. He didn't believe that God could change it.

Now, this egotistical usurper has only one chapter describing his splendid body—Ezekiel 28—and not even by name.

His given name, *Lucifer*, appears only in one place in the entire Bible, our next chapter's topic. We would not even know his original name if not for that. The once preeminent Lucifer now has no name. He is known only by his function: satan, or accuser. His newfound obscurity must grate the egotist who considered himself qualified to replace God.

THE BESPOILING OF LUCIFER

God judged Lucifer's *violence within*, and Lucifer gained two vastly distinct qualities.

Therefore I cast you as a profane thing
Out of the mountain of God;
And I destroyed you, O covering cherub,
From the midst of the fiery stones. (28:16)

Therefore I brought fire from your midst;
It devoured you,
And I turned you to ashes upon the earth
In the sight of all who saw you. (28:18)

40

Instead of alluring trading partners with his appearance, he profanely repulsed them. The fiery stones on which he once walked were now in the midst of him—a new part of his nature. Ezekiel, hearing this, could understand why God sorrowfully lamented this loss.

Once Lucifer walked those guardian stones, free to come and go as he pleased. Now he burns eternally from their fire within him. God made that fire an inescapable element of Lucifer's fallen nature. He was laid before kings, a serpent, a spectacle to be gazed upon, a horror to all who see (28:19).

In the place of his lovely music, he can only lie. He can only seduce with alluring speech. Jesus described Lucifer in John 8:44 when He confronted the Jewish leaders.

> You are of your father the devil, and the desires of your father you want to do. He was a murderer from the beginning, and does not stand in the truth, because there is no truth in him. When he speaks a lie, he speaks from his own resources, for he is a liar and the father of it.

THE TIME OF TWO KINGDOMS

When Lucifer was bespoiled by God, his ambitions did not cease. Thus, two kingdoms now existed where only one had been. The newly demoted satan, meaning accuser, brought his angelic nature from his former home, deformed by the fire within his midst. All his perfection was thenceforth dedicated to ruination. "*The thief does not come except to steal, and to kill, and to destroy.*" (John 10:10a). His will to sin became a fixed part of his nature; his ambition to dominate only grew.

John Milton wrote three lines in *Paradise Lost, Book I*, which capture satan's ambition to dominate.

> The mind is its own place, and in itself

> Can make a Heaven of Hell, a Hell of Heaven….
> Better to reign in Hell than serve in Heaven.

Now we know the fifth reason God laments the fate of Lucifer in Ezekiel 28. The mighty gatekeeper is cast out of heaven, exiled upon the Earth, consumed by fire within, and turned into ashes as a spectacle on the ground. Lucifer's original splendor was replaced with repugnance. He was now a horror and a dread under the rubber-necking gaze of his partner kings. What he thought his identity was now stripped from him. All that Lucifer once was, became darkness, fire, shame, and a horror.

Thus began the kingdom of darkness.

Discussion and reflection questions for Chapter Three can be found in the Reader Engagement Resources

---

CHAPTER FOUR

THE SIN OF LUCIFER

God revealed the source of Lucifer's sin. "*By the abundance of your trading You became filled with violence within*" (Ezekiel 28:16). But the prophecy doesn't define the violence, nor include his name and his partners. The Holy Spirit closes those gaps through Isaiah's prophecy in chapter 14.

THE WHY

Lucifer tried to replace God, and he had partners: that's what Isaiah 14 adds. Isaiah also specified the violence. *The anointed cherub who covers* acted to replace heaven's ruler, usurp God's position, and become God Himself. For his effort he became not God, but satan.

Why do we need to know this? Because satan still keeps trying to defeat God. To reclaim His Earth from the exiled satan, God created people as land-based mortal humans. The serpent despises the poor in spirit like us, and endeavors to replace us as Earth's rulers.

SAME FOR US

It's also why God was so emphatic to warn the Israelites, and us, about avoiding idol worship. We fall prey to those same heavenly beings who would compete with God in His exalted sovereignty. We'll explore this in more depth when we come to the heavenly events at Mt. Sinai.

Our enemy is sneaky now. The biblical knowledge of their needs and habits helps us withstand them. We do not want to be unaware of the devil's schemes.

Their bodies are now consumed with inexhaustible divine fire, so satan and his minions seek cooling relief. All moisture is consumed by the fire God put in them; to cool themselves, water is necessary. We will soon see this craving in many Scriptures: it's their only way to palliate their fiery inner torment. Human beings (like you and me) are water-based, and enemies see in us the moisture they crave. And if they can't be god of God, at least they want to be god of people.

Knowing the origin of the devil and his unseen partners enables our vigilance against his violence.

THE VIOLENCE

To reveal Lucifer's violence to Isaiah, God uses a type: the king of Babylon. Like the rulers of Tyre in Ezekiel, these empire-builders presumed themselves divine, making them a useful type for Lucifer. *"Your heart is lifted up, and you say, 'I am a god'"* (Ezekiel 28:2).

In Isaiah 14:12–17, God is the speaker and names Lucifer in His introductory exclamation. Filled with the emotion of contrast, the Lord again laments what the anointed cherub has become. Jesus revealed to John in Revelation 20 that satan would be locked up for 1,000 years. This prophetic look-back of Isaiah 14 describes the devil's current condition at the end of that millennium. It summarizes the cause of that fall and ends with quotes from satan's longtime subordinates.

How you are fallen from heaven,
O Lucifer, son of the morning!
How you are cut down to the ground,
You who weakened the nations!
For you have said in your heart:
'I will ascend into heaven,
I will exalt my throne above the stars of God;
I will also sit on the mount of the congregation
On the farthest sides of the north;
I will ascend above the heights of the clouds,
I will be like the Most High.'
Yet you shall be brought down to Sheol
To the lowest depths of the Pit.

Those who see you will gaze at you,
And consider you, saying:
'Is this the man who made the earth tremble,
Who shook kingdoms,
Who made the world as a wilderness
And destroyed its cities,
Who did not open the house of his prisoners?' (Isaiah 14:12–17)

In Ezekiel 28, the lament voices five divinity claims by the rebel. Likewise in Isaiah 14, five times God's lament cites Lucifer's ambition to replace Him:

I will ascend into heaven. I will exalt my throne above the stars of God. I will also sit on the mount of the congregation. I will ascend above the heights of the clouds. I will be like the Most High.

God perceived the poison purpose in Lucifer's heart: "*For you have said in your heart.*" He identifies the archangel's sin as a long-standing purpose—not merely a mood, whim, or passing thought.

THE OPPOSITE

BACKFIRE

Seriously? More qualified than God Himself? What seems nonsensical to us was persuasive enough to a third of the angels.

We must beware of minimizing the threat of pride's deception. That's why Jesus's Beatitudes pronounce the blessing for the poor in spirit, the mourning, and the meek—not the qualified, the capable, or the rich in spirit.

Where God's supremacy prompted Lucifer to think *I, I, I,* the holy angels think *You, You, You.* The Bible reveals their attitude and focus. Contrast Lucifer with the holy angels, in the Bible's largest recorded angel party with shepherds.

How mysterious it must have been to the holy angels to witness God Himself becoming a newborn baby human. The devil's jealousy raged, but these loyal angels burst into unified rejoicing about God's good will and favor upon mankind. Now, that same baby human would open *great joy to all people*—the same joy which the angels themselves felt.

And behold, an angel of the Lord stood before them, and the glory of the Lord shone around them, and they were greatly afraid. Then the angel said to them, "Do not be afraid, for behold, I bring you good tidings of great joy which will be to all people … .

And suddenly there was with the angel a multitude of the heavenly host praising God and saying:

"Glory to God in the highest,
And on earth peace, goodwill toward men!" (Luke 2:9–14)

Our song might begin with God meeting our needs or fixing our problems. The holy angels' song is about *Glory to God*. You, You, You—their song reveals their attention. The fallen satan burns with his jealousy of God's position. In contrast, the angels' joy is in God, His identity, and His favor.

The attitude of the holy angels is acutely clear in the archangel Gabriel (once Lucifer's colleague). One day, fifteen months before Jesus was born, aged Zacharias was the serving priest in the Temple. Gabriel appeared to him there and declared God's answer to their past prayers for a son. Although post-menopausal in age, Elizabeth his wife would become pregnant and bear a boy—the future John the Baptist.

But the old priest had a greater faith in the scientific evidence than Gabriel standing before him. He believed in his age, or sexual inabilities. If their physical intimacy was entirely in the past, they might even have stopped praying for a child.

This doubt was a subtle idolatry of the natural. It earned Zacharias a rare rebuke from an archangel.

But our attention is on Gabriel. He had been Lucifer's counterpart, yet none of Lucifer's violence was in Gabriel. His rebuke to Zacharias exhibited none of Lucifer's *I will* pride. He neither insulted nor punished the old priest. Instead, Gabriel gave him the proof that his skepticism wanted: muteness until the boy was born.

Movie angels might amp up their angelic nature, holiness, or raw power; they might shine brighter or talk in a deep bass with sound effects. Gabriel bases his credibility not on his archangel nature, but on Who he stands before, and Who sent him.

And the angel answered and said to him, "I am Gabriel, who stands in the presence of God, and was sent to speak to you and bring you these glad tidings. But behold, you will be mute and not able to speak until the day these things take place, because you did not believe my words which will be fulfilled in their own time." (Luke 1:19–20)

We see the angels' attitudes again when Apostle John recorded the worship in heaven. The violent *I-wills* of Lucifer and his partners are not present. The holy angels have an opposite attitude; their eyes are not on themselves, nor even upon us who are saved by Jesus. They have eyes for One only.

"Holy, holy, holy,
Lord God Almighty,
Who was and is and is to come!"

"You are worthy, O Lord,
To receive glory and honor and power;
For You created all things,
And by Your will they exist and were created."

"Worthy is the Lamb who was slain
To receive power and riches and wisdom,
And strength and honor and glory and blessing!"

"Blessing and honor and glory and power
Be to Him who sits on the throne,
And to the Lamb, forever and ever!"
(Revelation 4:8, 11, 5:9, 12, 13)

The unseen hosts of heaven are the opposite of Lucifer's prideful rebellion. We must also be the opposite of that *I will* ambition. With discernment for these opposites, we can identify who's who. When the *I will* of darkness exhibits itself in a Christian's heart, your *You, You* toward God can rise to replace it. Our love for Him exposes our *I, I, I*—and we can repent, unlike satan.

THE PENALTY

In his ambition, Lucifer imagined himself on God's throne. But instead of his ascent above the heights, God will lower him—not merely into the Pit, but to the lowest depths of the Pit. Isaiah is describing the end of time, and according to Revelation 20, God uses two stages to consign the fallen Lucifer to the Pit.

Revelation 20:3 reveals the first stage, which is both a partial and temporary enforcement. An unnamed angel throws Lucifer (now satan) into the waterless Pit. For 1,000 years he will remain there, unable to influence humanity. The millennial reign of Christ and the undying martyrs ensues. Not everyone is saved, but in the absence of the kingdom of darkness, people obey His rule.

The second stage begins with satan's final temporary release after the millennium. He will organize his greatest army in Earth's history. The vast majority of people then living will join him. Despite all the benefits of Jesus' rule, they will believe satan offers a better deal. The last war of satan's rebellion will take place, but will end in the devil's defeat forever.

That's when the eternal condemnation of Lucifer begins in Revelation 20:10. The lake of fire—different from the Pit but also waterless—becomes satan's eternal prison. With him in that hell will be everyone who declined to believe the gospel and respond with repentance and meekness.

In Isaiah 14:15, for that future enforcement, God uses the future tense: *you shall be brought down.*

TIMING

Isaiah 14 is God's address to satan just before the last rebellion in Revelation 20:7–8. But presently, the devil is not in that Pit. Instead, satan is a roaring lion, prowling the earth (1 Peter 5:8)—on our linear timeline.

The always-NOW of heaven is in play; God speaks from His timelessness into our time. On our calendar, Ezekiel 28 revealed when the unspoiled Lucifer was in God's Eden. That was before our creation, because he was already fallen when tempting Adam and Eve in their Eden.

God says in Isaiah 14 that satan weakened the nations, which only existed after the Tower of Babel in Genesis 11. In the past tense, God describes what satan has been doing ever since that nation-formation. His mockers in Sheol also use the past tense—*made the earth tremble, shook kingdoms, made the world as a wilderness and destroyed its cities* (14:16–17)

On our calendar, Isaiah 14 reveals Lucifer after that career of oppression and violence, and shortly before his eternal judgment. God shows us a time when satan's thousand-year imprisonment has just ended. From the time perspective of Isaiah 14, the next event is satan's last gasp effort (Revelation 20:7–8). After that, he will be a spectacle to all he once oppressed.

Those who see you will gaze at you, and consider you, saying: 'Is this the man who made the earth tremble, who shook kingdoms, who made the world as a wilderness and destroyed its cities, who did not open the house of his prisoners?' (Isaiah 14:16–17)

SATAN'S DEFIANCE CONTINUES

God replaced the cherub's original glorious nature with eternal consumption by the fiery stones. He also cast Lucifer to earth from the mountain of God. Yet these penalties did not suppress the devilish ambition. Instead, he defies God's judgment and continues to pursue his purpose: to replace God.

Hail horrours, hail
Infernal world, and thou profoundest Hell
Receive thy new Possessor: One who brings
A mind not to be chang'd by Place or Time.
The mind is its own place, and in it self
Can make a Heav'n of Hell, a Hell of Heav'n . . .

With rallied Arms to try what may be yet
Regaind in Heav'n, or what more lost in Hell?
(John Milton, *Paradise Lost*, Lines 221-270)

Jesus stated the devil comes to *steal, kill, and destroy*, hating the grace and mercy of God upon mankind. In stark relief, Jesus wants people to have abundant, overflowing life (John 10:10; cf 7:38–39). Just like us, Jesus had read Isaiah 14:12–17, one source of His knowledge about the devil.

God wants reconciliation with people. He takes costly actions to make it possible. In contrast, Lucifer intimidates, destroys, and imprisons people.

God desires for people to prosper and reproduce His image. He commanded us: "*be fruitful and multiply; fill the earth and subdue it*" (Genesis 1:28). He rejoices in men filling the earth with His productivity. But satan instead transforms *the world as a wilderness and destroys its cities.*

GOD TURNS THE TABLES

God seeks the fallen. The pattern of satan is far different: "*who did not open the house of his prisoners*" (Isaiah 14:17). God's productivity is part of our created nature but it threatens the stifling sovereignty of satan. To protect his power, the devil isolates people as prisoners he won't let go.

This explains satan's history of hatred for us. Our race of beings is painful for Lucifer and his allies. They tried to replace God and use ruling power to their liking, but they were cast out. To their horror, the seats they once held are now filled with a new race, the frailest of all: human beings.

BACKFIRE

Throughout the nine-book *Unseen* Series, we find this very frequent habit of our God. If anything is predictable, it is God refusing service to expectations, turning the tables, and flipping evil on its own head.

In people, God turns the tables and defies every heavenly expectation. He replaces the strong with the weak and the proud with the humble. He rewards the poor in spirit, the mourning, and the meek. No one feels it so acutely as satan.

Hannah sang about the topsy-turvy of God in her song (1 Samuel 2:1–10). Zacharias, repenting after the birth of John the Baptist, sang it as well (Luke 1:57–69). Mary also saw God's upside-down habits when the Son of God was a baby in her womb; she sang this praise.

> He has shown strength with His arm;
> He has scattered the proud in the imagination of their hearts.
> He has put down the mighty from their thrones,
> And exalted the lowly.
> He has filled the hungry with good things,
> And the rich He has sent away empty. (Luke 1:51–53)

Second Peter 1:4 must hurt the devil for the same reason. Lucifer was the proud, the mighty, the rich that Mary sang about. He attempted to replace God, assuming mistakenly that his preeminence was his nature. In fact, it was not his to keep nor his permanent possession; God alone established his exalted nature. Turning the tables on the high and mighty rebel, God exalts us, the meek and the lowly. Through our faith in His gospel promises, He gives us birth as living spirits—privileged to partake in the divine nature. The throne which the mighty Lucifer attempted to get by force, is ours by God's gift.

> By which have been given to us exceedingly great and precious promises, that through these you may be partakers of the divine nature.

LUCIFER BECOMES SATAN

God created Lucifer as the very seal of perfection. This is stated of no other being, angel or man. What happened? Some flaw in Lucifer overwhelmed his anointing for perfection.

Lucifer had exquisite qualities, but these did not prevent his fall. The Scripture reveals that being the seal of perfection included neither moral excellence nor integrity. Instead, his superiority was his beautiful nature of splendor.

> Your heart was lifted up because of your beauty; you corrupted your wisdom for the sake of your splendor. (Ezekiel 28:17)

Lucifer's perfect creation stopped where his will began. Make note: God's most exalted angel still had a free will for choices which God respects for eternity, just as He respects our choices. Lucifer misused his will to commit violence against the throne of God. Ever since, he wills to replace God.

Whatever perfection he had was limited to his nature. The corporeal and spiritual qualities of Lucifer were the limit of his perfection. It was an act of his will, pure and simple, that made him the eternal devil.

He still has the created angelic nature God gave him. That's why the Son of God actually dialogued with satan in the wilderness. Jesus did not insult or use dismissive speech. He affirmed the principle: do not dishonor what God once honored.

Lucifer has become satan, yet his failure does not excuse us from respecting God's original honor for him. In Ezekiel 25, God judged the nations for gloating after He punished Jerusalem. The same judgment awaits those who demean God's original beings, though fallen. It's why there was a Scripture for Paul to use when wicked Jewish leaders accused him in Acts 23:5. *"You shall not speak evil of a ruler of your people."*

Jude and Peter likewise caution us against dismissive disrespect for the fallen. It's worth repeating in our time when spiritual realities are dismissed as mythical fiction.

> Likewise also these dreamers defile the flesh, reject authority, and speak evil of dignitaries. Yet Michael the archangel, in contending with the devil, when he disputed about the body of Moses, dared not bring against him a reviling accusation, but said, "The Lord rebuke you!" (Jude 8–9)

Especially those who walk according to the flesh in the lust of uncleanness and despise authority. They are presumptuous, self-willed. They are not afraid to speak evil of dignitaries, whereas angels, who are greater in power and might, do not bring a reviling accusation against them before the Lord. (2 Peter 2:10–11)

STILL THAT WAY

God did not respond personally to Lucifer's original rebellion in heaven. Instead, He delegated to the archangel Michael (Revelation 12:7) who cast down the devil and his angels, all before our creation.

Since placing mankind on the earth, God does very little without our participation. The vast bulk of God's actions in the Bible are in partnership with man. We are the race created in His image to rule on His behalf.

God honors choice—a theme seen constantly in the *Unseen* Series. He desires that we, like Him, respect the choices of others—both the bad and the good.

In our time, respect for authority is at low ebb. Many Christians today also evidence disrespect for the angelic creation of satan and other rulers in the kingdom of darkness.

PATTERNS OF POWER

Lucifer's approach is to oppose power with power, to dominate with maximum power, and to imprison opponents. The original seedbed for this was his trading, where he did things for other angels and collected IOUs from them. We can deduce it was by such trading that he began using power over other beings to impose his will. His motto might have been, what good is power if you aren't using it *against* others?

God's approach, in contrast, could be called minimalist. His motto might be, what good is power if you aren't using it *with* others? No one is more able to impose His will sovereignly. Yet, He prefers to let mankind take part in what God wants done (Genesis 1:26ff). Chapter thirteen, "Unimaginably Bad" about Days Five and Six, will review that in more depth.

King Rehoboam manifested satan's pattern of power after succeeding his deceased father Solomon. The people's grievances required him to meet leaders from all twelve tribes of Israel. They wanted a reduction in forced labor conscriptions; these had skyrocketed for Solomon's building projects (1 Kings 12).

The wisest advisors listened to the people and advised Rehoboam to grant their request. "They are right, and if you lighten up, they'll serve you forever." But King Rehoboam also asked his young, hot-headed, and power-hungry friends. Their advice: "Show them you're in charge now! You'll lose power if you aren't hard."

Their advice resembled satan's motto: what's power for if you don't use it to control others? King Rehoboam's answer cost him the ten northern tribes. The kingdom that David built remained split until its final exile to Babylon in 587 BC, about 400 years later.

WHY WERE WE CREATED?

God totally dominates Lucifer and his dominion of darkness in the six days of creation. Chapter eleven will review this clearly in Scripture. Those six days culminated with our creation—six days you will never read in the old way again.

God created mortal humans for numerous reasons; studying them is of great value. One motive He had was so the Second Person of the Trinity could be born fully God and fully human. The Church of living human spirits was appointed to be His bride even before the foundation of the world. God's decrees when He alone existed are the subject of chapter eight.

As his replacements, we incite satan's jealousy and confirm his enemy status. The privilege of God's first partner will be ours. You might call it the world's first replacement warranty.

An excellent resource to explore eight biblical reasons that God created mankind is *Who Am I and Why Am I Here?* by Dr. Bill Hamon. For our purposes in this Book Three of the *Unseen* Series, the reason in focus is this: we are Lucifer's replacement.

God saw a virtue in replacing the fallen rebels with people. But He created us subject to sin; we are very costly for Him to love. How could that be beneficial? Lucifer, the seal of perfection, is replaced by us frail mortals; we are anything but perfect.

God uses His power minimally. He needs nothing, yet He creates beings for joint effort, to exercise power together on His behalf. What Lucifer sought to take by force, God willingly shares. What Lucifer was qualified to enjoy, our God gives to the unqualified. He created us that way, to see which of us will reciprocate His love. He cherishes the contrite heart and the penitent person with a will to repent toward God.

Yes, we are imperfect, mortal, and subject to sin. Our poverty of spirit deserves to be mourned. But in His hands, it is our primary qualification.

> For thus says the High and Lofty One
> Who inhabits eternity, whose name is Holy:
> "I dwell in the high and holy place,
> With him who has a contrite and humble spirit,
> To revive the spirit of the humble,
> And to revive the heart of the contrite ones." (Isaiah 57:15)

Jesus has now atoned for all our sin. The Holy God can live in the imperfect people He cherishes. Jesus' gift to His Church was the Holy Spirit's filling. With Him in us, we can respond to God as He deserves through the process of our lives.

> If anyone loves Me, he will keep My word; and My Father will love him, and We will come to him and make Our home with him. (John 14:23)

> For the eyes of the LORD run to and fro throughout the whole earth, to show Himself strong on behalf of those whose heart is loyal to Him. (2 Chronicles 16:9)

This befits those chosen "*before the foundation of the world*" (Ephesians 1:4), which we explore in chapter eight.

DEEP CONTRAST

Lucifer: perfect at his creation. Redeemed people: perfected in a process. Lucifer: established in the position due his perfect creation. Redeemed people: seated by grace in the heavenly realms as living human spirits. Lucifer become satan: unable to repent, unable to die. Redeemed people: dying after a process of perfecting repentance.

Satan: once privileged with fire, but now consuming fire is his judgment. Human beings: physically water-based, and surrounded by rivers supplying unending fertility. Satan: seeking coolness in the deep. The human race: land based.

No wonder Scripture calls attention to the jealousy and anger of the fallen Lucifer. What he sought by aggression, we receive freely. We who are low, God has raised into the heavenly realm; the exalted Lucifer, He has cast down to the lowest depth.

All this is public. All beings in the heavenly realms see Him do this. When they look at the thrones desired by Lucifer and his partners, they see only human beings—chief of which is Jesus in a resurrected human body.

> But God ... made us sit together in the heavenly places in Christ Jesus, that in the ages to come He might show the exceeding riches of His grace. (Ephesians 2.6–7)

Sadly, mankind rebelled like Lucifer had. For the first few thousand years of humanity, God responded by singling out people consecrated to His ways. That group included Abel, Enoch, Noah, then Abraham. From the line of Abraham, God chose a nation of people for consecration, including Joseph, David, the prophets, and remnant of Israel. God's choice of Israel as His vanguard against darkness comprises Book Five in the *Unseen* Series.

Finally came Jesus. He opened the door for vast numbers of humanity to follow as heirs—we who submit to Jesus Christ as Lord.

EXPLANATORY POWER

The explanatory power of these scriptural observations is very broad. Now we know why God created no more creatures in perfection, after Lucifer's failure. By creating people with freedom for good and bad choices, He preserved our ability to repent in meekness. Our consistent choices for sin are part of our imperfect creation. Thus, the Lamb was *"slain before the foundation of the world"* (Revelation 13:8), and the Holy Spirit is necessary for us to follow Christ (Joel 2:28–32).

It explains why the code key is poverty of spirit, not wealth of spirit like Lucifer's. God ordained this code key, and its meekness. With it, He induced the kingdom of darkness to engineer Jesus' crucifixion. They could not decipher any revelation that required poverty of spirit and its meek mourning. The enemies didn't know Jesus' death was the atonement that would release the Holy Spirit upon all flesh.

Had they known, they would not have crucified the Lord of glory. (1 Corinthians 2:8)

Originally, God welcomed Lucifer as the seal of perfection to tread around the throne, but with us—the poor in spirit—God does something even better. He lives in us.

And I will pray the Father, and He will give you another Helper, that He may abide with you forever—the Spirit of truth, whom the world cannot receive, because it neither sees Him nor knows Him; but you know Him, for He dwells with you and will be in you. (John 14:16–17)

Our focus has been on one enemy, the devil—the spoiled Lucifer, now become fire and malevolence. But Paul said we wrestle against rulers, plural, as we saw in chapter one. Where did Lucifer's partners come from? And what is his relationship with them?

Discussion and reflection questions for Chapter Four can be found in the Reader Engagement Resources

CHAPTER FIVE

REBEL PARTNERS

Ezekiel 28 identified Lucifer's trading as the origin of his iniquity. We used Tyre's commercial prowess to review how the archangel used IOUs in his widespread trading. As his pattern of power, Lucifer held those IOUs over others—but who? Angels would have been the only victims available prior to our creation.

We have seen God's description that satan has partners. But how? Some law or principle must govern how angelic beings can work together with satan. The devil and his partners have patterns in their relationships, but what are they?

The Bible reveals these governing laws of darkness, not by plain statement, but by presuming them. When we identify what Scripture presumes in its statements, we discover the principles of satan's kingdom. These discoveries must satisfy the test of Explanatory Power, providing a better explanation for what we read in Scripture and experience in our lives.

THE DEVIL IS JUST ONE

The devil has a body, as discussed thoroughly in chapters two and three. He is not omnipresent and can only be in one place at a time. Jesus tacitly affirmed this limitation in His letter to Pergamum. *"I know your works, and where you dwell, where Satan's throne is."* (Revelation 2:13) It's in a place, because satan, like us, is in one spot at a time and moves from place to place.

Peter's teaching cited previously also presumes the physical limit on satan. The devil walks about in his body, one place at a time.

Be sober, be vigilant; because your adversary the devil walks about like a roaring lion, seeking whom he may devour. Resist him, steadfast in the faith, knowing that the same sufferings are experienced by your brotherhood in the world. (1 Peter 5:8–9)

Our lexicon as Christians includes phrases such as "satan attacked me;" comedian Flip Wilson coined the phrase, "the devil made me do it." We quickly blame our personal troubles on the devil. Such thinking believes that we individually are satan's primary occupation.

We must also believe—falsely—that satan is everywhere all the time, like God. If satan is the only perpetrator, we must also believe that satan is omnipresent.

Neither of those beliefs is true. Peter said that the same suffering affects every Christian in the world. With a physical body limiting him to one place at a time, satan requires partners to conduct his worldwide stealing, killing, and destroying.

Someone tempted or troubled is right to identify evil as the cause, but it is unlikely to be the devil himself. In fact, only three people in the Bible have direct interaction with satan: David, Jesus, and Judas. Even Apostle Paul's thorn in the flesh was only a messenger from satan.

Peter describes a global devouring. To cause Christians' worldwide suffering, the kingdom of darkness has to use a delegation system. The prowling satan requires partners. It's the only explanation that reconciles the global presence of evil with God's exclusive omnipresence.

PARTNERS IN REBELLION

Revelation 12:3–4 symbolically reveals Lucifer had partners in his rebellion. When Lucifer's partners were expelled with him from God's courts, heaven's population decreased by thirty-three percent.

And another sign appeared in heaven: behold, a great, fiery red dragon having seven heads and ten horns, and seven diadems on his heads. His tail drew a third of the stars of heaven and threw them to the earth.

We saw in chapter three that Lucifer was reshaped and his body re-formed with fire, because of his iniquity. But he was not the only angelic being to suffer these alterations. Using the image of stars, Revelation 12:4 signifies that a third of the angels fell with Lucifer.

HOW TO READ THE BOOK OF REVELATION

It's important to note: John recorded Revelation—he didn't author it. The book is organized by Jesus, whose angel led the apostle through its cascading flow of visions. His authorship is stated very clearly in the first two sentences of the book.

The Revelation of Jesus Christ, which God gave Him to show His servants—things which must shortly take place. And He sent and signified it by His angel to His servant John, who bore witness to the word of God, and to the testimony of Jesus Christ, to all things that he saw. (Revelation 1:1–2)

Commentators over the centuries have handled this book in wild ways. For example, in our lifetime, a well-respected scholar argued that Revelation was written not by John the Apostle, but by John the Baptist.

To make sense of John's Revelation requires meekness which knowledge and study cannot supply. As discussed in Book Two, God's Word is in code, and the code key is not alphabetical, but attitudinal. The devil and his partners are eminently knowledgeable, with millennia of experience in deception. But they cannot mimic meek humility, or any of the Beatitudes.

The book of Revelation is an encrypted communication. As with any good cryptography, God's enemies act upon their misinterpretation—exposing their enemy stance.

Jesus intended this, as He said in Revelation 22:11.

THEIR END COMETH

It doesn't help our understanding that we've been led to think, wrongly, that Revelation provides a timeline for the end of all things. While there are clear sequences established for some events it describes, the time, the identity, and the expected manifestation are unclear. In fact, the end of the world is portrayed more than three times. The Millennial Reign of Christ, around which so many divisions among Christians have centered, receives only two verses.

He who is unjust, let him be unjust still; he who is filthy, let him be filthy still; he who is righteous, let him be righteous still; he who is holy, let him be holy still.

We have anxiety about the events of our times; the anxious search for security seduces us to squeeze Revelation into our boxes. We sometimes act like children, unable to say, "I don't know," so we make up some answer to explain what God reveals in it.

This betrays a lack of meekness. Revelation came from the mind of Jesus, who organized His revelation as He saw fit. If anything, the book of Jesus' revelation shows how much higher are His thoughts than ours (Isaiah 55:8).

> It is the glory of God to conceal a matter, but the glory of kings to search it out a matter. (Proverbs 25:2)

The book of Revelation is about specific future events. But God designed it perfectly to conceal what the events are. But after they occur, we will say, "So that's what Revelation was talking about!"

No one who is damned for eternity will be able to claim, "I never knew!" Jesus revealed Revelation so we would know what is coming and submit to Jesus at any cost. That's why Jesus assures overcomers: every cost we pay will be made right.

OUTLINE OF REVELATION

Chapters 1–3 are the letters of Jesus to seven specific churches, but why? In Jesus' mind, His letters fit with a book which reveals what is about to happen. These letters teach how the Lord Jesus judges, punishes, and rewards both churches and Christians. First Peter 4:17 says that judgment begins with the household of God, and the seven letters exemplify that.

Chapters 4–5 describe the worship in heaven. Jesus is the Lamb slain from the foundation of the world. When he takes the seven-sealed scroll from the Father's hand, it initiates the cascade of events.

In chapters 6–7, He breaks seal by seal. Although never unrolled, its contents never "read," the scroll releases events of disaster upon the earth—culminating in the end of the world (Revelation 6:17).

Chapters 8–11 uses seven trumpets to repeat a sequence resulting in the end of the world (11:15–19). A break from these cyclic retellings comprises chapters 12–15, describing the war in heaven, the birth of God's people, the expulsion of satan from heaven, and the spillover of heaven's war onto earth.

Chapters 16–18 uses seven bowls to reveal the third telling of the end-time events. This cycle includes the demolition of our system of trading, symbolized by Babylon in Revelation 17–18.

Finally, chapters 19–20 tell of the penultimate battle, and the last 1,000 years of earth. After these, God's enemies mount a massive ultimate attack—but God sends fire which devours them (20:7–9). After their failed assault, God's enemies receive a complete, total, and permanent punishment in the lake of fire.

Chapters 21–22 close the book. Apostle John sees the completely new heavens and earth, with full communication between the two. All the saved overcomers are in God's direct company. So dramatically different is the new, our longtime standbys are no longer needed—the sun and the moon.

THE WAR IN HEAVEN

The contextual overview gives "the 30,000 foot view" of God's revelation to John. The war in heaven fits into that big picture. He wants us capable to serve as Jesus' soldiers, and thinks we need to know what happened before the creation of human beings. We want to fight knowledgeably at His side. Apostle Paul wrote, *"lest satan should take advantage of us, for we are not ignorant of his devices."* (2 Corinthians 2:11). That's why God revealed more details in Revelation 12.

Now a great sign appeared in heaven: a woman clothed with the sun, with the moon under her feet, and on her head a garland of twelve stars. Then being with child, she cried out in labor and in pain to give birth.

And another sign appeared in heaven: behold, a great, fiery red dragon having seven heads and ten horns, and seven diadems on his heads. His tail drew a third of the stars of heaven and threw them to the earth. And the dragon stood before the woman who was ready to give birth, to devour her Child as soon as it was born. She bore a male Child who was to rule all nations with a rod of iron. And her Child was caught up to God and His throne. Then the woman fled into the wilderness, where she has a place prepared by God, that they should feed her there one thousand two hundred and sixty days.

And war broke out in heaven: Michael and his angels fought with the dragon; and the dragon and his angels fought, but they did not prevail, nor was a place found for them in heaven any longer. So the great dragon was cast out, that serpent of old, called the Devil and

Satan, who deceives the whole world; he was cast to the earth, and his angels were cast out with him. (Revelation 12:1–9)

This symbolic passage expresses actual truth about actual events. The woman giving birth obviously correlates to Jesus' mother, Mary. Clothed in sun with the moon for her footstool, a global impact is conveyed. Thus, this symbol has long been interpreted as the birthing of God's people.

Jesus, as the first-born (Romans 8:29), is the "*male Child who was to rule all nations with a rod of iron*"—fulfilling the Messianic Psalm 2:9. He will delegate His authority to His Church, which is why Jesus used the Greek word *ekklesia* ("ruling assembly") wherever you read the word *church*. In his name, we will judge the angels and the nations on His behalf (1 Corinthians 6:2–3).

COMING FEATURES

In Book Nine of the *Unseen* Series, *Nobody Sees This Victory Yet: The Destruction of Darkness*, we will see the one time that Jesus Himself leads the fight.

God does not deign to fight against the rebels. Verse 7 tells who does all the fighting: "*And war broke out in heaven: Michael and his angels fought with the dragon; and the dragon and his angels fought.*" Lucifer is contesting God's position of Lord of all, but God takes no action in the war of Revelation 12.

This is appropriate. God's exalted worth as the Lord of everything means that fighting a created contestant is beneath His dignity. Instead, Michael and his angels do all the fighting. By this test, the holy angels prove their willingness to fight their angelic companions, and their loyalty to God's exalted preeminence.

TWO TIME REALMS

For us, time is linear, sequential, and directional. Ezekiel 28 says God cast Lucifer out of heaven before creating us people. But in this passage, the order is reversed. First, the baby Jesus is born of a woman, and afterward comes the war in heaven with the rebels' expulsion. The solution to this puzzle of time sequence is the eternal NOW. Chapter eight, *Before the Foundation of the World*, explores the NOW in the Bible.

We memorialize Jesus' birth on our holiday calendar. Like Good Friday and Easter, we commemorate the historical events of our faith. But with the symbols of Revelation 12, God reveals these actual occurrences are not only in our linear timeline. They also occur eternally—in the NOW of the timeless unseen realm.

THE DRAGON SWAPS PLACES

The passage specifies the dragon's identity. He is *"that serpent of old"* from Genesis 3; he symbolizes the devil and satan. Revelation 12:8–9 describes four explicit consequences of his rebellion.

First, after they lost the war against God, Apostle John records, *"nor was a place found for them in heaven any longer."* This cannot mean God permanently barred them from heavenly realms. The Bible reveals they still interact with God's realm.

For example, satan continues presenting himself to God, in Job chapters 1–3. The prophet Zechariah sees satan accusing the high priest Joshua in God's presence (Zechariah 3:1). Jesus assumes this as well, warning that satan asked God's permission to sift Peter (Luke 22:31). And as we saw, Paul names them *"spiritual forces of wickedness in the heavenly realms."*

If not the heavenly realms, what place are they deprived of? The Greek word gives the answer: no place of honor was found for them any longer. Verse eight uses the word τόπος, transliterated *topos*. (Our word topographical uses it, meaning "writing of places.")

Jesus chose the same word in John 14:2, *"I go to prepare a place* (topos) *for you."* Places at a feast are another time He uses *topos*—and does so with multiple meanings.

> So He told a parable to those who were invited, when He noted how they chose the best places, saying to them: "When you are invited by anyone to a wedding feast, do not sit down in the best place, lest one more honorable than you be invited by him; and he who invited you and him come and say to you, 'Give place to this man,' and then you begin with shame to take the lowest place. But when you are invited, go and sit down in the lowest place, so that when he who invited you comes he may say to you, 'Friend, go up higher.' Then you will have glory in the presence of those who sit at the table with you. For whoever exalts himself will be humbled, and he who humbles himself will be exalted." (Luke 14:7–11)

Jesus' selection of the parable was not random. The feast guests esteemed themselves so highly they chose the best place. Likewise, these angelic rebels sought the highest places in heaven. But God said, *Give place to this man.* They lost their place of privilege in heaven.

Fallen people are in the least place, but He saves those who are willing. He moved human beings up to the places forfeited by His angelic enemies. With shame, they *take the lowest place.* In stark contrast, *we have glory in the presence of those who sit at the table with you.*

Ephesians 2:6 and Zechariah 3:7 affirm this replacement.

THEIR END COMETH

Again we see that the previous, angelic occupants who rebelled against God were expelled from their τόπος places, and replacing them, we the meek and humble are lifted up to take their τόπος places. As Mary sang in Luke 1:52, *He has put down the mighty from their thrones, and exalted the lowly.*

The theme repeats: the home they forfeited is becoming ours.

[God] raised us up together, and made us sit together in the heavenly places in Christ Jesus.

If you will walk in My ways,
And if you will keep My command,
Then you shall also judge My house,
And likewise have charge of My courts;
I will give you places to walk
Among these who stand here.

To us, He says, *Friend, go up higher.*

THE DRAGON'S NEW PLACE

Second, Revelation 12 affirms Ezekiel 28. When God cast out satan from heaven, where did he go? The unwelcome news is that satan was cast to Earth. That's where God next creates us—right in the devil's new domain.

Being cast down and prowling Earth aligns with the typological revelation in Ezekiel 28 and Isaiah 14. Peter describes this in 1 Peter 5:8. *"Your adversary the devil walks about like a roaring lion, seeking whom he may devour."* Lions devour by killing, chewing, and ingesting. But the devil devours using a roaring deception.

THE DRAGON'S NEW WORK

The third statement about the dragon: he is satan *who deceives the whole world.* The apostles warned frequently about deceivers. Jesus prophesied in Matthew 7:15 about wolves in sheep's clothing who came to Christians and churches to deceive them.

It's justifiable to say satan deceived the whole world from Genesis 3 alone, as Paul teaches in Romans 5:12–19. All of us were in the DNA of Adam and Eve; by deceiving them, he deceived us all. But deception has characterized all satan's strategies to protect his dominion over Earth.

Jesus described the devil as *the father of lies* and permitted no excuse for the religious leaders who followed his deception (John 8:44). So deceived were they, Jesus could call the devil their father without any argument from them.

The devil's skill as a deceiving liar is clear throughout history, and even after Jesus reigns personally on Earth. For one thousand years, Christians will live without death, ruling the world on His behalf. Simultaneously, satan suffers a thousand-year lockup, absent and ultimately forgotten.

> He [an unnamed angel] laid hold of the dragon, that serpent of old, who is the Devil and Satan, and bound him for a thousand years; and he cast him into the bottomless pit, and shut him up, and set a seal on him, so that he should deceive the nations no more till the thousand years were finished. But after these things he must be released for a little while.
>
> And I saw thrones, and they sat on them, and judgment was committed to them. Then I saw the souls of those who had been beheaded … And they lived and reigned with Christ for a thousand years. (Revelation 20:2–4)

Even after satan's long absence, and despite the worldwide blessings of Christ's reign, all humankind falls prey to his deceptive prowess. He tricks our entire mortal race into joining his attack upon the few remaining Christians huddled in Jerusalem.

> Now when the thousand years have expired, Satan will be released from his prison and will go out to deceive the nations which are in the four corners of the earth, Gog and Magog, to gather them together to battle, whose number is as the sand of the sea. They went up on the breadth of the earth and surrounded the camp of the saints and the beloved city. (Revelation 20:7–8)

The devil's skill at deceiving couldn't be clearer.

THE DEVIL'S NEW PARTNERS

Jesus spoke about *"the devil and his angels"* (Matthew 25:41). That partner association is the fourth revelation of Revelation 12:8–9. *"His angels were cast out with him."* As John watches, he sees *"His tail drew a third of the stars of heaven and threw them to the earth"* (12:4). This has long been interpreted as the third of heaven's angels who joined Lucifer's rebellion.

They are on Earth now, but where? The Bible's teaching is they rule nations under satan. Nation-claiming by fallen angels receives full attention in Book Four of the *Unseen* Series, titled *Nobody Sees These Enemies: How to Discern and Disarm Unseen Tempters*.

Most nations named in Ezekiel's journal no longer exist. Why did the Holy Spirit inspire these chapters and preserve them for us today? Because studying them reveals how the hierarchy of darkness works.

God judged Ammon, Moab, Edom, and Philistia in Ezekiel 25. Tyre occupies chapters 26–27. Egypt receives the next four. God describes each nation's offense as if they were a unit. Each people group expressed one identity because they are types for satan's rebel-partners.

These behaviors befit the principalities who serve satan. That's why God preserved the prophecies about ancient nations that have disappeared—nations claimed by fallen rebels. Their personal reactions to the fall of Jerusalem voiced the glee of their angelic dominators. For example, Ammon's principality saw opportunity in Judah's destruction and exile.

> Because you said, 'Aha!' against My sanctuary when it was profaned, and against the land of Israel when it was desolate, and against the house of Judah when they went into captivity … Because you clapped your hands, stamped your feet, and rejoiced in heart with all your disdain for the land of Israel. (Ezekiel 25:3, 6)

HOW LUCIFER RECRUITED REBEL PARTNERS

In Ezekiel 28, Isaiah 14, and Revelation 12, the Holy Spirit reveals satan's origin. We've seen Lucifer's heavy-handed, self-exalting behaviors. In Isaiah 14 God illuminates the partners' resentment for satan. How does such an oppressive behavior win allies? Why did they ever join him?

Angels are very sensitive to obligations. Honor is the code of conduct for both holy and fallen angels. Book Eight of the *Unseen* Series, *Nobody Sees These Friends: Partners in the Unseen*, explores this sensitivity in depth.

With facts from Scripture, we have proposed that Lucifer would bind angels with IOUs. They would be obligated, and their angelic honor activated. Lucifer called in those IOUs when he arose against God. The angels who owed him joined him.

People do this when blackmailed into unexpected cooperation with sinister crooks. With the devil also, we fall into obligations through his deceptive tricks. Afterward, he and his partners can manipulate us like puppets. It's no leap of logic to surmise that any angels who gave him an IOU would find it being used against them.

This method is pictured in Absalom's rebellion. He had a devilish recruitment plan to convert King David's loyal subjects into his rebels. The covering cherub's pitch was like Absalom's. We can reverse engineer satan's recruiting habit.

> After this it happened that Absalom provided himself with chariots and horses, and fifty men to run before him. Now Absalom would rise early and stand beside the way to the gate. So it was, whenever anyone who had a lawsuit came to the king for a decision, that Absalom would call to him and say, "What city are you from?" And he would say, "Your servant is from such and such a tribe of Israel." Then Absalom would say to him, "Look, your case is good and right; but there is no deputy of the king to hear you." Moreover Absalom would say, "Oh, that I were made judge in the land, and everyone who has any suit or cause would come to me; then I would give him justice." And so it was, whenever anyone came near to bow down to him, that he would put out his hand and take him and kiss him. In this manner Absalom acted toward all Israel who came to the king for judgment. So Absalom stole the hearts of the men of Israel. (2 Samuel 15:2–6).

Israelites brought lawsuits to David. Similarly, angels desired admission to God on His throne. To get it, they had to deal with the covering cherub, Lucifer. Absalom sat in the gate and intercepted the supplicant Israelites. He stole the hearts of David's subjects with promises of better treatment. It's easy to picture Lucifer promising angels a better treatment than they could get from God. In fact, Lucifer's *I will* assertions in Isaiah 14 resemble sales promises.

Imagine the conversations in his many sanctuaries, like campaign promises. "Join me. I'll sit on God's mountain, go where I want, and you will be my chief officials." Thinking Lucifer would win, these rebel partners expected patronage jobs. They would be his lieutenants throughout heaven. "Once Lucifer is God, I'll have access because he owes me for helping him."

Ezekiel 28 describes events and relationships prior to the creation of people. Yet verses 17 and 19 refer to kings and peoples. Who were they? Interpretation with this grid identifies them: they are the angels to whom Lucifer had promised rulership, and the angels those subordinates might have recruited.

In his sanctuaries distant from the fiery stones on the mountain of God, Lucifer thought his nascent rebellion would remain secret. He stupidly disdained the omniscience of God.

The Bible doesn't reveal satan's partners with propositions but with pictures and patterns. This template of interpretation provides significant explanatory power for many Scriptures.

THE DISCIPLES THOUGHT IN IOUs

The disciples showed the same IOU pattern of thought. They wanted to help Jesus ascend His throne, rule Israel, and demolish Roman rule. That's a reason Peter protested Jesus' statements about His death: they seemed like failure prophecies, completely opposite to the disciples' expectations.

> From that time Jesus began to show to His disciples that He must go to Jerusalem, and suffer many things from the elders and chief priests and scribes, and be killed, and be raised the third day. Then Peter took Him aside and began to rebuke Him, saying, "Far be it from You, Lord; this shall not happen to You!" (Matthew 16:21–22)

Jesus told one rich man to release his affectionate idolatry of wealth. Unwilling, the rich man left sad, so Jesus said a camel could go through the eye of a needle quicker than a rich man could enter heaven.

> Then Peter answered and said to Him, "See, we have left all and followed You. Therefore what shall we have?" (Matthew 19:27)

Why did Peter object? The disciples believed the wealthy had a better chance at ruling in the Messiah's kingdom. More wealth meant better bargains with the king, more respect, and greater influence. But if not even a wealthy man can get in, how could the disciples? They had nothing, in direct consequence of leaving everything to follow Him.

That is IOU thinking. The chances of the rich were worse than expected. What could the impoverished disciples offer to get into the kingdom of heaven? Following Jesus had left them poorer than ever.

James and John showed the same IOU thinking. They expected an earthly kingdom and asked for favored positions. Lucifer's partner angels could have thought likewise: "let us be your second-in-command."

Then James and John, the sons of Zebedee, came to Him, saying, "Teacher, we want You to do for us whatever we ask." And He said to them, "What do you want Me to do for you?" They said to Him, "Grant us that we may sit, one on Your right hand and the other on Your left, in Your glory." (Mark 10:35–37)

Jesus rebuked them with training about servant leadership. Churches promoting servanthood use Jesus' teaching often. Well we should, without neglecting His veiled rebuke of darkness.

Lucifer's pattern of power is lording it over his partners; Jesus warns against that. Jesus' kingdom has no place for the jealousy and one-upmanship of the kingdom of darkness. Partners in His kingdom are far different from the partners in satan's.

And when the ten heard it, they began to be greatly displeased with James and John. But Jesus called them to Himself and said to them, "You know that those who are considered rulers over the Gentiles lord it over them, and their great ones exercise authority over them. Yet it shall not be so among you; but whoever desires to become great among you shall be your servant. And whoever of you desires to be first shall be slave of all. For even the Son of Man did not come to be served, but to serve, and to give His life a ransom for many." (Mark 10:41–45)

LUCIFER'S FOUNDING LIEUTENANTS

These angelic partners in rebellion did become Lucifer's lieutenants. Isaiah 14 refers to the king of Babylon (14:4), but when Isaiah penned this, Babylon did not have a king. It was not an empire in Isaiah's time; far from conquering, Babylon was a vassal of the Assyrian Empire.

Yet Isaiah 14:9–11 talks about kings vanquished by Babylon, through its conquests long in the future. Ahead of their time, God uses these kings as types. They symbolically represent satan's subjugated principalities. Isaiah 14 reveals that satan had partners.

Isaiah 14 also reveals their function: as partner kings under his dominion. They claim nations and people groups. Apostle Paul described these founding members of satan's dominion in Ephesians 6:12 with the word *principalities*, as discussed in chapter one. Paul's revelation of unseen wicked rulers, plural, would have support from this passage. Paul said we stand against satan, but wrestle against these rulers; this passage explains his foundation.

Isaiah 14 also reveals that justice will be done upon the kingdom of darkness. All its rulers will be down in the Pit.

KINGDOM THINKING

Jesus said, "*Blessed are the poor in spirit, for theirs is the kingdom of heaven.*" (Matthew 5:3). The first clause is the condition of the blessedness; the second tells why that is a blessed condition.

We don't quickly grasp the ruling authority signified by the why in Jesus' statement. Ours is the kingdom, like princes whose family owns the kingdom. Subject only to our King, our authority is total. Every citizen of heaven looks to us as its royalty.

Most of humanity has lived under kings, but America is a republic. Our democratic methods have prevented us from living under kings (at least in name or title). Our election cycles depose our authorities. These precious gifts from our founding fathers have obscured our understanding of kingship and dominion.

Kingdom is not familiar to us. Kings of old live only in our mythology or history. To us, today's monarchs are holdovers from bygone days, nothing more than tradition, and irrelevant. We class the British royals with celebrities, not with rulers. This disdain for royalty deflates our own identity as God's regents on earth.

The devil runs a kingdom of his own. Our poor understanding of kingdom authority gives them opportunity. We easily dismiss them as we do the British royal family. But this impairs our vigilance against the tyranny of an evil unseen king. Our eyes for unseen domineering are undeveloped.

THE FAMILY OF DARKNESS

Fiction and crime journalism give us a concept that conveys darkness' violent threat: the crime family. Thankfully, most of us know of it only from entertainment fiction or news reporting.

Their pattern uses bribery to control, threats to dominate, and violence to enforce. Words are never genuine, and they blame broken commitments on other's failures. Relationships are all conditional; those who perform poorly are demoted, at best. The crime family's web of control makes every participant into a prisoner.

Even the head mobster is a prisoner of competitive fear from within and without. Isaiah 14 reveals how the head mobster of darkness came to be mocked by his former subordinates.

THE JUDGMENT OF DARKNESS

Trombones have music stands, on the stationary part. The "time trombone" of the prophets held "music" they read, but what they saw and wrote was sometimes on the mobile part of the trombone. As if the prophets' music was near and far in rapid succession, moving in and out, God revealed events with thousands of years between. The date of the far-off events was not always revealed.

The time trombone is in full force in Isaiah 14. Writing in the 720s BC, Isaiah speaks as if a kingdom 150 years in the future has already conquered many kings. The music stand goes further out, and all those future kings are described in a conversation at the end of time, which summarizes the activity of the kingdom of darkness since its founding.

The setting is after the completion of God's judgment. God's artistic method is a description of their last reunion, in the Pit of their eternal punishment.

> Hell from beneath is excited about you,
> To meet you at your coming;
> It stirs up the dead for you,
> All the chief ones of the earth;
> It has raised up from their thrones
> All the kings of the nations.
> They all shall speak and say to you:
> 'Have you also become as weak as we?
> Have you become like us?
> Your pomp is brought down to Sheol,
> And the sound of your stringed instruments;
> The maggot is spread under you,
> And worms cover you.' (Isaiah 14:9–11)

Isaiah's prophecy reveals that satan's judgment includes the mocking of his long-time subordinates and prison inmates. How unified are they, in fact?

Discussion and reflection questions for Chapter Five can be found in the Reader Engagement Resources

---

CHAPTER SIX

DIVIDED PARTNERS

The fallen angels were satan's original partners in rebellion. Under him, they were the founding crime family of darkness.

But Lucifer's urge to ascend was irrepressible. The iniquity in his heart—the five *I wills* of Isaiah14:13—did not vanish because he was cast out of heaven, but strengthened instead. Are we surprised that he betrayed the loyalty of his fellow founders? These original rulers in the kingdom of darkness testify that he oppressed them.

MOCKING

God will judge the devil. When that happens, the principalities and rulers he discarded along the way will mock him.

Those who see you will gaze at you,
And consider you, saying:
"Is this the man who made the earth tremble,
Who shook kingdoms,
Who made the world as a wilderness
And destroyed its cities,
Who did not open the house of his prisoners?" (Isaiah 14:16–17)

Nations have come and gone; kingdoms have shaken up. Only a very few nations from Isaiah's time exist today. The nations and cities of earth are always bubbling up and declining.

This cycle of rise and fall has a spiritual basis. Beginning after Babel, one of satan's partner principalities claimed each nation. These are "*the rulers of wickedness in the heavenly realms*" in Ephesians 6:12. The people groups of earth jumble up over time, because the hierarchy of darkness gets jumbled.

God claimed a nation as well: Israel, still manifesting His long-suffering and loyalty. Book Four of the *Unseen* Series is *Nobody Sees This Israel: God's Vanguard Against Darkness.*

The evil ruler of darkness promotes and demotes his subordinate principalities. Nations fall out of influence and cease to exist. Each occurrence manifests satan's demotion for its unseen ruler. Millennia of this pattern signify countless demotions among satan's rebel partners.

As a consolation in their damnation, these rebel partners have wielded power over nations and people groups. Yet under their leader's ruthless domination, it never lasts. The devil treats them like disposable dirt.

These angelic beings are damned eternally because of his rebellion. Add to that the long history of heartless abuse by satan. In Isaiah 14:16–17 above, God reveals that these demoted partners mock their once-great dominator. Doubtless, satan's ruthless disloyalty stored up their angelic resentment against him. God uses a type to tell us about them: the kings in Isaiah's future, conquered by the king of the future empire, Babylon.

His rebellion against God merited eternal fire. And for his constant betrayal of his angelic partners, satan earned their mocking disdain. Those he once humiliated will stare at his eternal humiliation.

EGGSHELLS

God reveals that the judgment of Lucifer includes the mocking of his former subordinates. In this prophecy of Isaiah, the dead kings call the judged Lucifer "*the one who shook kingdoms.*"

We might think of violation of national sovereignty or borders, but not in this passage. Their disdain was payback for the dominion they lost because of satan's abuse. The devil brought destruction upon the lands and the people these fallen partners had claimed.

He took prisoners and would not release them (14:17). Isaiah's symbolic kings care only about their own experience; they do not care about imprisonment of their human prey. The rulers of darkness are describing how satan oppressed them; the prisoners uppermost on their minds are themselves—not people.

74

When 14:12 identifies Lucifer, it also describes his track record: *"you who weakened the nations."* His partners knew his motto firsthand. "What good is power if you don't use it to oppress?"

The principalities and their assigned regions could never satisfy satan's domineering expectations permanently. These unseen kings walked on eggshells under satan, constantly threatened by his iron-fisted discipline, self-exalting rule, conditional favor, and quixotic capriciousness. One by one, satan weakened these unseen kings and undercut their dominions. The best result they could hope for was mere demotion.

PARTNERS IN DOOM

Isaiah knew about the afterlife incompletely. Only with Jesus did God fully reveal it. Jesus was the first to teach a heaven for the saved and a hell for eternal punishment (Matthew 25:46, *et al*). Without that revelation, Isaiah 14 reveals satan's prison. It's not for people. The devil's lockup is for those who serve him—*the house of his prisoners.*

Despite the devil's abuse for the rulers of this dark age, they are on thrones even in death (14:9). In contrast, Lucifer comes under their disdain. The devil receives the greatest dishonor.

His kingdom-claiming partners continue as *dignitaries*, even in the afterworld, as Peter wrote. They are those *principalities and rulers of darkness of this age* against whom we wrestle, as Paul wrote.

After a career across millennia, satan destroys every unseen partner who enters agreements with him. God's judgment on the devil will represent the payback of those betrayed partners. God paints the scene of satan's final judgment in Isaiah 14:18–21. All the kings Babylon would one day conquer are His types for the many partners satan betrayed.

All the kings of the nations,
All of them, sleep in glory,
Everyone in his own house;
But you are cast out of your grave
Like an abominable branch,
Like the garment of those who are slain,
Thrust through with a sword,
Who go down to the stones of the pit,
Like a corpse trodden underfoot.
You will not be joined with them in burial,

Because you have destroyed your land
And slain your people.
The brood of evildoers shall never be named.
Prepare slaughter for his children
Because of the iniquity of their fathers,
Lest they rise up and possess the land,
And fill the face of the world with cities.

DELIVERED TO SATAN

The devil tempted Jesus in the wilderness with three attempts, all failed. One offering he made to Jesus may have been the tempter's least favorite: "*all the kingdoms of the world.*" Have you wondered how Jesus and satan could see all the kingdoms of a spherical globe from a high mountain?

> Then the devil, taking Him up on a high mountain, showed Him all the kingdoms of the world in a moment of time. And the devil said to Him, "All this authority I will give You, and their glory; for this has been delivered to me, and I give it to whomever I wish." (Luke 4:5–6)

Many Southern Americans know the advertising slogan, *See Seven States from Lookout Mountain.* Whether it's Appalachia, the Rockies, or Mount Everest, the devil's mountain could not display all the world's kingdoms.

Even if satan only showed the then-known kingdoms, no mountain on earth would suffice. A different explanation is required unless the devil is omnipotent or the kingdoms are omnipresent—which they are not.

The most plausible explanation is that when satan showed Jesus the kingdoms, he wasn't showing their geographical territories, but their kings. Showing the kings is identical to showing the kingdoms. What satan offered Jesus for a temptation was the glory and positions of his rebel partners. I can't imagine they would like that.

Jesus' tempter says all the kingdoms of the world were *delivered* to him, but by whom? The passage doesn't tell us, but the early church fathers devoted a lot of debate to understand it. Many believed that Adam and Eve were the ones who delivered it to satan, when they fell. Others believed it was God Himself who delivered the kingdoms to satan. Others wrote satan was lying or exaggerating—but Jesus did not dispute satan's claim.

Our grid in the *Unseen* Series is that satan collects IOUs deceptively, to gain power over angels and people. He installed his rebel partners as his unseen rulers of wickedness, to maintain an iron grip on nations and people groups. They owed him for their privileges.

His partners were the ones who claimed all the kingdoms of men at Babel. To satisfy their IOUs, "*the rulers of wickedness in the heavenly realms*" delivered their dominions to satan. He then bribed Jesus with their dominion of the whole world's kingdoms.

THE KINGS OFFERED TO JESUS

How would satan have given these to Jesus? What was his plan for the transfer?

It wouldn't have been a real estate closing. The earth is the Lord's (Psalm 24:1); darkness could claim only the dominions, not the lands.

The devil could have transferred ownership of the IOUs. Thinking Jesus to have the same power policy as he did—against others—satan was offering Jesus power to manipulate the spiritual rulers.

It's easy to imagine satan being devious to Jesus. Agreements with the devil always have fine print. After his bribe had been accepted, satan could exile all the ruling principalities to his prison. It would force Jesus to implement His own command structure for unseen dominion.

After all, satan had imposed a hierarchy of control upon his partners in darkness. When satan taunted Jesus, "if you are the Son of God," Jesus would have heard the taunt to do likewise, or even better.

Wisely, Jesus recognized that satan's agreements have built-in tricks. He knew that all the kingdoms of the world would become His anyway, and that He would indeed have a global command structure for seen and unseen alike.

> And there were loud voices in heaven, saying, "The kingdoms of this world have become the kingdoms of our Lord and of His Christ, and He shall reign forever and ever!" (Revelation 11:15)

> And they sang a new song, saying:

> "You are worthy to take the scroll,
> And to open its seals;
> For You were slain,
> And have redeemed us to God by Your blood
> Out of every tribe and tongue and people and nation,

And have made us kings and priests to our God;
And we shall reign on the earth." (Revelation 5:9–10)

CONDITIONAL PARTNERS

Because of their angelic sensitivity to obligations, satan uses IOUs against his partners. He operates them like puppets. The devil thought he could rope Jesus into this system.

Although they were his original partners, he has no loyalty to them. The devil juggles his principalities. The constant rise and fall of nations manifests demotion and promotion in the unseen realm.

A principality can have an iron grip on its territory, and yet the capricious oppressor replaces it with another. He causes cities to be destroyed when a territory is transferred between the unseen principalities.

To offer Jesus the kingdoms, satan summoned all his principalities and dark rulers to congregate and appear to Jesus. For Jesus to see them all—a very large number—required a prime vantage point, the high mountain.

And the partner-kings had a vantage point also: from satan's bargaining table. In his bribe to tempt Jesus, they would have recognized satan's willingness to dump them and give their dominions to Jesus.

JESUS KNEW DARKNESS

Scripture reveals the foregoing, not directly but indirectly. Patterns, types, and pictures comprise types, which depict the workings of the kingdom of darkness.

We must test these interpretations, including measurement by other Scriptures.

We have seen that Apostles Peter and Paul, as well as Jude, teach truths that require this typological interpretation of the Old Testament. Apostle Paul wrote "*we are not ignorant of the devil's devices*" (2 Corinthians 2:11), but sadly, we cannot say the same thing in today's churches.

Jesus provides confirmation as well. He converses with critics about demonic activity in Luke 11:14–26. Critics nearby saw him cast a demon out of a mute man's life. These religious watchmen found no joy in a mute person speaking again. Instead, they imposed a dismissive explanation that excused them from following Jesus.

"*He casts out demons by Beelzebub, the ruler of the demons*" (11:15). Jesus cites their criticism in 11:18, "*you say I cast out demons by Beelzebub.*" As seen in Book Two of the *Unseen* Series, the heart chooses and the mind excuses.

The name used by the religious critics was a then-popular name for the devil. In a dismissive way, it meant "Lord of the dung-flies." These critics, desperately protecting their own authority, attempt to disarm Jesus' public following. Saying He is a plant of Beelzebub, they dismiss the mute man speaking. They tell people that Jesus serves satan, and tricks the Jews by casting out demons.

The critics said only a ruler of demons could command demons. Their theological bankruptcy about God's power for the same is striking. But Jesus doesn't correct their underestimate of God's power. Instead, He addresses their wrong thinking about the kingdom of darkness.

> But He, knowing their thoughts, said to them: "Every kingdom divided against itself is brought to desolation, and a house divided against a house falls. If Satan also is divided against himself, how will his kingdom stand? Because you say I cast out demons by Beelzebub." (11:17–18)

DIVISION CRIPPLES

Abraham Lincoln used Jesus' principle in Luke 11:17–18. After receiving the 1858 Republican Party nomination to run for President against Stephen Douglas, candidate Lincoln used this phrase in his acceptance speech:

> "A house divided against itself cannot stand." I believe the government cannot endure permanently half slave and half free. I do not expect the Union to be dissolved—I do not expect the house to fall but I do expect it will cease to be divided. It will become all one thing or all the other.

Like Lincoln, we wanted the *Union* to stand, but Jesus doesn't use the phrase in that positive way. We do not want *the kingdom of darkness* to stand, but to fall. Jesus stated this as a principle of reality.

He could read Isaiah 14 just like we can. There, God used types of Babylon's conquered kings to portray the force of division latent in the kingdom of darkness. Alerted by this, Jesus doubtless found additional evidence when He cast out demons. Still today, relying on our divine authorization (Matthew 16:19), deliverance ministers bind evil spirits to actions that divide them. Jesus knew that darkness would fall, because He had seen evidence of its division.

We, in contrast, will stand because in Him we are one.

Christians talk as if the rulers of darkness walk in lockstep with one another. To hear us tell it, the devil and his partners synchronize with unanimity and agreement. But this mistaken belief requires Jesus to mean, "the kingdom of darkness will stand because it is not divided." This is at odds with everything Scripture foretells about its ultimate demise.

Knowing from Scripture that it would fall, Jesus is affirming that the kingdom of darkness is divided against itself. It will fall.

ONE, OR NOT

The division in darkness is why Jesus wanted us, His Church, to be one organic unity. Jesus' ambition for us contrasts dramatically with satan's desire for his kingdom. Rather than oppress or dominate, God the Son prayed His followers would be one. On the night before His crucifixion for our sins, our unity was of utmost value to Jesus. The price He paid certainly earned it, fair and square.

> Holy Father, keep through Your name those whom You have given Me, that they may be one as We are ... I do not pray for these alone, but also for those who will believe in Me through their word; that they all may be one, as You, Father, are in Me, and I in You; that they also may be one in Us.... I in them, and You in Me; that they may be made perfect in one. (John 17:11, 20–23)

But within satan's kingdom, Jesus saw divisive forces embedded. Seeing how readily satan offered his partners' kingdoms to Jesus, He knew its division started at the top. He would have expected their discord from the Isaiah 14 prophecy. For us, Jesus desired oneness, but for them, Jesus had a different ambition: division.

JESUS' REBUTTAL: WHO'S THE PLANT

Jesus rebuts the accusation that He is an enemy plant. But His logic does not rely on the principle He just stated. He does not use the principle of division as His defense.

The logic of His defense is in the question He asked the Jewish leaders. *"And if I cast our demons by Beelzebub, by whom do your sons cast them out?"* (11:19)

They say Jesus casts out demons as an agent of satan. Yet they and their disciples had also cast out demons, so the natural question is obvious. How do the students of the critics cast out demons?

Jesus didn't wait for their answer because His question rhetorically contains its own answer: "not by God." He knows they can't admit that. But if the critics responded, "we cast them out by God," it reveals their jealousy is the only basis for attacking Jesus. They won't admit that either. The passage records no attempt to answer Jesus.

The question, *"by whom do your sons cast them out?"* reveals Jesus' discernment. When the Jewish leaders cast out demons, they really were tricksters and plants of Beelzebub. They accused Him falsely of what they themselves were actually doing.

SAME TODAY

We see in our own political world the same tricks. One leader or party will accuse his opponent of doing something wrong—something the opponent is innocent of, but which the accuser is guilty of.

Why didn't Jesus use the division principle to say He can't be a plant of the enemy? Because He knew that satan's disguised servants really can drive out satan's demons. The answer in His question presumes that reality: "yes, the kingdom of darkness can drive out demons."

The division principle simply forecasts the outcome: that divided kingdom will fall. The kingdom of darkness is not unified in lockstep. Jesus' question shows His knowledge that demons can trick us by pretending to cast one another out. The Jewish leaders are, in fact, plants of Beelzebub. Beelzebub's kingdom is divided against itself, and it will fall.

The religious critics accuse Jesus of a spiritual crime for which they are in fact the guilty party. Their accusation disguises the origin of their power to cast out demons. Jesus pinpoints the damning evidence when he says their own sons will be their judges (11:19).

DIVISION SHOWS

Jesus provides another evidence in Matthew 7:21–23. There He reveals that evildoers who do not know Him will cast out demons. Jesus' statement teaches us His discernment: the demons can be driven out by their wicked unseen rulers.

The deceptive tactics of darkness continued after Jesus founded the Church by pouring out His Spirit. In Acts 19:13, we see evidence of this division within darkness many decades later.

> Then some of the itinerant Jewish exorcists took it upon themselves to call the name of the Lord Jesus over those who had evil spirits, saying, "We exorcise you by the Jesus whom Paul preaches." Also there were seven sons of Sceva, a Jewish chief priest, who did so.

IF THIS IS THE COUNTERFEIT, WHAT MUST THE REAL BE?

Book 5 is *Nobody Sees This Israel*, and Book 7 is *Nobody Sees This Church*. Both address sorcery in depth.

Can people who are not filled with the Spirit of God drive out demons? Many scriptures assume they can, such as those cited here.

But if the counterfeiters can do it, we Christians must be even more powerful for expelling demons.

The Jewish exorcists and Sceva's seven sons drove out demons, falsely using Jesus' name. What success they had was entirely by the permission of satan. Paul testified from experience about the trickery of darkness, and warned the Corinthian Christians about the deception.

> For such are false apostles, deceitful workers, transforming themselves into apostles of Christ. And no wonder! For Satan himself transforms himself into an angel of light. Therefore it is no great thing if his ministers also transform themselves into ministers of righteousness, whose end will be according to their works. (2 Corinthians 11:13–15)

JESUS' REBUTTAL: WHO'S THE POWER

In Luke 11, Jesus gave the principle of a kingdom standing if undivided, falling if divided. But He used that predictive grid to challenge the religious critics themselves, not for His own defense. The power He displays when He releases captives from satan's house: that was His defense.

> But if I cast out demons with the finger of God, surely the kingdom of God has come upon you. When a strong man, fully armed, guards his own palace, his goods are in peace. But when a stronger than he

comes upon him and overcomes him, he takes from him all his armor in which he trusted, and divides his spoils. (11:20–22)

Jesus' accusers are, in fact, the plants of Beelzebub. His reply to them is an all-out assault. First, He used the *principle of division* to expose them. Then, Jesus prophecies the fall of darkness based on that principle. He finally uses the *principle of power* when He says, "*the kingdom of God has come upon you.*"

The principle is power, because in referring to the devil, Jesus describes him as the proprietor of the palace. Just as the mocking kings of Isaiah 14:17 stated above, the devil won't let his prisoners go.

Jesus says satan guards his own palace like a strong man. The reason Jesus can cast out demons is not because He is a plant of darkness, but because He has more power. He and His followers are the someone stronger. We overcome the devil and his possessiveness.

You are of God, little children, and have overcome them, because He who is in you is greater than he who is in the world. (1 John 4:4)

OUR STRENGTH AGAINST DARKNESS

Picture in your mind the image Jesus uses above: "*he takes from him all his armor in which he trusted.*" An armored man was a common sight to Jesus' listeners. Each Roman occupier in their streets wore helmet, hauberk, buckler, and shield. What would Jesus' Jewish listeners imagine when He said that?

In their mind's eye, they would walk up to that Roman soldier, really close—close enough to physically remove his armor. And not only close enough, but with such intimidating power that the Roman soldier offers no resistance. Instead, the powerful soldier lets the Jew touch him and pluck the armor off piece by piece, without resisting at all. This picture must have been electric to Jesus' hearers!

Yet there is more strength. After the occupying soldier is completely disarmed and dis-armored, something happens next. Jesus

THIS IS FOR US

Jesus' indication that He is the someone stronger, and in us continuing His overcoming power, is not a justification for bad-mouthing God's enemies. They are still angelic in nature, which the NT apostles affirm.

says the someone stronger takes the possessions that the soldier guarded.

This teaching takes place in a conversation about the devil. As mighty as his public relations campaign projects him, his strength is inferior to ours. His palace and his goods are ours for the taking.

AS SEEN TODAY

Are there Spirit-filled people casting out demons today? Yes.

Other than in movies? Yes, movie demons are demonstrative for ticket sales. Sadly many people are welcoming evil to oppress them through the entertainment they select.

Jesus authorized us to cast out demons. Many thousands of trained deliverance ministers have helped millions of people that way.

Training is essential for deliverance ministers to avoid the trickery of darkness. My wife and I received our training from several sources.

ChristianInternational. com is the site for training in quick deliverance.

continued on next page

From beginning to end, Jesus' defense is not about unity and division. It is about power. It is not about the preservation of the kingdom of darkness, but about its fall. He teaches we will be its plunderers and take what they have been guarding: people.

IT ALL FITS

Jesus taught little about satan, the strong man. His focus was to liberate satan's prisoners, and to plunder darkness. And that fits His selection of Isaiah 61 to introduce His ministry in Luke 4:17–19.

And He was handed the book of the prophet Isaiah. And when He had opened the book, He found the place where it was written:
"The Spirit of the Lord is upon Me,
Because He has anointed Me
To preach the gospel to the poor;
He has sent Me to heal the brokenhearted,
To proclaim liberty to the captives
And recovery of sight to the blind,
To set at liberty those who are oppressed;
To proclaim the acceptable year of the Lord."

After rising from death, Jesus must have told the disciples about His three days of physical death. That's how Apostle Peter could write, "*He went and preached to the spirits in prison*" (1 Peter 3:19). Apostle

Paul tells both the visit and the result in Ephesians 4:8–9. It's also a good example of Paul's reverse engineering to an unstated but necessary truth.

"When He ascended on high,
He led captivity captive,
And gave gifts to men."

Now this, "He ascended"—what does it mean but that He also first descended into the lower parts of the earth?

Jesus was the someone stronger for you and me. He plucked off satan's armor. He plundered the house of satan's prisoners—you, me, and everyone with faith that follows Jesus.

OUR KINGDOM STANDS

Lastly, this interpretation of Luke 11:17–18 accords with Jesus' emphatic command to love one another (John 13:34–35). We are in the kingdom of light. If it's true that a divided kingdom can't stand, then we are to love one another, so our kingdom does stand. Apostle John affirms this clearly in 1 John 2:9–11.

RestoringTheFoundations.org is the site for training in disciplined, permanent deliverance. The Catholic Church also has long experience with demonic oppression; they have authorized priests (and authors) for that ministry. KatieSouza.com is experienced at deliverance for groups.

If this is really happening, why don't you see it on the news or hear about it in your church? Some cultures are acutely aware of evil spirits, but in Western culture, our materialistic naturalism prohibits belief in evil spirits. And once delivered, people don't seek publicity about their past oppression!

He who says he is in the light, and hates his brother, is in darkness until now. He who loves his brother abides in the light, and there is no cause for stumbling in him. But he who hates his brother is in darkness and walks in darkness, and does not know where he is going, because the darkness has blinded his eyes.

The hate for a brother marks someone as part of the kingdom of darkness. It is divided, and it will fall. Love for one another signals that we are the kingdom that shall stand.

THE PARTNERS MOCK SATAN

No wonder satan's former partners gloat after God judges him. Long oppressed by him, receiving no loyalty from him, the principalities mock satan in Isaiah 14:10–11. They speak out of their resentment for him: "*Have you become as weak as we?*" In 14:11, they gloat over the demise of his original musical body, which we saw in Ezekiel 28. These principalities were the kingdoms whom he had shaken; theirs, the people he had slain and the cities he had destroyed.

Lucifer's humiliation includes becoming an object of horror on which his longtime subordinates gaze disdainfully. They see the greatness of his fall from his original musical body, now covered in worms and maggots. He who purposed to ascend to the highest seat is now brought low to the lowest spot—all in front of those he oppressed. He had sought the highest honor, but in the end, is the most dishonored, with not even a grave to call home. The slaying which satan once practiced on the earth and its inhabitants is finally practiced upon him; and everyone in hell sees it.

> Like the garment of those who are slain, thrust through with a sword, who go down to the stones of the pit, like a corpse trodden underfoot. (14:19)

PLURAL, NOT SINGLE

Apostle Paul did not single out satan as the one we wrestle against, but the unseen rulers who apply the destruction of darkness. The types of Isaiah 14 support Paul's revelation from experience: the principalities and rulers are plural.

Paul warned us to stand against satan's tricks, yes—but our wrestling is with his subordinate rulers. He does not imply that satan's influence was less than theirs. Quite the contrary, satan could weaken them and shuffle their assignments (Isaiah 14:17). Paul knew that we were far more likely to run into satan's nation-claiming subordinates than satan himself.

Paul speaks from experience. He penetrated many new territories and people groups with the gospel. Paul's preaching in each nation met with new antagonism from its unique dark ruler. This apostle knew we wrestle against satan's partners because he was God's first principality penetrator.

The book of Acts describes Apostle Paul's travels. Each place he went, they worshiped different "gods," *a.k.a.* their unseen principalities. As he spread the gospel and planted churches, each place resisted uniquely. Jesus' own statement to the Pergamum church shows how the kingdom of darkness exercised localized control (Revelation 2:12).

These rulers for satan trick earth's people groups into agreements. Using chokepoints and bottlenecks, they want every nation damned. They began this strategy after God divided the nations by language at Babel—reviewed extensively in Book Four of the *Unseen* Series. On the strength of those chokepoint agreements, they deploy their cannon-fodder demons to oppress people individually.

But the Church pierces the hold of satan's subordinates. When we minister to a person, we wrestle against these unseen potentates. When we advance the gospel's influence in their territories, it is those evil spiritual rulers who oppose our efforts by any means. Threatened by the Church, satan's partners must intimidate and harass. They must wrestle us into discouragement and resignation, or face satan's angry disloyalty.

The kingdom of darkness is not the only plural body in Paul's statement about wrestling. We, the Church, are plural as well, and we are the ones who take the fight to the dark rulers. Often we have succumbed to the resistance of darkness, but not always. The Church is global because many Christians did not succumb, but wrestled the principalities into defeat.

So shall we in our time. With Paul, Peter, the apostles, and every Christian through the ages, we wrestle as one.

Finally, my brethren, be strong in the Lord and in the power of His might. Put on the whole armor of God, that you may be able to stand against the wiles of the devil. For we do not wrestle against flesh and blood, but against principalities, against powers, against the rulers of the darkness of this age, against spiritual hosts of wickedness in the heavenly places. (Ephesians 6:10–12)

Discussion and reflection questions for Chapter Six
can be found in the Reader Engagement Resources

CHAPTER SEVEN

FIRE AND WATER

Each chapter of this book is increasingly challenging to write. The subject of heaven's inhabitants and structure is lofty and humbling.

Most challenging of all is editing. I rewrote every paragraph at least once to lower the complexity. I chose words for their ease of understanding. Yet God reveals the unseen realm under a veil of mystery. Our available vocabulary isn't ready for what the Bible reveals in its shade. Our grid of interpretation has trouble yielding to concepts that are foreign.

I ask you, reader, to process and test each insight for its explanatory power of other Bible revelations. Deuteronomy 29:29 describes the attitude needed to explore the Scripture.

> The secret things belong to the LORD our God, but those things which are revealed belong to us and to our children forever, that we may do all the words of this law.

He placed no limits on what we could ask, but instructs us in humility when our puzzles linger unsolved. All His answers for us are in there—but not immediately evident. God invites us to a treasure hunt in His Word.

The direct revelation God gave us about the unseen realm is sparse. There are 1,189 chapters in the New King James translation of the Bible. Of those, how many contain explicit reference to the physical structure of heaven? Exodus 24, Ezekiel 1, 28 and Revelation 4, 21 and 22—six chapters, half of one percent.

Careful reading of the Bible always pays dividends because there is indirect revelation—the things that are assumed about the unseen world of spirit. God's infrequent references to that spirit world are His invitation to us treasure hunters. He has hidden mysteries in His Word for us to enjoy—both the search and the arrival, both with Him in us. The low-hanging fruit doesn't satisfy overcomers; we want to go higher up and further in, more intimate with Him at every step.

We please God when our hunger for Him drives us into His Word. For our safety, He doesn't reveal everything at once, but assures us we'll understand it over time. Christian readers have an unsurpassed resource within: He lives in us and explains it to us.

> But the anointing which you have received from Him abides in you, and you do not need that anyone teach you; but as the same anointing teaches you concerning all things, and is true, and is not a lie, and just as it has taught you, you will abide in Him. (1 John 2:27)

THE FIRE OF HOLINESS

God's holiness consumes all who embrace sin—so much so that He Himself is a consuming fire (Hebrews 12:29). Speaking to Lucifer after his fall, God revealed there were once fiery stones around His throne (Ezekiel 28:14). Only once did a human witness God's fiery throne area, in Daniel's vision of Judgment Day.

> His throne was a fiery flame,
> Its wheels a burning fire;
> A fiery stream issued
> And came forth from before Him. (Daniel 7:9–10)

Ezekiel has visions where fire symbolizes God's judgment, using *fire* forty times. He witnessed fire passing among the four cherubim, which they scattered over Jerusalem in judgment (10:2). When God uses fire, it expresses His holiness. Fire executes His judgment.

He established this pattern *"before the foundation of the world,"* the subject of the next chapter. That's when an everlasting fire was prepared for all God's future enemies—the devil, his angels and demons, and all who align with them. Lucifer was the first revealed case where God used fire for His wrath, when He installed consuming fire into Lucifer's nature.

> And I destroyed you, O covering cherub,
> From the midst of the fiery stones . . .

Therefore I brought fire from your midst;
It devoured you,
And I turned you to ashes upon the earth
In the sight of all who saw you. (Ezekiel 28:16, 18)

God transformed Lucifer and his partners with fire, one consequence of their sin. Yet theirs was not the only physical transformation. God put something new where the fiery stones had once been. Heaven itself was reshaped.

BURNING BUT NOT CONSUMED

God's fiery holiness is supernatural. It has an inexhaustible quality yet doesn't consume. Moses saw this when God called him in Exodus 3:2–3.

And the Angel of the Lord appeared to him in a flame of fire from the midst of a bush. So he looked, and behold, the bush was burning with fire, but the bush was not consumed. Then Moses said, "I will now turn aside and see this great sight, why the bush does not burn."

God is an ever-consuming fire with wrath upon those who refuse Him. It does not go away. His fiery wrath is inexhaustible because it doesn't destroy a soul that He has created. His wrath at their disdain for Him burns them eternally, yet without a final consumption.

The entire span of the Bible reveals that God creates and sustains all—even the fire of hell. By His power, God Almighty simultaneously holds all rebels in unending existence. His wrath both holds them in existence and consumes them.

God is a just judge,
And God is angry with the wicked every day. (Psalm 7:11)

The Lord has made all for Himself,
Yes, even the wicked for the day of doom. (Proverbs 16:4)

For our God is a consuming fire. (Hebrews 12:29)

For by Him all things were created that are in heaven and that are on earth, visible and invisible, whether thrones or dominions or principalities or powers. All things were created through Him and for Him.

And He is before all things, and in Him all things consist. (Colossians 1:16–17)

All things were made through Him, and without Him nothing was made that was made. (John 1:3)

Upholding all things by the word of His power.(Hebrews 1:3)

You created all things,
And by Your will they exist and were created. (Revelation 4:11)

AS SEEN TODAY

In our day, there is little reverence for God and His holiness. Our Christianity toys with His abundant grace and comes very close to the disdain that earns His eternal wrath. Jesus warned us this would happen when He said *the love of many will grow cold* (Matthew 24:12).

Such an inexhaustible fire doesn't destroy a person. Instead, it desiccates them with eternal, inescapable dryness. We began with Apostle Paul's teaching about the unseen rank and file of darkness. How did he recognize them? What knowledge did he have from the Bible and from experience?

Water and the dryness of its absence are primary clues. By recognizing the moisture motive of our unseen enemies, we can penetrate the mystery of their identification. When we spiritualize these forces or discount their physical angelic needs, we miss such clues.

DRAGON OF FIRE AND WATER

In Revelation 12, Apostle John sees *a fiery red dragon*, and is told plainly that the dragon symbolizes satan (12:9). This dragon, the fallen Lucifer, symbolizes his transformation. Lucifer became fire personified after his degrading by God.

This antagonistic enemy hates humankind and is consumed with animosity toward the newborn male child. The holy angels protect the mother and child, but the dragon persecutes the helpless pair and all their descendants. He spews his fiery nature; he uses water as well.

So the serpent spewed water out of his mouth like a flood after the woman, that he might cause her to be carried away by the flood. (Hebrews 12:15)

The dragon of Revelation 12 is not the first in Scripture to project evil power with water. In Daniel 11:22, a vile ruler replaces a series of rulers whose evil is only mediocre: "*With the force of a flood, they* [all who oppose him] *shall be swept away from before him and be broken.*"

FALLEN ANGELS AND MOISTURE

All the fallen spirits, whether angels or demons, crave moisture. Wetness is their most prized commodity. Jesus knew their habits and described their motive in Luke 11:24. Jesus says the unclean spirit cannot find rest in dry places. The unspoken truth: unclean spirits require moisture to rest.

When an unclean spirit goes out of a man, he goes through dry places, seeking rest; and finding none, he says, "I will return to my house from which I came."

God moved the fiery stones from His throne area, and moved them into Lucifer's nature and that of his partners. In place of their previous condition, an inward fiery nature torments them inescapably. God's enemies crave cooling relief—which only moisture can provide to them.

Is this reverse-engineered understanding supported by the Bible? Yes, by many Scriptures—as cited throughout the *Unseen* Series. The punishment afflicting them is fire within their midst. They refuse relief from God; they insist on doing things their way. Naturally, these fallen angels would use their powers to quell their inner fire.

Opposing God earned them an eternally parched dryness. Yet the same misplaced confidence persists which led them to rebel against God. They try to quell the fire themselves, and seek cooling moisture from any source.

Meek people recognize this pattern of self-provision—an ever-present sin pattern.

This has explanatory power for many biblical facts. The Almighty Creator prepared hell before *the foundation of the world.* He created it as an unending punishment for all who disdain Him: dryness, desiccation, and fire with no source of cooling moisture.

The devil, who deceived them, was cast into the lake of fire and brimstone where the beast and the false prophet are. And they will be tormented day and night forever and ever. (Revelation 20:10)

Jesus' parable about the rich man and the beggar Lazarus affirms the dryness which accompanies God's wrath—so dry that even a drop of water is highly prized.

Then he cried and said, "Father Abraham, have mercy on me, and send Lazarus that he may dip the tip of his finger in water and cool my tongue; for I am tormented in this flame." (Luke 16:24)

The insatiable desire of darkness to cool off has profound impact for interpreting Creation itself, as chapters 10–12 will soon uncover.

DEMONIC CRAVING FOR PEOPLE

The devil had a prison, as we saw in Isaiah 14. In it are two groups whom he imprisons: fallen angels and demons. The distinction is a major subject of Book Four, *Nobody Sees These Enemies: How to Discern and Disarm Unseen Tempters*.

God's name for the prison in Zechariah 9:11 is "*the waterless pit*"—a dry place. It was the Abyss which the demons named Legion feared most greatly. Their request to Jesus in Luke 8:26–33 is best explained by their dread of dryness. Their craving for moisture also explains the pigs running into the sea.

Then they sailed to the country of the Gadarenes, which is opposite Galilee. And when He stepped out on the land, there met Him a certain man from the city who had demons for a long time. And he wore no clothes, nor did he live in a house but in the tombs. When he saw Jesus, he cried out, fell down before Him, and with a loud voice said, "What have I to do with You, Jesus, Son of the Most High God? I beg You, do not torment me!" For He had commanded the unclean spirit to come out of the man. For it had often seized him, and he was kept under guard, bound with chains and shackles; and he broke the bonds and was driven by the demon into the wilderness. Jesus asked him, saying, "What is your name?" And he said, "Legion," because many demons had entered him. And they begged Him that He would not command them to go out into the abyss. Now a herd of many swine was feeding there on the mountain. So they begged Him that He would permit them to enter them. And He permitted them. Then the demons went out of the man and entered the swine, and the herd ran violently down the steep place into the lake and drowned.

The text itself gives no clue as to why the swine ran down into the sea. No known Jewish belief would explain this. But we can understand based on Jesus' description of demons seeking rest in Luke 11:24. They want moisture to cool off their inner torment of fire. Just as Jesus said, demons do all within their power to get it.

The demon seeking rest and Legion's request to enter pigs are actual behaviors revealing their actual motives. Their preferred source for the cooling wetness is people. The poor Gadarene man was the best source in the region. Not just one demon but hundreds found rest in him. The pigs were nearby the entire time. The sea was right at hand all the while. Yet the many demons preferred the man.

Jesus' appearance needed no interpretation for these demons, who knew immediately the man was about to be off limits for them. They had to go somewhere and knew only two alternatives existed: either stay on earth somehow, or go into the dreaded, dry abyss.

Their worst alternative was a return to the abyss, satan's prison. The cruel, power-hungry satan is merciless and utilitarian with his underlings. He steals, kills, and destroys them, just as he does people.

If they couldn't have a human being, the second best was nearby: *the large herd of swine.* The rich man in Jesus' parable craved a single drop of water on his tongue. Likewise, the demons in the Gadarene man craved even the least possibility of moisture. Those pigs looked promising enough. But the pigs had less tolerance of demons than people had, and opted for the body of water below the cliff rather than live with demonic torment.

Jesus visited that very prison after His death, prior to His resurrection. These same demons may have had a second encounter with Jesus if 1 Peter 3:19 is any guide. Ephesians 4:8–10 was Paul's teaching about the harrowing of hell. We review this thoroughly in Book Four of the *Unseen Series, Nobody Sees This Enemies: How to Discern and Disarm Unseen Tempters.*

95

TESTIMONIES OF CHRISTIANS

Experiences of Christians in subsequent church history are consistent with this. The first of two examples is Anthony the Great (251–356 AD), regarded as the first Christian monk. He lived for decades in the desert east of the Upper Nile, three days' journey from people. He dwelt in the desert and fasted for lengthy periods until believers began bringing food to him.

In that dry place, his body was the only source of moisture. He endured constant onslaughts from demons and evil apparitions. Of course this has a biblical precedent: Jesus' forty days in the dry wilderness.

A second example closer to our time is Emmanuel Eni, a Nigerian Christian and prophet who converted from satanic religions. He testifies about visits to darkness. Although all Christians do not accept his fantastic testimony, it affirms the importance of moisture for darkness. Prior to his salvation, his visits to the kingdom of darkness always occurred underwater, off the seashore.

Several Scriptures reveal that the hideout for evil rulers is the ocean. As unexpected or troublesome as this may seem, God's shaded mysteries in the Bible all lead us to such a conclusion.

WICKED RULERS FROM THE SEA

Apostle John sees in Revelation that the sea is a storehouse. These rulers of wickedness emerge from the sea, not the land. Daniel also sees the horrible beasts coming from the sea. In both cases, the earth-shaking, global enforcers of evil arise fully grown. All the development and preparation took place in the ocean, and the beast emerges fully ready to command mankind.

> And four great beasts came up from the sea, each different from the other. (Daniel 7:3)

> Then I stood on the sand of the sea. And I saw a beast rising up out of the sea, having seven heads and ten horns, and on his horns ten crowns, and on his heads a blasphemous name. (Revelation 13:1)

RIVERS, THE SEATS OF DARKNESS

Moisture is important also for Babylon, judged in Revelation 17–18. The empire was five centuries past when John recorded his vision. Its original geographical setting makes it a symbol in Revelation 17–18 for satan's trading patterns.

"*Come, I will show you the judgment of the great harlot who sits on many waters*" (17:1). This harlot is Babylon the Great. The angel identifies the waters for John. "*Then he said to me, 'The waters which you saw, where the harlot sits, are peoples, multitudes, nations, and tongues*" (17:15). Why is Babylon depicted as sitting on waters? How do "waters" symbolize peoples, multitudes, nations, and tongues?

The ancient Babylon in 600 BC sat astraddle the Euphrates River, which flowed through it. The Euphrates River flowed into new channels, winding away from the great city. For 2,300 years, Babylon's ruins lay forgotten and buried until discovered in the 1800s.

Cyrus the Great started this redirected flow. To conquer Babylon in 539 BC, his army dug new channels for the river. When it suddenly flowed away from the city, the soldiers walked in at night through the gates which had once permitted the water to flow in and out.

In Revelation 17, Babylon symbolically represents satan's godless system of trading, just as Tyre had. Like the original Babylon, it sits on waters. Traders mourn its demolition.

They threw dust on their heads and cried out, weeping and wailing, and saying, "Alas, alas, that great city, in which all who

COMING FEATURES

In Revelation 17–18, Babylon sits on three seats; one is waters. A change in the allocation triggers its destruction. Book Nine, *Nobody Sees This Victory, Yet: The Destruction of Darkness*, considers the meaning of all three seats in depth.

AS NOT SO MUCH SEEN TODAY

Today, consumer goods come by rail, air, truck and digital delivery. Our dependence upon water for trade is not as evident as before. Many generations had only two delivery methods: waterways or animal transport.

In his seminal 1812 book on capitalism, *The Wealth of Nations*, early economist Adam Smith showed that ports for sea trade directly correlated to national wealth.

had ships on the sea became rich by her wealth! For in one hour she is made desolate." (Rev. 18:19)

Lucifer's sin originated in his trading. In Revelation 17–18, Babylon and its trade symbolize satan's influence on the commerce of earth.

Notably, Babylon sits on waters.

TORMENT

Every Scripture about the judgment of God's enemies speaks of fire or its consequences. Jesus knew about the terrible fiery torment awaiting the fallen angels and demons—and they knew it as well. In Matthew 8:29, two men oppressed by an army of demons fell down at Jesus' feet. "*And suddenly they cried out, saying, 'What have we to do with You, Jesus, You Son of God? Have You come here to torment us before the time?'*" The kingdom of darkness could read the Bible and knew their fate of torment. It sounds as if they also knew the time set for their destiny to be enforced..

> And the smoke of their torment ascends forever and ever; and they have no rest day or night, who worship the beast and his image, and whoever receives the mark of his name. (Revelation 14:11)

> The devil, who deceived them, was cast into the lake of fire and brimstone where the beast and the false prophet are. And they will be tormented day and night forever and ever. (20:10)

WATER

The rebels' nature remained angelic, but they could never undo the fiery burning within. God had permanently installed it in them. Therefore, fire and water play prominent parts in heaven after Lucifer's fall. Upcoming chapters eleven through thirteen discuss the waters of Genesis 1–3. Book Four of the *Unseen* Series ties the Flood to the heavenly role for water.

Water and the desiccation by fire have great explanatory power for the Bible. Understanding this interplay enables us to identify the works of darkness.

THE NEW PAVEMENT

The Bible contains several eyewitness testimonies about God's throne. Other than Daniel's vision of a river of fire, each reports seeing a watery pavement. Why didn't the Bible witnesses see fiery stones around God's throne? According to Ezekiel 28:14, we would expect to see them if nothing had changed them.

But we know a change occurred. The fiery stones Lucifer once walked upon were all installed in him. They fuel an eternally consuming inward burning. But what replaced the fiery stones?

Now, surrounding God's throne are both liquid and solid water. Each eyewitness of physical heaven saw God's throne on a pavement described as sapphire, or a crystal sea. Both resemble or relate to water. John witnessed rainbows around God's throne, a result of water and light.

They saw the God of Israel. And there was under His feet as it were a paved work of sapphire stone, and it was like the very heavens in its clarity. (Exodus 24:10)

The likeness of the firmament above the heads of the living creatures was like the color of an awesome crystal, stretched out over their heads. (Ezekiel 1:22)

Which is it: crystal or sapphire? Both are firm and translucent. These visions of God's throne area defied the vocabulary of the ancients. To us, however, they resemble something common.

Picture an ice skating rink after the Zamboni has resurfaced it. What would an ancient Middle Eastern person see? What words would he or she use to describe it? The only choice is analogy, because they had no direct experience with an extensive structure of ice. The Bible eyewitnesses describe heaven's physical structure with analogies: sapphire and crystal.

If it had been us, we would recognize the pavement as ice, but not in the warm Middle East prior to refrigeration. They could only describe a newly resurfaced ice rink by its likeness. The words available to them would be pavement, a sapphire, a firmament, a crystal sea.

They might describe it by its effects. When earthly light and ice meet, refraction can form rainbows. Imagine the God of light Himself enthroned on an ice rink. The rainbows would be dazzling, stunning, like lightning.

Where the fiery stones once paved the platform are now ice, water, and rainbows.

He who sat there was like a jasper and a sardius stone in appearance; and there was a rainbow around the throne, in appearance like an emerald … Before the throne there was a sea of glass, like crystal. (Revelation 4:3, 6)

THE WATER OF LIFE

If indeed water replaced fire around God's throne, as a crystal ice pavement, many Scriptures involving water become more understandable. One such is Psalm 46:4–5, describing a river in Jerusalem. There was no physical river on that mountain. The river is the presence of God, like water.

There is a river whose streams shall make glad the city of God,
The holy place of the tabernacle of the Most High.
God is in the midst of her, she shall not be moved;
God shall help her, just at the break of dawn.

Another is Jesus' declaration at a Jerusalem festival about us whom He fills with His Holy Spirit. He uses the same image used throughout the Old Testament. God's blessing is like the irresistible flow of water.

Jesus's declaration is the first to tell how this flow becomes implanted within us: believing in Him. When He frees us from His wrath and fills us with His love, His Holy Spirit will fill us. Rivers, plural, signify the abundant impact of His presence in us. His blessing and holiness irresistibly spill out in every situation of our lives. Like many waters, His love flows and gives life wherever we go.

"He who believes in Me, as the Scripture has said, out of his heart will flow rivers of living water." But this He spoke concerning the Spirit, whom those believing in Him would receive; for the Holy Spirit was not yet given, because Jesus was not yet glorified. (John 7:38–39)

THE WATER AND THE FIRE

Ezekiel's prophecies include the fire of God. Fire dominates his call during his first vision. In chapter one, he describes the mighty cherubim using fire seven times. The fire represents God's wrath against those who disdain Him. In 10:2 and 6, the glory of God departs the Temple in Jerusalem and destructive fire is spread over it. Babylon—an actual empire at the time and the tool God used to exile Israel—is judged by God's fiery wrath as well.

> I will pour out My indignation on you;
> I will blow against you with the fire of My wrath,
>
> And deliver you into the hands of brutal men who are skillful to destroy. (Ezekiel 21:31)

Yet even amid God's fiery judgment, Ezekiel sees the sapphire pavement (1:26, 10;1). As Apostle John did in Revelation 4, Ezekiel describes the surroundings of God with rainbows, a result of light and moisture. God's wrath (the fire) and kindness (the watery surroundings) are inseparable; the prophet saw both—as must we.

> And above the firmament over their heads was the likeness of a throne, in appearance like a sapphire stone; on the likeness of the throne was a likeness with the appearance of a man high above it. Also from the appearance of His waist and upward I saw, as it were, the color of amber with the appearance of fire all around within it; and from the appearance of His waist and downward I saw, as it were, the appearance of fire with brightness all around. Like the appearance of a rainbow in a cloud on a rainy day, so was the appearance of the brightness all around it. This was the appearance of the likeness of the glory of the Lord. (Ezekiel 1:26–28)

Ezekiel then begins to refer water and dryness in the judgments that God exacts, most notably in Egypt's case. God speaks of Egypt having rivers, and cites the pride of the Pharaohs who claim the Nile as their handiwork. His judgment is to dry up the rivers; only the Nile remains today.

> I will make the rivers dry,
> And sell the land into the hand of the wicked;
> I will make the land waste, and all that is in it,
> By the hand of aliens.
> I, the Lord, have spoken." (Ezekiel 30:12)

The prophet did not hold back in shame about God's holiness. But the prophecy of judgment by fire decreases over the course of his forty-eight chapters. Late in his prophetic ministry, God transports Ezekiel physically on two occasions to witness a restoration of wetness.

A chapter dear to many saints is Ezekiel 37. God transports Ezekiel in his body to an unnamed valley where the prophet sees innumerable bones, dissembled skeletons of a long-dead army. These bones Ezekiel describes not as lifeless, dead, or old which we might. Instead he writes, "*and indeed, they were very dry*" (37:2). Yet God brings these very dry bones fully to life. Interpreting the experience for Ezekiel, He identifies the method He uses.

I will put My Spirit within you, and you shall live. (Ezekiel 37:14)

Second, God takes Ezekiel to a high mountain where he witnesses a new Temple (chapters 40–46). He is given a guide and a measuring rod, and God instructs the prophet to *"declare to the house of Israel everything you see"* (40:4)

From within the new Temple, he witnesses water flowing (47:1). The stream widens and deepens into a river. Growing deeper and wider with no tributaries, the river symbolizes the life-giving waters that flow from God living in people by His Spirit. It is the Scripture that Jesus cited at the Jerusalem festival, above.

When it reaches the sea, its waters are healed.... Wherever the rivers go, will live.... Everything will live wherever the river goes. (Ezekiel 47:8–9)

MORE WATER SCRIPTURES

God's blessing is symbolized by water and His wrath by fire. This simple recognition provides deep insight for understanding the Bible, beginning with the garden of Eden. God's blessing on people always involves water or water-based structures.

When God created our first parents, He also planted Eden for them on Earth (Genesis 2:8). We have ten verses describing this garden. Our curiosity would like many more, yet, of the ten verses, He devoted five to its waters. As sparse as the revelation of Eden is, God used half to describe its waters.

Now a river went out of Eden to water the garden, and from there it parted and became four riverheads. The name of the first is Pishon; it is the one which skirts the whole land of Havilah, where there is gold. And the gold of that land is good. Bdellium and the onyx stone are there. The name of the second river is Gihon; it is the one which goes around the whole land of Cush. The name of the third river is Hiddekel; it is the one which goes toward the east of Assyria. The fourth river is the Euphrates. (Genesis 2:10–14)

We've already seen that Jesus used abundance of water to symbolize being filled with the Holy Spirit. Even before His declaration to the Jerusalem feast-goers, Jesus made an evocative statement to the woman at the well.

Jesus answered and said to her, "If you knew the gift of God, and who it is who says to you, 'Give Me a drink,' you would have asked Him, and He would have given you living water." ... "Whoever drinks of this water will thirst again, but whoever drinks of the water that I shall give him will never thirst. But the water that I shall give him will become in him a fountain of water springing up into everlasting life." (John 4:10, 13–14)

BLESSING WATER, JUDGMENT DRYNESS

The fire that burns within darkness's rulers consumes all moisture and leaves them waterless. In contrast, it's said that human bodies are six-tenths water. That's why people are prime targets for darkness.

If water represents the flow of God's blessing upon us and through us, its opposite represents God's judgment and wrath. Like many beloved Scriptures, Psalm 1:3–4 gains new meaning with these facts as it describes seeking God in His Word. Its moisture is blessing and fruitfulness; just as Jesus said, our impact produces the fruit of His blessing everywhere we go. But dryness like windswept wheat husks results from His judgment.

He shall be like a tree
Planted by the rivers of water,
That brings forth its fruit in its season,
Whose leaf also shall not wither;
And whatever he does shall prosper.

The ungodly are not so,
But are like the chaff which the wind drives away.

To the woman at the well, Jesus identified knowing Him as a satisfaction for every thirst. God revealed the opposite to the prophet Amos. Rejecting God means our thirst is never satisfied. The Lord identifies thirst with a famine of hearing His voice, in Amos 8:11–13.

> "Behold, the days are coming," says the Lord God,
> "That I will send a famine on the land,
> Not a famine of bread,
> Nor a thirst for water,
> But of hearing the words of the Lord.
> They shall wander from sea to sea,
> And from north to east;
> They shall run to and fro, seeking the word of the Lord,
> But shall not find it.
>
> In that day the fair virgins
> And strong young men
> Shall faint from thirst."

SUMMARY OF FIRE, DRYNESS, AND WATER

Lucifer's fall began with his jealousy of God's position. His actions to depose God Almighty confirmed his fate. The fiery stones he once walked as gatekeeper to the throne of God are now eternally installed within his very nature. In place of his splendor is now a thirst and famine which satan can never satisfy.

Where fiery stones once symbolized God's remote inaccessibility now stands a cooling water environment—a pavement of ice and clouds producing glorious rainbows.

God not only made heaven moisture dominant. He also created us substantially composed of moisture. He placed our first parents in a watery Eden. The sounds of gushing water filled it, together with the aromas and glistening of its river-borne minerals.

Since Jesus' ministry, human beings can be born again as living spirits. God seats us with Jesus in the heavenly realms, and welcomes us into a throne room which is icy, cool, refracting light into rainbows, and sparkly. All these water elements of the unseen serve to manifest the satisfaction of direct access to God with no gatekeeper. Lucifer and his partners forsook the presence and voice of God; their famine is eternal and their fire unquenchable.

THE PENALTY OF JEALOUSY

God not only sustains these enemies in their eternal punishment. He also amplifies the penalty by provoking their jealousy: He shows them cooling moisture at every turn. In His parable about the callous rich man in hell, Jesus revealed the visibility of heaven. The devil, all his hierarchy, and all his prisoners can see the moisture in heaven.

> And being in torments in Hades, he lifted up his eyes and saw Abraham afar off, and Lazarus in his bosom. Then he cried and said, 'Father Abraham, have mercy on me, and send Lazarus that he may dip the tip of his finger in water and cool my tongue; for I am tormented in this flame.' But Abraham said, 'Son, remember that in your lifetime you received your good things, and likewise Lazarus evil things; but now he is comforted and you are tormented. And besides all this, between us and you there is a great gulf fixed, so that those who want to pass from here to you cannot, nor can those from there pass to us.' (Luke 16:23–26)

Visual provocation of his original jealousy is part of satan's penalty. Lucifer chose jealousy, and jealousy he will have eternally. His jealousy must be at a fever pitch.

Inwardly burning fire motivates the kingdom of darkness to seek cooling moisture. The explanatory power of this simple revelation is comprehensive. The habits exhibited by the kingdom of darkness, both in Scripture and today, seek relief from their inner burning.

It was all by God's design. The Bible reveals that the fate of the fallen was sealed before they were even created, as we will now see.

Discussion and reflection questions for Chapter Seven
can be found in the Reader Engagement Resources

CHAPTER EIGHT

BEFORE THE FOUNDATION OF THE WORLD

The Bible reveals unseeable, unknowable, and untouchable realities. Otherwise we would not know them. Our visible rules, buildings, and activities do not identify us who are the Church. Apostle John saw what we are: the bride of Christ in Revelation 21:1–3. His bride is the very image of an intimate relationship with God Almighty.

> Now I saw a new heaven and a new earth, for the first heaven and the first earth had passed away. Also there was no more sea. Then I, John, saw the holy city, New Jerusalem, coming down out of heaven from God, prepared as a bride adorned for her husband. And I heard a loud voice from heaven saying, "Behold, the tabernacle of God is with men, and He will dwell with them, and they shall be His people. God Himself will be with them and be their God."

The bride of Christ is the fellowship of human spirits made alive. We were each born again by faith in Jesus and filled with His Holy Spirit. We are the only ones on earth capable of wrestling against evil spiritual rulers as Apostle Paul said in Ephesians 6:12.

The uncontrollable life of living human spirits vexes religion and its practitioners. His Bible is no mere moral code, nor are we merely religious adherents. We are God's wind on Earth, as Jesus described us to Nicodemus in John 3:6–8.

That which is born of the flesh is flesh, and that which is born of the Spirit is spirit. Do not marvel that I said to you, 'You must be born again.' The wind blows where it wishes, and you hear the sound of it, but cannot tell where it comes from and where it goes. So is everyone who is born of the Spirit.

The devil is no mere irritant. He and his kingdom are what we replace. In the Bible, God reveals our unseen purpose as the race of man: to rule Earth with Him and dislocate the unseen usurpers. He seeks only one qualification: a poverty of spirit that yields our obedient faith to the Son of God.

Precisely because of our meekness and lack of qualification, Jesus called Himself the Son of Man as if to say, "I am like them, and that's My purpose, too."

SPIRIT "TRAVEL" IN SCRIPTURE

Through the types and symbols of Ezekiel, Isaiah and John, God the Spirit has revealed the origin of the devil and the kingdom of darkness. The fall of Lucifer and his partners preceded our creation. To receive God's revelation in the Bible is like time travel; it tells us what we would have noticed if we had been there. What if the garden of Eden were rediscovered! We might board a train or ship to our rediscovered first home—geographical travel. But for God's Word, we don't need to travel physically because the Bible takes us back, in time, and before time.

THIS IS FOR US

Talking about time travel shakes me a little bit; possibly you. In the nine-book *Unseen* Series, we are not talking about being good Christians or trying harder. If you are stuck there, then get unstuck.

In this chapter, we have an ancient Bible discovery awaiting us—older than Eden and preceding Earth's creation. The Scripture's words take us even further back than the angels' creation. Through God's revelation, we can travel to the reality before He created anything else at all.

In fact, this revelation is far more than the fictional time travel in entertainment. In what follows from the Bible, you will see Creation with your spirit's eyes. This travel will just happen. There's no train whistle, no "all aboard." Your spirit will know.

LIVING HUMAN SPIRITS

Our bodies are on Earth's timeline. But as followers of Jesus Christ, our spirits, like the wind, are not controlled by our bodies.

Jesus repeatedly used an analogy to reveal our standing to us: as Father:Me so I:you. This is called the divine analogy. In Luke 22:29, He used it to describe our authority. "*I bestow upon you a kingdom, just as My Father bestowed one upon Me.*" Apostle Paul believed Jesus' statements and worded it this way: God "*made us sit together in the heavenly places in Christ Jesus*" (Ephesians 2:6).

For many Christian readers, being a spirit is a new way of understanding the Bible. Our privileges as spirits indwelt by God are undeserved and unearned. Christian intimacy with God requires us to mature as spirits, which Jesus told the woman at the well.

The true worshipers will worship the Father in spirit and truth; for the Father is seeking such to worship Him. God is Spirit, and those who worship Him must worship in spirit and truth. (John 4:23–24)

God's authority is unlimited, and He exercises it through us who follow Him. Jesus identified the limit on our spirits' authority in Matthew 16:19.

Whatever you bind on earth will be bound in heaven, and whatever you loose on earth will be loosed in heaven.

"Whatever:" Lord Jesus means there is no limit. Our authority is total. Book One of the *Unseen* Series provides further exploration: *Nobody Sees This You: How to Live as a Spirit in the Unseen Realm.*

Please note that religion and Church are two different systems. I regret to say that religion suppresses our spirit identity, the same way that religion crucified Jesus. In our immaturity as a Church, religion has long infected us; it serves as an emissary of our enemy. Book Seven describes it—*Nobody Sees This Church: Resisting Darkness.*

BEFORE THE FOUNDATION OF THE WORLD

Let's travel to the reality that is outside time. The Bible reveals that our Triune God took three specific actions preceding the creation of anything else, including time itself. All reality stems from them, so I call them reality actions.

The Bible has one phrase for these: *before the foundation of the world.* As you'll see shortly, "the world" is not earth or society or humankind. "The world" is everything besides God Himself.

Maturing as Christians requires our Bible interpretation grid to improve. We continually yield to ever-improving explanations of its content. God's reality acts undergird all creation; they have critical explanatory power for the Bible and penetrate every word.

We, the Church, are destined to overcome and replace Earth's unseen usurpers. Our acceptance of God's three outside-time decisions is of sweeping importance to this destiny. All the Bible makes far more sense to you after understanding them.

Action One: God chose us who are saved and prepared a kingdom for us.

Action Two: Jesus was crucified.

Action Three: An eternal fire was prepared for all God's enemies, angelic and human alike.

Apostle John wrote that his gospel concerned what was in the beginning. Jesus existed before anything else existed. To disclose God's initial actions to John and His other disciples, Jesus coined the phrase, *before the foundation of the world.*

As we will see, God guided the word choice of the New Testament authors in using this terminology. The maturing Christian and church receive this critical knowledge of the unknowable unseen.

WORD CHOICE REVEALS GOD

God is a verbal God. His choice of words in the Bible is very significant. He committed Himself to the limits of vocabulary, culture, and translation. We plumbed this deeply in Book Two of the *Unseen* Series, *Nobody Sees This Unseen Realm: Unlocking Bible Mysteries.*

We might have preferred that the Son of God maintained a deathless life on Earth. That was not God's plan. Instead, He took Jesus' resurrected body back into the unseen. He then poured out His Spirit, who left us a book which He inspired. That book is our Bible—God's Word, through human authors in human language.

He reveals Himself in the Bible—a book that transcends the confused languages of Babel itself. My wife wrote about His miraculous care in compiling the Book He gave us. Her title is *The Bible: The Real Life of a Book*, by D.D. Renfroe.

Such studies as the *Unseen* Series must not second-guess the Scripture's deeply experienced translators. When God committed to a book in human language, He also committed to translation. The industry of Bible translation is proven, trustworthy, and important. We honor those who have dedicated their lives to know and translate its ancient languages. Our purpose is to understand God's word choice, not to correct or dispute its translators.

JESUS' WORD CHOICE

Jesus' disciples preserved His teaching in the New Testament. Of course, they honored Him by using the words He chose. We honor Him likewise when we study His word choice, in this case *before the foundation of the world*.

The Spirit of wisdom and revelation rewards our study with knowledge of the unseen realm. Jesus came to reveal it to men, as He told Nicodemus after using the wind example to describe us.

> If I have told you earthly things and you do not believe, how will you believe if I tell you heavenly things? No one has ascended to heaven but He who came down from heaven, that is, the Son of Man who is in heaven. (John 3:12–13)

Jesus' word choice is meaningful because His vocabulary was broad. He was a native Aramaic speaker. From His Jewish upbringing, He learned Hebrew. He grew up learning Egyptian as a child until Herod the Great died. In His first career as a carpenter/contractor, Jesus would have learned Greek while building the Greek city Sepphoris, now excavated, only five miles from Nazareth. And the disciples wrote the New Testament ("NT") in the dominant language of the day—Greek.

Jesus revealed God's three before-time reality actions with specific Greek words with known meanings. We also know the alternative words He did not choose. We study His phrase, *before the foundation of the world*, to test our existing grid of Scripture. By faith in Him, our spirits can verify the reality His word choice reveals.

BEFORE

Before anything existed, heaven or earth or time itself, there was God.

In the beginning was the Word, and the Word was with God, and the Word was God. He was in the beginning with God. All things were made through Him, and without Him nothing was made that was made. (John 1:1–3)

"Before" and "beginning" both imply a timeline—ours, in fact. The time in which all physical creation exists is linear, sequential, and directional.

Linear means that we experience only one moment at a time. Those moments are one after the other—sequential, and never simultaneous. And they always go in one direction only. The present moment becomes past history; the past never becomes the present. Future never precedes present or past.

Our language and thought patterns are all time-bound because it is all we know. That's why Jesus' phrase uses the word *before*. We can neither experience nor describe any other time-reference. Yet God chose human communication to package His revelations. God speaks the eternal in our time-confined language.

Our timeline did not exist until God created it. What He reveals about the foundation of the world preceded the creation of our time.

Neither He nor His actions are bound to our time. What He does is not limited to a sequential, directional, and linear timeline—no more than His resurrection body was inhibited by walls or distance.

THE FOUNDATION

Before the foundation of the world is the phrase that Jesus coined. The Greek language of the New Testament uses the words καταβολῆς κόσμου. We transliterate them *kataboles* ("foundation") *kosmou* ("of the world").

Foundations in everyday use pertain to buildings. The Greek word for such foundations was θεμέλιον, *themelion* in our alphabet. The New Testament authors used that word to denote the support structure for something heavy. The structural foundation is often literal, such as Acts 16:26 when an earthquake shook Paul's prison on its foundation. Figurative use also occurs, as in Romans 15:20 where Paul expresses his policy not to build on someone else's foundation. Both use *themelion*.

Jesus chose *themelion* when warning us about the figurative foundation of our lives in Luke 6:47-49.

Whoever comes to Me, and hears My sayings and does them, I will show you whom he is like: He is like a man building a house, who dug deep and laid the foundation ["themelion"] on the rock. And when the flood arose, the stream beat vehemently against that house, and could not shake it, for it was founded on the rock. But he who heard and did nothing is like a man who built a house on the earth without a foundation ["themelion"], against which the stream beat vehemently; and immediately it fell. And the ruin of that house was great.

Another word for foundation is the καταβολῆς (*kataboles*) which Jesus used in His phrase, *before the foundation of the world*. That is the only time that Jesus used *kataboles*. When His disciples penned the New Testament, they followed His word choices.

OF THE WORLD

The phrase under study includes *the world*, and two Greek words were available for this as well. Jesus and the New Testament writers used both words.

For land, dirt, real estate, and physical earth as a location, the word used was γην, *gen* in our alphabet. For example, Jesus' third beatitude uses it. "*Blessed are the meek, for they shall inherit the earth*" (*gen*, Matthew 5:5).

The second choice was the one in Jesus' phrase: κόσμος, *kosmos*. Used many times in the NT, it's easily seen in John's gospel. Jesus came into the world (1:9), and takes away the sin of the world (1:29). He is the savior of the world (4:24) and the light of the world (8:12)—for just a few instances. In each case, John uses the root word *kosmos*.

In our language, it is the word cosmos, which sounds the same. For the people of the Bible just as for us, cosmos is everything that exists. It comprehensively designates all reality.

THE DISCIPLES PRESERVED JESUS' WORDS

The New Testament ("NT") recorded three occasions when Jesus used His unique phrase, in Matthew 25:34, Luke 11:50, and John 17:24, respectively.

Come, you blessed of My Father, inherit the kingdom prepared for you from the foundation of the world.

The blood of all the prophets which was shed from the foundation of the world.

You loved Me before the foundation of the world.

The authors used Jesus' phrase exactly, just as they followed His word guidance in other areas. When they intended land, dirt, real estate, or earth, they used γην, *gen*. If a structural foundation was the meaning, their choice also was θεμέλιον, *themelion*. And when His disciples discussed God's three actions above, they used the same phrase Jesus did: *before the foundation of the world*, καταβολῆς κόσμου.

Jesus' disciples also imposed His words on the Scriptures they quoted from the Old Testament ("OT"). It was the entire Bible available to them. Jesus and His disciples both cited it frequently in our New Testament. The NT authors quoted the Greek translation of the Hebrew Scriptures. History credits a group of seventy Jewish scholars for the translation work, so the resulting Greek OT is called the Septuagint (from their word for seventy).

The Scripture is God's Word, even when the only portion was the OT. It is God's Word, even after translation into other languages. Yet when the New Testament writers quoted their Septuagint Bible, they changed its wording to fit what they learned from Jesus. Inspired by the Holy Spirit, the disciples gave greater weight to Jesus' word choices because they, like us, knew Him to be the complete revelation of God in flesh.

MATTHEW'S WORD CHOICE

An example is in Matthew's gospel. All four gospels describe Jesus' habit of teaching in parables; Matthew records a sampling in chapter 13. When he explains Jesus' method with a quotation from the Septuagint, Matthew changes the wording to fit Jesus' word choice.

All these things Jesus spoke to the multitude in parables; and without a parable He did not speak to them, that it might be fulfilled which was spoken by the prophet, saying:
   "I will open My mouth in parables;
   I will utter things kept secret from the foundation of the world."
(Matthew 13:34–35)

Matthew's gospel emphasizes the many ways that Jesus fulfilled Scripture prophecies. The prophecy Matthew cited here is Psalm 78:2, but Matthew reworded it to follow Jesus' word choice. In the Septuagint Psalm 78:2 uses these words: ἀπ' ἀρχῆς (*apo arches* in our alphabet), meaning "from the beginning." Matthew's citation changes that to ἀπὸ καταβολῆς κόσμου *(apo kataboles kosmou)*, meaning "from the foundation of the world." The meaning is not altered. Matthew's rewording follows Jesus' leadership in his word choices—even overwriting Scripture citations with Jesus' exact words.

This word-choice discovery escorts us deeper into the unseen realm. The events described by Jesus' phrase were outside time. Our study takes us into that eternal NOW.

PAUL'S WORD CHOICE

Like Matthew, Apostle Paul also uses both the Greek words for "foundation." His letter to the Ephesian church contains both. Using *themelion* for a building's foundation, Paul explains how apostles and prophets are the foundation of the Church (2:19–20).

But Paul uses Jesus' exact phrase in his overflowing wonder of the gospel. Ephesians 1:3–6 is the longest sentence in the Greek New Testament, and includes the word choice of Jesus: καθὼς ἐξελέξατο ἡμᾶς ἐν αὐτῷ πρὸ καταβολῆς κόσμου—translated *He chose us in Him before the foundation of the world.*

CONSISTENT WORD CHOICE

Apostolic influence follows Jesus' word usage in the letter to the Hebrews. In 4:3, God's works were finished from the foundation of the world (*kataboles kosmou*). Hebrews 11 also uses the structural word about Abraham's hope; he waited for *"the city which has foundations* [themelion], *whose builder and maker is God"* (11:10).

Like Matthew and Paul, Apostle Peter also follows Jesus' choice of words for this revelation, describing Jesus' appointment in 1 Peter 1:20. *"He indeed was foreordained before the foundation of the world* [kataboles kosmou], *but was manifest in these last times for you."* And Apostle John uses *kataboles kosmou* in Revelation 13:8 and 17:8.

All who dwell on the earth will worship him, whose names have not been written in the Book of Life of the Lamb slain from the foundation of the world.

And those who dwell on the earth will marvel, whose names are not written in the Book of Life from the foundation of the world.

THE REVELATION

The Scriptures above reveal God's three reality actions "before" He created our timeline. But these actions are not before, after, or during. They are the underlying reality God decreed prior to any creating, because they are before the foundation of the entire cosmos.

The reality formed by God's three decrees contain and surround everything created. Time exists as one of many elements within God's three actions. These abiding reality actions are determinative for the unseen realm as well.

Action One: God chose us who are saved and prepared a kingdom for us.

Action Two: Jesus was crucified.

Action Three: An eternal fire was prepared for all God's enemies, angelic and human alike.

God spoke to forty-four Bible authors over a 1,500-year period. Each received a partial revelation of the unseen realm. That's why the Bible can be studied as mere history and preached as religious rules without seeing the unseen realm. Often a scholar, preacher, or leader locks in on a favorite section of the Bible. As the saying goes, they miss the forest for the trees. The heavenly realities are revealed by Scripture taken as a whole.

But the Bible's composition completed only in its last 100 years. Prior to its completion, God's reality actions were only partially revealed. Bible books taken individually do not clarify that God built existence itself upon these three truths.

God's entire scriptural revelation was progressive. He revealed to mankind in stages over time. The incarnation of Jesus fully manifested the Second Person of the Triune God. The writings about Him finalized the Spirit's selection of Bible contents.

EXAMPLE: HELL

One of God's reality decrees before anything else was made was the preparation of hell. Nine of every ten Bible references to hell are from

Jesus' lips. He described Judgment Day and hell in Matthew 25:31–46. Please note: He who came first as the suffering Savior will return in His body as the Judge of all men. You and I are accountable to Him; He alone will decide our eternal destination.

> "When the Son of Man comes in His glory, and all the holy angels with Him, then He will sit on the throne of His glory. All the nations will be gathered before Him, and He will separate them one from another, as a shepherd divides his sheep from the goats. And He will set the sheep on His right hand, but the goats on the left. Then the King will say to those on His right hand, 'Come, you blessed of My Father, inherit the kingdom prepared for you from the foundation of the world *(kataboles kosmou)*: for I was hungry and you gave Me food; I was thirsty and you gave Me drink; I was a stranger and you took Me in; I *was* naked and you clothed Me; I was sick and you visited Me; I was in prison and you came to Me.'
>
> "Then the righteous will answer Him, saying, 'Lord, when did we see You hungry and feed *You*, or thirsty and give *You* drink? When did we see You a stranger and take *You* in, or naked and clothe *You*? Or when did we see You sick, or in prison, and come to You?' And the King will answer and say to them, 'Assuredly, I say to you, inasmuch as you did *it* to one of the least of these My brethren, you did *it* to Me.'
>
> "Then He will also say to those on the left hand, 'Depart from Me, you cursed, into the everlasting fire prepared for the devil and his angels: for I was hungry and you gave Me no food; I was thirsty and you gave Me no drink; I was a stranger and you did not take Me in, naked and you did not clothe Me, sick and in prison and you did not visit Me.'
>
> "Then they also will answer Him, saying, 'Lord, when did we see You hungry or thirsty or a stranger or naked or sick or in prison, and did not minister to You?' Then He will answer them, saying, 'Assuredly, I say to you, inasmuch as you did not do *it* to one of the least of these, you did not do *it* to Me.' And these will go away into everlasting punishment, but the righteous into eternal life."

Jesus presents two destinations. The first is what we think of as heaven: *"the kingdom prepared for you before the foundation of the world."* How important it will be to hear those words over us!

The second is hell, described as *"the everlasting fire prepared for the devil and his angels."* There, Matthew records one Greek word, αἰώνιον *(aionion* in our alphabet) synonymous with Jesus' *before the foundation of the world.* Both heaven and hell are of the same quality: before time, outside time, and after time.

Have you heard someone say the Old Testament God is a God of wrath, and the New Testament God is the God of love? This self-justifying dismissal of the entire Scripture is immature reading, at best. In fact, the Old Testament has only one revelation of hell. Almost all Bible references to hell are from the lips of Jesus in the New Testament. No wonder—why else would He incarnate as man and die to save us?

In Jesus, salvation by faith was at hand. Only then did God reveal the existence of hell. God's revelation in Scripture is progressive. In contrast to the people of old, we have it all. We are accountable to honor and to live in all that He reveals—the reason for Christian discipleship.

TIME: BEFORE, NOW, AND ALWAYS-NOW

God created everything, including the linear time that limits natural humanity. God is uncreated; He has always been. He is unlimited by what He created, including time. God is neither part of nor limited by time. All that He revealed is from His perspective outside our linear timeline. This is hard to imagine and may not be clear.

But the preceding review of Jesus' phrase makes one thing very clear: He wants us to know what God did *before the foundation of the world.* Jesus coined the phrase for that reason.

He desired for us to understand the unseen realm and how we live in it. In the Bible, God reveals the history of that world. Because His reality actions precede the foundation of the cosmos, they make everything else possible. The visible realm that all people live in depends upon God's three timeless decrees. The Scripture all makes sense when viewed from the eternal NOW of that spirit world.

The Christian, as someone born of the Spirit, receives the right to become a child of God (John 1:12). Jesus used His own example and the divine analogy to teach about being God's child. Like Him, we can see what our Father shows (John 5:19) and hear what our Father says (John 12:49–50). Book One of the *Unseen* Series explores our spirit existence in depth; it is titled *Nobody Sees This You: How to Live as a Spirit in the Unseen Realm.*

God is outside time. His vocabulary defies placement on humanity's linear timeline. His reality actions preceding Creation are eternally NOW:

they are not linear, sequential, or directional. Always-now is the time experience of the unseen realm where we live as spirits.

These always-NOW decrees of God touch our timeline throughout human history. When the seen and unseen come close without a veil, we see the touch points of the unseen realm. One example is Jacob's ladder, but we need not look that far back to find such a touch point of the unseen, which is occurring today on earth.

Typological interpretation of Scripture with meekness opens our eyes to the unseen. The reality actions of God determined the destiny of both His kingdom and the enemy kingdom of darkness.

Our spirit nature was part of God's decree before the foundation of the world. As we understand this, we become more effective against God's unseen enemies. Just as God chose us in Christ before the foundation of the world, likewise, the eternal fire was prepared for satan and all who align with him.

Living as born-again human spirits disarms their ability to scare us with death, decay, and the passage of time. By God's reality action decrees, we have a superior destiny to theirs. God enthroned us living human spirits in the unseen realm. Promoting us, the weakest, is His way of showing all spirits, friend and foe, that He is love.

> But God ... made us sit together in the heavenly places in Christ Jesus, that in the ages to come He might show the exceeding riches of His grace in His kindness toward us in Christ Jesus. (Ephesians 2:4–7)

Now that we have thoroughly reviewed the calamity of heaven, we are well-equipped to understand the calamity of Earth.

Discussion and reflection questions for Chapter Eight can be found in the Reader Engagement Resources

---

PART TWO

THE CALAMITY
OF EARTH

CHAPTER NINE

THE TEST ABOUT ORIGINS

God declares that we who love Him must undergo tests and trials. He uses the kingdom of darkness, as discussed in Book One of the *Unseen Series*. The prophet Zechariah recorded God's determination to test us. Apostle Peter also takes it up in his first letter.

> I will bring the one-third through the fire,
> Will refine them as silver is refined,
> And test them as gold is tested.
> They will call on My name,
> And I will answer them.
> I will say, 'This is My people';
> And each one will say, 'The Lord is my God.' (Zechariah 13:9)

> You have been grieved by various trials, that the genuineness of your faith, being much more precious than gold that perishes, though it is tested by fire, may be found to praise, honor, and glory at the revelation of Jesus Christ. (1 Peter 1:6–7)

Such tests include the debates about the origin of everything—Creation. For nearly two hundred years, the materialistic naturalism of our society has tested our obedience to the Word of God. We are tested not only for our bravery to present gospel truth faithfully. He also tests our maturity by the manner in which we communicate it.

And a servant of the Lord must not quarrel but be gentle to all, able to teach, patient, in humility correcting those who are in opposition, if God perhaps will grant them repentance, so that they may know the truth, and that they may come to their senses and escape the snare of the devil, having been taken captive by him to do his will. (2 Timothy 2:24–26)

THE STATE OF DEBATE

Does Genesis chapter 1 describe the creation of the universe in six twenty-four-hour days? From conservative Christians to atheist scientists, from creationists to evolutionists, everyone thinks it claims to.

Theologians have used the Latin phrase *ex nihilo*, "out of nothing." It means Genesis 1 tells God's creation of all physical reality, from nothing, by His speech alone: *and God said*. As for the time frame, the text itself uses the word *day* repeatedly.

Some accept a middle ground of compromise between the two sides. They play with the definition of *day* or try to synthesize Genesis 1 with theoretical astrophysics. But what use is the middle ground between two inaccurate sides?

Consider how people act in arguments and debates, even in families. Lines are drawn between black and white. Polarized positions exert a centrifugal force, creating a no-man's-land that no adherent can cross.

Likewise, almost two centuries of such debate over evolution have crystallized, even petrified, the two sides. Creationists versus evolutionists: each has its preferred set of "undeniable" evidence. If the question of origins is a test, what's our grade?

DARKNESS'S TRICK

As the *Unseen* Series progresses, a powerfully effective strategy of darkness becomes clear. It is the pressure to be right, and it is a trick. Christians are very susceptible. Sidestepping blunt force temptation, darkness feeds our fear of being wrong. The unseen enemies we wrestle promote rules of right and wrong that disarm us and favor them. Anyone can see how pressure to be right makes us rigid, argumentative, unloving, and tyrannical.

John 17 relates Jesus' last prayer before His crucifixion. He asked the Father that we would be one. His request didn't include that we would be right. The most important truths are abundantly clear in the Bible, but He left much for us to process through. The devil's origin and the preceding eight chapters are just one of many examples.

Christians are free to think, with the liberty of asking questions. Our agreement is not that we are right in everything. We are free to be wrong because Jesus disarmed satan the accuser; He nailed the written code to the cross (Colossians 2:14–15). Our agreement is that knowing Him is our highest pursuit. When God is our first love, we disarm our unseen accusers more every day.

> And this is eternal life, that they may know You, the only true God, and Jesus Christ whom You have sent. (John 17:3)

God committed to the human process of translating His Word into all the languages of the world. By necessity, He also committed to our human process of inquiry. Using our puzzles and questions, He pulls us into the Bible. With receptivity, we grow gradually to understand His Word. Some are fast and some slow, but we are all gradual.

If we believe that Jesus' death covered our sin against God, we also must accept that He will forgive us for immature conclusions from the Bible. Jesus blessed hungering and thirsting for righteousness, not rightness (Matthew 5:6).

Look at the twelve disciples Jesus chose. They were no scholars and had much to learn. But they followed Jesus and hungered throughout the process of learning from Him. That's the mark of a disciple—not correctness.

RESIST THE TRICK

I have worked hard in this writing, the hardest I've ever done. To publicize a new interpretation of the six twenty-four-hour days is challenging to my skills of persuasion. Some will dismiss it, while others will passionately embrace it and argue for it.

Both groups must resist the trick of darkness, the pressure to be right. Christians and the Church have been consistently vulnerable to it. Instead, it's better to adopt the attitude of John the Baptist when Jesus' ministry outshone his own calling. Jesus affirmed it after His public comments about John's ministry.

A man can receive nothing unless it has been given to him from heaven. (John 3:27)

I thank You, Father, Lord of heaven and earth, that You have hidden these things from the wise and prudent and have revealed them to babes. (Matthew 11:25)

God laid puzzles throughout His Word to entice us as a group of His appointed kings, plural. Together we plumb the Scriptures to see and solve the mysteries. It is a defining act of our sanctifying unity, which Jesus prized so highly as His last request before crucifixion.

It is the glory of God to conceal a matter,
But the glory of kings is to search out a matter. (Proverbs 25:2)

Behold, how good and how pleasant it is
For brethren to dwell together in unity!

It is like the precious oil upon the head,
Running down on the beard,
The beard of Aaron,
Running down on the edge of his garments.
It is like the dew of Hermon,
Descending upon the mountains of Zion;
For there the Lord commanded the blessing—
Life forevermore. (Psalm 133)

Sanctify them by Your truth. Your word is truth. (John 17:17)

RECEPTIVITY TO GOD

Rigidity about God always short-circuits receptivity to God. We tightly grip our favorite templates for interpreting Scripture. It puts us in dangerous company; so did the leaders who crucified Jesus.

You search the Scriptures, for in them you think you have eternal life; and these are they which testify of Me. But you are not willing to come to Me that you may have life. (John 5:39–40)

Uncurious Christians ignore our own Father's choice of words. Our love for Scripture becomes subordinate to our comfortable understanding. Hardened positions dull our Bible reading.

Leaders can gain a vested interest in their conclusions, which stifles their meekness before the Word of God. Entrenched reputations cannot tolerate being less than correct. Ego prohibits exploration.

Revisit the basics with me for new, open-minded receptivity to God's word choices in Genesis 1. We will use the same Inductive Bible Study principles and advanced Bible logic which I outlined in Book Two of the *Unseen* Series.

As if it were a person, let's interrogate the long-named "Creation account" with this questioning receptivity. We are safe with our Father. Our questions are no threat to us or to Him. God deserves to be asked; His Word can stand it.

Let's ask Genesis chapter one: Do you actually claim to reveal how God created physical reality?

EVOLUTION VERSUS CREATION

Charles Darwin first proposed his theory of evolution and natural selection when he published *On the Origin of Species* in 1859. It directly challenged the traditional Christian understanding of six days' creation by God. Ever since, long-held Christian cosmology has debated the so-called "hard and fast conclusions of science."

The debate is a shell game. We'll soon see that neither position is right about Genesis chapter 1. As a result, argument over evolution has detoured God's Church. The kingdom of darkness used it to cloud biblical revelation and enhance our pressure to be right.

Darkness could only do so with Jesus' permission as the Lord of His Church. He stated in the Scriptures above that He tests His people. His seven letters to churches emphasize it also (Revelation 2–3). God permits the debate about evolution and creation. It is a test for us. He wants to prove and mature His Church.

THE SHELL GAME

The *shell game* is a carnival event, which has given rise to an alternate meaning. When we decide that someone is tricking us with fake options, we call it a shell game.

The carnival operator has three cups ("shells") upside down with an object under one shell. He shifts them conspicuously, right in front of the player. After the shells are shuffled, the player attempts to guess where the hidden object is.

There's a prize for success, but we all know the trickster controls the player entirely. Rapid reshuffling and sleight of hand conceal and deceive the player.

THE TWO SHELLS

Academia began taking a secular direction well before 1859. Some seminaries and churches followed the trend as well. "Scholars" gained respect by arguing against the trustworthiness of Scripture. The magnetism of Darwin's new theory drew them to one side in the new debate.

Another side formed for the authority of the Bible. Many preachers and theologians defended traditional Christian belief in the six-day creation.

In 1909, leaders for orthodox Christian doctrine published a four-volume series of essays. They named the collection *Fundamentals*, giving rise to the nickname Fundamentalist. Today it is an *ad hominem* insult which liberal folks use for a Christian who respects the authority of Scripture.

This debate is a shell game. The kingdom of darkness promotes it to hide the truth; they insinuate half-truths into the premises of each side.

UNDER THE EVOLUTION SHELL

Under shell one, evolutionary theory has several truths and desirable qualities. Microevolution has actually been observed. Advocates often show a truthful compulsion to know our origins. Their dedication to science has stimulated archaeology and produced beneficial discoveries. Their religious fervor for an untestable theory reveals the faith impulse God implanted in us. Christian proponents of evolution often have an evangelistic motive to reduce offense to the gospel of Jesus Christ.

But these do not redeem their disrespect for God's revelation, which they vocally disdain. Their arguments are replete with wrong ideas about Him. They also use poor logic, with unprovable presuppositions. From proven microevolution between species, they jump to macroevolution from genus to genus and family to family. This fallacy argues from the small to the large.

Worst of all, a faith in evolution theory is counterproductive to faith in Jesus and His gospel of the kingdom.

UNDER THE CREATIONIST SHELL

Under shell number two are those holding the traditional understanding of creation. They defend the integrity of the Bible record and propagate a high regard for the Bible's trustworthiness and authority. This position finds a divine purpose for our creation in God's image. Creationists consider God's Word superior to science in non-spiritual matters.

However, their interpretation of Genesis 1 leaves them in a weak, fixed position. Their argumentation betrays the influence of preconceptions. The necessity to defend against evolution pushes Christians into the traditional corner.

The kingdom of darkness stokes the fire of uncompromising and rigid uniformity. While it is often needed for defense, it becomes a fearful burden of pressure to be right.

Those so pressured hold it over fellow Christians also. Criticism and ostracism can result for someone who voices the problems in traditional Christian cosmology. That is one reason the previous eight chapters about the devil's origin are rare teaching.

The traditional interpretation of Genesis 1 leaves no room for the kingdom of darkness. Under the cloak of the two hardened positions, our enemies have insinuated falsity into our truths. They will be evident in chapter ten.

UNDER THE COMPROMISE SHELL

There is a third shell in this shell game. Christians who hold to the integrity of Scripture seek a middle ground. Some interpret the Genesis 1 days as geological epochs.

The inescapable fact is that all highly respected translations have *days*, not epochs. The original words of Genesis 1 are *days*, not long periods of time or ages. Its author also wrote about evening, morning, seasons, and years. God's revelation in Genesis 1 is very attentive to time.

But the middle ground proponents adopt the time theories of geology and astrophysics. They subordinate God's revelation and choice of time words. This poor foundation of trust in man's reason cripples their compromise.

The Genesis 1 sequence cannot accommodate modern geological presuppositions. The sun and moon come on Day Four after Day One's light and the grasses of Day Three. Even the rhythm of morning and evening precedes the creation of the heavenly bodies. The compromise requires too many mental pretzels to work.

Another middle ground assertion is that Genesis 1 is not literal, but poetic. Unquestionably, there is refined poetic order in the chapter. But to believe that men's discoveries are superior to God's specific word choices only begs for more problems.

This three-shell game has several benefits for the kingdom of darkness.

WHAT DARKNESS FEARS

The devil leads the crime family of darkness. Wetness that cools their inescapable burning is their craving. Earth is their exile, which they seek to rule for their own benefit. The kingdom of darkness therefore correlates with moisture-seeking behaviors.

God created mankind to dislocate them, the subject of Part Three, *The Calamity of Darkness*. Slowly tending us from our own fall in Eden, He maintained a remnant of people who loved Him.

Jesus' accomplishments opened the door globally. The Church was born with the pouring out of the Holy Spirit.

Now the unseen criminals see the Church as the greatest threat to their rule of Earth. They are correct; we are. God's Word reveals to us and to them that His Church of living human spirits dethrones them on Earth.

THE DEBATE DARKNESS WANTED

Ever since, disarming, disabling, and distracting the Church has been job number one for darkness. The debate about origins has performed that job for the last century and a half, with several benefits for them.

First, when positions solidify at opposite extremes, rigidity replaces receptivity to the Holy Spirit. We are living spirits, filled with the Spirit of God Himself. That is how we rule on His behalf. But when we become rigidly defensive, a cloak of righteousness replaces our supple attentiveness to God. So He permits our tests to continue.

Second, the leaders of the Church rightly sought to defend truthful doctrine. But Darwin's premises and advocates governed the debate. We responded intellectually, painting Christians into a defensive corner.

The Christians' focus on fighting evolutionary theory left society to drift. The pressure for right thinking on evolution alienated people who disagreed. The defenders of Scriptural authority had previously been society's thought leaders. In mere decades, they were a shrinking opposition.

The progressive and social gospel movements arose into the leadership vacuum. Churches who saw little benefit arguing about Creation turned to the mounting social problems of the increasingly industrial society. They detached Church from the Bible. Progressive pragmatists came into the leadership stature once held by orthodox theologians.

Truthful thinking is critically important, and pragmatic service equally so. But the net result of our Christian response to evolution has been the demotion of truth and a withered influence upon culture. Western society became increasingly unhinged from the Bible.

Third, darkness used the shell game debate to encourage mockery of the Church and the Bible. Events such as the trial of an evolution teacher in Dayton, Tennessee, played into the hands of media who labeled it the Scopes Monkey Trial.

The fourth benefit is most damaging. The kingdom of darkness set the boundary lines for the debate. They asserted superiority over the very ruling body appointed to dislocate darkness. With it, darkness engineered the false intellectual debate between two sides with rigid loyalty to half-truths. Are we surprised?

WHAT GOD WANTED, PART ONE

God's method to reveal Himself to mankind has taken the form of a Book: the Bible. My wife's book describes the miracle of its composition, compilation, protection, and promulgation: *The Bible—The Real Life of a Book* by D.D. Renfroe.

We could never know about Creation or Eden without the Bible. Yet, as important as it is, the Bible has only three chapters about it—out of 1,189 chapters. God has the same stinginess in His chapters about heaven, described in only two chapters.

But the Bible has plenty of revelation about God's central motives in the Creation. Those motives are a treasure to anyone who wants to fulfill their purpose as a human being.

First, God's primary desire for humankind is partnership with Him. Yes, He wants us to know about the origins of everything—but for a purpose, to be His partners.

Thus says the Lord:

"Let not the wise man glory in his wisdom,
Let not the mighty man glory in his might,
Nor let the rich man glory in his riches;
But let him who glories glory in this,
That he understands and knows Me,
That I am the Lord, exercising lovingkindness, judgment, and righ-
teousness in the earth.
For in these I delight," says the Lord. (Jeremiah 9:23–24)

"As You sent Me into the world, I also have sent them into the world.…
I have declared to them Your name, and will declare it, that the love with
which You loved Me may be in them, and I in them." (John 17:18, 26)

For whom He foreknew, He also predestined to be conformed to the
image of His Son, that He might be the firstborn among many brethren. (Romans 8:29)

Second, God revealed His Creation so that we could fulfill His earthly
purpose for the race of men. His pronouncement of our purpose on Earth
was the pinnacle event of Genesis 1. He made us to replace Earth's previous dominators, who (as we shall shortly explore) were the exiled satan
and his fellow principalities.

Let Us make man in Our image, according to Our likeness; let them
have dominion over the fish of the sea, over the birds of the air, and over
the cattle, over all the earth and over every creeping thing that creeps
on the earth.… Be fruitful and multiply; fill the earth and subdue it;
have dominion over the fish of the sea, over the birds of the air, and
over every living thing that moves on the earth. (Genesis 1:26, 28)

This understanding of human purpose is why Apostle Paul could char-
acterize our existence this way in Ephesians 6:12.

We do not wrestle against flesh and blood, but against principalities,
against powers, against the rulers of the darkness of this age, against
spiritual hosts of wickedness in the heavenly places.

WORLDVIEW

Jesus revealed the three reality actions prior to the foundation of the cosmos (reviewed in chapter eight). Discussion about the cosmos discloses our worldview. Each person interprets reality with beliefs formed early in life. From infancy, we build a grid for explaining and controlling our surroundings. These grids comprise untestable, unprovable premises and presuppositions—*a.k.a.* our worldview.

One worldview dominates our modern society: materialistic naturalism. This grid of reality presumes a closed universe, in which every cause and effect is potentially explainable by observable forces. By implication, therefore, nothing happened and no one existed before the so-called Big Bang. Materialism cannot admit unseen causes, so spiritual reality is never welcome; that would be an open universe. "Closed" means no influence upon the universe from outside it, presuming without proof that there is no unseen reality.

The naturalist worldview requires only reason, time, and discovery to explain everything. Meanwhile, it tolerates religions to fill gaps of explanation until science can close the gap. This gives rise to the pejorative term for faith, "God of the gaps."

This worldview dominates the modern grid of reality. Once we become Christians, that doesn't vanish from us. We all still carry the deceived worldview into our maturing process. This is by God's design as part of our testing. Will we mature as living spirits? Jesus challenges us to grow up, like He did the disciples who interpreted His warning in exclusively earthly terms.

> Then Jesus said to them, "Take heed and beware of the leaven of the Pharisees and the Sadducees." And they reasoned among themselves, saying, "It is because we have taken no bread." But Jesus, being aware of it, said to them, "O you of little faith, why do you reason among yourselves because you have brought no bread? Do you not yet understand, or remember the five loaves of the five thousand and how many baskets you took up? Nor the seven loaves of the four thousand and how many large baskets you took up? How is it you do not understand that I did not speak to you concerning bread? —but to beware of the leaven of the Pharisees and Sadducees." (Matthew 16:6–11)

Discipleship to mature as a Christian gradually challenges our childhood grid in the same way. The Holy Spirit makes us more like Jesus and extracts us from the dark grip of materialistic naturalism. Paul described the process in 2 Corinthians 5:11 and 10:4–5.

> Therefore, from now on, we regard no one according to the flesh. Even though we have known Christ according to the flesh, yet now we know Him thus no longer ... For the weapons of our warfare are not carnal but mighty in God for pulling down strongholds, casting down arguments and every high thing that exalts itself against the knowledge of God, bringing every thought into captivity to the obedience of Christ.

Jesus said that everyone who believed Him would be born as a spirit. Spirit birth puts the Christian into the unseen realm of spirit living; our spirits are free from the limits upon our flesh. But not everyone who claims to be Christian follows Jesus into such discipleship. Instead, religion and the rapture become their means of feeling secure.

Christians can preserve the familiar worldview that has little room for the unseen. God reveals true reality in the Bible, but our reluctance to yield hampers our unseen warfare. We are born anew as living human spirits, but remain in the grip of our long-held, anti-spirit worldview. This single fact explains many Christian frustrations.

RELIGION OF SCIENCE

Our language, research, and educational systems have a religious faith: only visible physical reality exists. Materialistic naturalism is a religion, with faith in science that cannot be justified scientifically.

Our world is addicted to human reason and scientific method. Their tortured explanations require more faith than God does. Evolutionary theory is a good example of a ginned-up controversy that stretches credulity.

Science is good. As a method, science utilizes repeatable, verifiable, and predictable experimentation. That's how scientists and researchers developed the artificial parts in my heart, and the medicines that keep me well. We thank God for all who use scientific method to improve our lives.

Of course, that method is impossible for the untestable, such as God. Therefore, the religion of science excludes the unseen realm. It has to because unseen causes aren't subject to scientific experimentation. Their pride is at stake.

God uses a telling phrase describing our unseen enemies in Job 41:34. "*He is king over all the children of pride.*" Using the religion of science, our unseen enemies obscure their existence. For the modern template of reality, the only cosmos is the physical one. Of course in that grid there are no demons. In the religion of science, everything is completely explainable by physical forces. Its believers religiously insist the untestable cannot exist.

With this deceptive worldview, you can place your faith in Jesus, yet mature slowly. The trained-in skepticism about unscientific reality retards your spiritual growth. This worldview puts Jesus and God in the same category as Santa Claus and the Easter Bunny.

The Word of God does not yield its secrets to scientific skeptics but to followers of Jesus. Living by materialistic naturalism puts the Christian in agreement with darkness. Its sinister authors prefer to act secretly and obscure that there even is a different worldview.

IF THIS IS THE COUNTERFEIT, WHAT MUST THE REAL BE?

Science is a method which prospers in the hands of the Holy Spirit's people. When scientists use their method to argue with what He has revealed, their theories are handicapped from the get-go. But when the scientific method is used in agreement with what He has revealed, we accelerate the fulfillment of His desire for us to dominate the earth.

This is in fact the case with everything men can do. We can do it in argument with Him, or in agreement with Him.

The Bible worldview is an open universe in which God is an independent actor, accountable to no one. In the true reality, our interpretive template says spirit is superior to flesh.

THE REQUIREMENTS OF SCIENCE

Evolution is defended as scientific truth, in defiance of its theoretical status. Its proponents condescendingly look down on religious faith as a lesser pursuit, willfully blind to their own religious faith—in science. Among the defenders of evolutionary theory are many Christians who have adopted its principles as the best explanation of physical reality. They often do so by compartmentalizing: science has its purpose, and faith has a different purpose. This book is intended as a judgment on no one, but an invitation to revisit what God has revealed.

All new explanations face requirements. One is testing. We can test the new explanation in several ways. Scientific experiments are one type of test. We can also compare the new understanding to other observed realities. But not every new explanation comes from science. Revelation is another source of new understanding. Revelation and science are not at odds and cannot be compartmentalized, because the God who reveals what can't be seen is the same God who created the scientifically observable. The nine-book *Unseen* Series presumes the ability of the reader to test the new explanations of the Bible's revelations.

Science is a method of discovery and verification by testing. The scientific method relies upon an experimentation process. Scientific theories are validated by experiments changing only one variable at a time. People who use this method are called scientists. They produce theories and hypotheses by observing repeatable, predictable physical processes.

That is one reason that evolution is only a theory. It cannot be validated by experimentation because the required period of observation—millions of years—exceeds the time that mankind has been available to observe. Scientific method is limited to the physically observable. It cannot produce any knowledge of the unseen realm, which can only be revealed. It also cannot rule out anything about the unseen realm.

The testing of theories can take another form: the effective explanation of other observable events. Watson and Crick could not see DNA, but the theory of DNA's presence in all living cells explained other, observable realities. No one can see atoms, but their presence powerfully explains things that actually happen, from medicine, to weapons, to electricity.

The effective use of scientific method is also a group effort: the experiments that validate hypotheses must be repeatable and verifiable by others. Therefore science is not monolithic; its conclusions can never be "hard and fast." Previous explanations are modified by later discoveries.

EXPLANATORY PROCESS

This maturing process of ever-new explanations is installed in humanity. Our constant drives to explore, innovate, and solve are part of being made in God's image. Each generation thinks its explanations are the best, and resists their followers who attempt improvements.

The rigidity of some Christians who defend the Bible is a discrediting quality. Scientists exhibit equally rigid insistence that their explanations are the best—defying the very presuppositions of scientific discovery. Both sides of the Creation versus evolution debate discredit themselves when they dogmatically resist that drive to explore, common to all people and all endeavors by God's design.

PHILOSOPHY OF OBSERVATION

People interpret observations by using prior assumptions; *a priori* is the Latin phrase. These are presupposed truths that cannot be established by testing through repetitive experimentation. They are accepted by faith which belies the scientific pride in logic and reason. All scientific observations are affected by the *a priori* beliefs. All scientific theories have largely theoretical, untestable foundations.

For example, neither you nor anyone can verify that the report of our five senses is the actual world that exists. It is untestable. This huge field of philosophy is called epistemology, from the Greek words for *faith* and *word*. This branch of thought explores what faith is needed for us to navigate life with our senses.

René Descartes ("day-CART," 1596–1650) addressed the reliability of our senses with a thought experiment: what if the ruler of the universe was an evil genius? What if he was fooling us into thinking we exist at all? His considerations gave us the well-known conclusion, "I think, therefore I am."

PHILOSOPHY OF REVELATION

We don't have to pretend to be scientists if we are not. But we are not their fool, either. Just because science says it's so, doesn't make it so. Their grid for interpretation is faith-based. It may not be Christian faith or any known religious doctrine, but it is a religious faith, nonetheless. All scientists interpret their observations using untestable, faith-based *a priori* beliefs.

We respect scientists' work and contribution to humanity. We can welcome the results of the scientific method without bowing to the religion of science. Its beliefs and conclusions are used to bludgeon dissenters—until an influential person wants different conclusions. Nowhere in recent history has this been more evident than with vaccination scandals.

In these pages I write as I live, with an *a priori* belief: the Bible is the Word of God, divinely authoritative, uniquely inspired, and entirely trustworthy, with the total accuracy appropriate to its intentions. Unlike the presuppositions of the scientific community, our *a priori* belief has been thoroughly tested and found valid by people of every culture and every century.

That inspired Bible enables us to know what occurred before the creation of time. The revealed events—such as the fall of Lucifer—are unobservable, untestable, unrepeatable events, known to us only by God's revelation. However, like DNA and other such untestable realities, we can test our understanding in another way. Does our interpretation have explanatory power for what we actually experience? If more of life and reality are explained by our new understanding, its stronger explanatory power makes it the preferred understanding. The new discoveries in God's Word force the modification of previous understanding.

WHAT GOD WANTED, PART TWO

Why would God permit the publication and promulgation of satan's lies about evolution? Let's ask the bigger, simpler question behind that one: why does God permit the enemy to bother us? Apostle Peter wrote the answer in 1 Peter 1:6–8. He wrote from knowledge; Peter had more recorded encounters with satan than any other apostle.

> Now for a little while, if need be, you have been grieved by various trials, that the genuineness of your faith, being much more precious than gold that perishes, though it is tested by fire, may be found to praise, honor, and glory at the revelation of Jesus Christ, whom having not seen you love.

God permits the enemies to test His Church. Some Christians live as if their purpose is the pursuit of personal fulfillment. We certainly are fulfilled, but that is not our purpose.

God created us to be His partners in His great enterprise. This eternal enterprise predates Creation and outlasts it. He wants you to be part of it with Him, both with your life in your earthly body and for eternity afterwards.

Evolutionary theory is one such test. Our response to it is also part of the test. Darkness and sinful humankind use evolution as their distracting shell game to obscure Bible truth.

How will we respond?

PROTECTING THE OLD

The Christian public follows gifted leaders. We receive the fivefold leadership as Jesus' gift to His Church. "*He Himself gave some to be apostles, some prophets, some evangelists, and some pastors and teachers*" (Ephesians 4:11). We prosper by following their leadership.

Yet even these gifted leaders can settle for inadequate Bible grids. Sometimes, the cost of improvement affects so many in their organizations. And there may not be time or stamina to investigate new Bible paradigms. We Christians place many demands upon those who minister to us.

If a monk made one stroke wrong when hand-copying the Bible, the error was replicated every time another monk used that edition. Likewise, if a leader is unable or unwilling to find better Bible explanations, the deficient template can be reinforced, replicated, and unchallenged.

This book focuses on our templates for Genesis 1, but the pattern applies to all our Bible reading. We use our leaders as cover for our incomplete Bible template. After all, if unsolved Bible puzzles don't bother them, why should the puzzles bother us? But it's one of the tests we all undergo. Will we pursue God?

Protecting existing explanations is a powerful motive that we all share. Every generation prefers their old wineskins, when God wants to pour out new wine of understanding (Mark 2:12–22). God tests each generation for receptivity.

In contrast, consider the meek person. The maturing Christian can honor leaders without using them as an excuse to settle for existing explanations. As we grow in meekness, we fall in love with God, no matter the cost. We worship Him, no matter the challenge to our existing ideas. Like Moses said to the Lord on Mt. Sinai, "*Please, show me Your glory*" (Exodus 33:18). Meekness and knowing God go hand in hand. That's why someone like Joshua added this footnote to the dispute of Aaron and Miriam.

(Now the man Moses was very humble, more than all men who were on the face of the earth.) (Numbers 12:3)

It's God's Word, not ours. In meekness, we yield all our Bible templates to Him. To do otherwise is to group ourselves with the Bible students who crucified Jesus. But unlike them, our repentance from stubbornness makes us ready for corrected understanding. Hungering and thirsting for righteousness, we are eager to improve our explanations. This never stops.

Paul described to Timothy this continual effect of the Bible. Included is the process of continual improvement in our Bible grids, templates, and expectations.

All Scripture is given by inspiration of God, and is profitable for doctrine, for reproof, for correction, for instruction in righteousness, that the man of God may be complete, thoroughly equipped for every good work. (2 Timothy 3:16–17)

Discussion and reflection questions for Chapter Nine
can be found in the Reader Engagement Resources

CREATION IN FOUR STEPS

The traditional Christian doctrine of creation in six days is a misreading of Genesis 1. This dramatic statement is simple to support from the text itself.

But as the saying goes, simple doesn't mean easy. Relinquishing an interpretation held so long by so many is hard. Whatever we read, we bring a grid of expectations. Without thought, we dismiss what doesn't fit into the expected template.

There are several signals of defects in our Bible grid. For one, its mysteries defy penetration. Bible puzzles resist solution; explanations sound contrived and complex. All this, we tolerate in order to protect our preferred interpretations.

Meanwhile, the Holy Spirit whispers, "Come up here" from the Bible pages. We know that there is more if we will but come.

NOT POETIC

In chapter nine's shell game, the compromise shell tries to reconcile the creation/evolution debate. Some interpret it only as poetry; they say the poetry is the revelation, not the events. The language of Genesis chapter 1 is undeniably poetic in structure. If it is *only* poetic, some feel relieved from pressure to take it literally.

Others in the compromise shell try to reconcile popular astrophysics with creation. To them, the days in Genesis 1 represent billion-year epochs. As they see it, the events may be literal, but definitely not in twenty-four-hour days.

Reconciliation is good, but these attempts limit Genesis 1 to poetic interpretation *only*. Seeking explanations is good—unless we limit them by what others like. To limit the creation account to poetic revelation is indefensible. Nothing in Genesis 1 restricts it to poetic interpretation.

The chapter includes no signals to read it as poetry *only*; to do so imposes a limit which the chapter does not claim. Any motive for restricting Genesis 1 to poetic revelation must originate in the reader.

The language is plain and purposely chosen. No one forced the use of time words; their inclusion was purposeful. Other time words were available; seasons and years are mentioned in Genesis 1. The six days are each described as a cycle of evening and morning. Every respected translation uses the word "day" for these reasons.

Worldwide evidence supports this. Embedded in every society is the seven-day week. Genesis chapter one explains its origin. There, God clearly describes a seven-day sequence of events.

God purposely chose to reveal Himself in a book containing His Word. God's actual choice of words matters. Our response to those choices is serious.

Genesis 1 makes no apology and offers no rational justification. To the contrary, the chapter methodically describes events at the beginning of the world we know. The language is clear: in six days, God worked to eliminate all the formless, dark void, and rested on the seventh.

For hundreds of years, Christians have interpreted Genesis 1 using the Christian doctrine of six-day creation. But is that a correct reading of the text itself?

OLD TEMPLATE

The traditional Christian doctrine of Creation ignores the plain language of Genesis 1:1–2. We know that we Christians can be out of sync with the Scripture's plain meaning. That's why we study it constantly, to align more closely with our Father.

In the beginning God created the heavens and the earth. The earth was without form, and void; and darkness was on the face of the deep. And the Spirit of God was hovering over the face of the waters.

Before the six-day sequence even begins, the earth already exists. The deep exists. Waters exist. The Holy Spirit interfaces with the deep waters of the earth.

These are physical realities preceding the six days. The language is clear and convincing: the six days of Genesis 1 are not the initial creation. When the six days begin, creation has already occurred.

To believe the six days are the initial creation, we must ignore verse 2 because there is no explanation. To excuse ourselves, we take cover behind some scholar or theologian. No matter who it is, to insist that the six days are creation from nothing does not explain Genesis 1:2. Something *was* there before the six days started: the formless void of earth and its deeps.

We inherited a polarized choice from the last two centuries. Our forebears told us to believe *either* creation from nothing in six days *or* evolutionary theory. The simplest instinct tells us evolution is logically unprovable at best. The petrified terms of debate left us only one choice: interpret Genesis 1 traditionally.

Numerous interpretation difficulties arise, and their solutions require twists of logic that defy credulity. These twists signal defects in our grid for interpreting Genesis 1.

How could day and night, grass, and trees, precede the creation of the sun and moon? Why would God create the world and leave it formless and void? What is the firmament, and how are there waters above it? To avoid adjusting our grid of interpretation, we don't see the unsolvable puzzles it produces. We just ignore them.

Authors and teachers argue for creation against the erosive disbelief of evolution. To expose unbelief is good. But arguing that the six days of Genesis 1 reveal creation from nothing is a handicap.

Mental gyrations are necessary, which earns disrespect from our opponents. The complex explanations make pretzels using tortured logic. That's why our argument for creation has lost ground and gained few adherents. The Church was discredited for two hundred years while godless evolution became the religion of our society.

The six days are not original creation. The Bible's plain revelation in verses 1 and 2 disallows that interpretation. When the six days begin, creation has already occurred.

NEW TEMPLATE

By studying the devil's origin, we become equipped to demolish his arguments. The kingdom of darkness is defenseless against God's Bible truth in our mouths.

> For though we walk in the flesh, we do not war according to the flesh. For the weapons of our warfare are not carnal but mighty in God for pulling down strongholds, casting down arguments and every high thing that exalts itself against the knowledge of God, bringing every thought into captivity to the obedience of Christ. (2 Corinthians 10:3–5)

Our effectiveness increases as we align more closely with God's Word. This includes an improved grid to interpret Genesis 1. God's blitz attack on darkness shows us their weaknesses, and alerts us to His weapons, such as Paul described above.

Genesis 1 is far more important than the traditional explanation can see. It is no less valuable simply because it doesn't tell the original creation event. Quite the opposite—the six days reveal far more of the unseen world.

We wrestle against principalities and rulers; knowing their history strengthens our warfare. The improved creation grid in this book reveals how God binds these enemies. Our purpose becomes much easier to implement in the unseen realm.

Genesis 1 is not the only Creation passage; a four-step process is revealed and affirmed throughout the Bible. Previous chapters reviewed many Scriptures including Ezekiel 27–28, Isaiah 14, and Revelation 12. Together they reveal the coordination of God's actions in Genesis 1 with His plan for the kingdom of darkness. This understanding provides far more explanatory power for the six days.

This four-step process began in Genesis 1:1, God's original creation. Subsequently, and by God's leave, the exiled rebels deformed and emptied all its original contents. They caused the formless, dark, and watery void of Genesis 1:2.

But God withdrew their permission to dominate and ruin Earth to their liking. Beginning with 1:3, He reclaimed the ruined Earth in six twenty-four-hour days. The crowning creation was us—the only creatures ever made in His image and likeness—as Lucifer's replacements.

We can test this Bible grid. The resulting explanatory power unlocks many Scriptures.

RESULTING EXPLANATIONS

This plain reading of Genesis 1 yields far more explanatory power for the entire Bible. It unlocks revelation about the origin, purpose, and policies of satan's crime family.

Genesis 1:2 describes the ruined Earth. The Holy Spirit found it to be *"without form, and void."* Who caused that? The kingdom of darkness caused this formlessness and emptiness. Thus, this explanation accords with Jesus' statement about satan in John 10:10a, *"The thief does not come except to steal, and to kill, and to destroy."*

The revelation that creation occurred long before the six-day reshaping also explains how *"darkness was on the face of the deep."* Have you heard this explained away as a poetic description of a world without light? Why wouldn't God just write, "it was totally dark" or "there was no light?"

The spillover of war from the unseen caused Earth's condition. The darkness and the deep both match the work of satan and his partners in rebellion. This is exactly the explanation provided in the three origin Scriptures.

This war not only explains why God reshaped Earth. It also emphasizes why He made us, and why in His image. We are the ones to reclaim His dominion over Earth from darkness.

> Let Us make man in Our image, according to Our likeness; let them have dominion over the fish of the sea, over the birds of the air, and over the cattle, over all the earth and over every creeping thing that creeps on the earth. (Genesis 1:26)

THE HOVERING SPIRIT

Genesis 1:2 also says *"the Spirit of God was hovering over the face of the waters."* Is this only poetic language? We must not dismiss God's word choices.

Why *hovering*? It's poetic to talk about *the face of the waters*. But why choose *face*? Why are there *waters*?

The Earth was covered with water, also called the deep. The kingdom of darkness has reformed it to cool themselves from their inner burning. That explains many Bible puzzles. Two examples are Leviathan and his identity (Job 41, Isaiah 27), and Jesus' revelation of the demons' craving (Luke 11).

How do the waters have a *face*? This is not accidental. We fill in what we think it means: *surface*. Then why didn't the author of Genesis use *surface*? He had that word available. The ark floated on the *surface* of the waters (7:18). Moses also used it when the manna fell on the surface of the ground (Exodus 16:14). But instead of surface, *face* is used in Genesis 1:2.

What is our face for? It is the part of our head that is forward-facing. It is our center of perceiving and expressing, of nourishing and sensing, of interfacing and of isolating. We relate with no body part more greatly than with our face. We even call it "interfacing."

God reveals later in Genesis 1 that the firmament had a face, and the Earth has a face. Why wouldn't the Scripture simply say, "over the waters?" If it had to be a body part, why not "skin of the waters?" To us, water and sky are inanimate physical objects; why does the Bible use *face* for them?

After ruining the earth, the kingdom of satan turned their dispassive, disengaged, and dismissive face toward God.

Several Scriptures tell us why the Third Person of the Triune God was hovering. He searches for someone to relate to, and identifies who is on God's side. Two examples are 2 Chronicles 16:9 and Zephaniah 1:12.

> For the eyes of the Lord run to and fro throughout the whole earth, to show Himself strong on behalf of those whose heart is loyal to Him.

> And it shall come to pass at that time
> That I will search Jerusalem with lamps,
> And punish the men
> Who are settled in complacency.

Apostle John is also shown how the Spirit of God ranges the earth, in Revelation 4:5, 5:6.

> Seven lamps of fire were burning before the throne, which are the seven Spirits of God.... having seven horns and seven eyes, which are the seven Spirits of God sent out into all the earth.

Apostle Peter reveals that God is "*not willing that any should perish but that all should come to repentance.*" (2 Peter 3:9). The searching Spirit was hovering over the face of the waters. He was available to the rebels who ruined God's beautiful Earth. After such an opportunity to interface, satan and the kingdom of darkness are without excuse for their continuing opposition to God.

The hovering Spirit of God received no response. This fulfilled the plan God had made before the foundation of the world.

WHY FOUR STEPS?

There is only one way this grid can be accurate: that God enacted His creation plan in steps. In chapter eight, *Before the Foundation of the World*, we reviewed three decisive decrees God made before any creating—when only He existed. Those decrees required these four steps. Why did He follow a step-by-step process? Because His decrees must be fulfilled.

He declared them outside time, before creating the heavens and the earth. The creation we now inhabit was the end result of that process. Reverse engineering from His eternal decrees, the step-by-step sequence of creation becomes quite evident.

THE FOUR STEPS IN THE TOTAL CREATING PROCESS

Step one: create a physical universe. God executed that step in Genesis 1:1. "*In the beginning God created the heavens and the earth.*" Earth was necessary to receive Lucifer and his angels, who had yet to rebel.

Step two: the rebellion in heaven and their exile to Earth. We saw God's revelation about it in Ezekiel 28, Isaiah 14, and Revelation 12.

Therefore I cast you as a profane thing out of the mountain of God ... I cast you to the ground ... I turned you to ashes upon the earth. (Ezekiel 28:16, 17, 18)

So the great dragon was cast out, that serpent of old, called the Devil and Satan, who deceives the whole world; he was cast to the earth, and his angels were cast out with him. (Revelation 12:9)

How you are fallen from heaven,
O Lucifer, son of the morning!
How you are cut down to the ground. (Isaiah 14:12)

The rebellion was definitely going to happen. It was lamentable, a cause of grief for God. Yet He did not act preemptively to prevent it. Before the foundation of the cosmos, He had decreed unending fiery wrath upon enemies—before they even existed.

Step three: the ruination of Earth by rebels. Seeking relief from the inward burning God implanted into them, they turned this entire globe into a dark and watery deep. He permitted their destruction of His original Earth.

Step four: restore the demolished creation. God reclaimed dominance from the rebels of darkness. It is this step that has a six-day schedule. The kingdom of darkness didn't know or track days before God began. To satan and his angels, they would know only a relentless tempo with staccato terror and painful effect.

In the six lightning-fast days, He completely reshaped what darkness had imposed upon Earth. The damage they did, He reversed. The free rein they once enjoyed, God suddenly tightened. Like we put pigs in a pigpen, Almighty God hemmed in the kingdom of darkness. Never again would they be allowed to ruin God's physical universe.

The four steps culminate with a reproducing image of God upon the earth: us.

SATAN FULFILLS THE MUST

Many children ask why God created the devil or let him live. Anyone should wonder why, and the four-step process explains it. The kingdom of darkness must exist to fulfill His verbal decrees when He alone existed.

Psalm 138:2 says God honors his word above his name. This is a dramatic statement about His priorities. Executing what He says receives His greatest attention. Even the honor of being called by His right name is subordinate to His Word. Permitting Lucifer's rebellion and ruination of Earth is the consequence of God's priority structure.

The decrees of God before the foundation of the world must be fulfilled. Jesus knew the Father's priority structure, and justified His own words by saying *"the Scriptures must be fulfilled"* (Mark 14:49, *et al*). God permitted darkness to ruin and frustrate His creation, in honor of His own decrees.

THE SCHEDULE

Genesis 1 provides no schedule for the first three steps in God's creation process. No Bible teaching requires them to be completed in a certain time frame. Only step four has a schedule: six twenty-four-hour days.

During those one-hundred-forty-four hours, God manhandled the kingdom of darkness. Previously, as God watched, the fallen Lucifer and his angels had ruined all that He had made. But His power far exceeded theirs, as they learned all over again. He manhandled all that they had done, and He did it in summary fashion.

From their viewpoint, the six days would feel like an ambush. In rapid succession, one major surprise after another disrupted their comfy, cozy, and dark cooling pool. They could not contest His actions, nor could they resist His assault. By His rapid completion of step four, God attacked their home with staccato rapidity. It would be both fearsome and humiliating for the enemies of God.

OTHER SCRIPTURES ABOUT SIX DAYS

In the Ten Commandments, God explains why the Sabbath is a commandment, in Exodus 20:11.

> For in six days the Lord made the heavens and the earth, the sea, and all that is in them, and rested the seventh day. Therefore the Lord blessed the Sabbath day and hallowed it.

In Genesis 1, God named each day's result of His reshaping. The firmament He named Heaven. Earth was His name for the dry ground. The gathered waters were called Seas. He created all their contents in those six days. None of these include the original, unexplained stage one, which occurred long before the six days.

The New Testament agrees with Genesis 1 that God created everything. Its writers also hold to the six-day sequence recorded there; Hebrews 4:4 is an example. Jesus affirmed what Genesis relates about Adam and Eve. But nowhere in the New Testament are we taught that the events of the six days are the creation event.

STEP ONE: CREATE THE HEAVENS AND THE EARTH

This was the only step preceding the fall of Lucifer. We have one verse about it. No schedule is given, no method explained. None of the results are detailed. Not even the governing physical laws are described; we cannot assume they mirrored the observable ones we know.

In the beginning God created the heavens and the earth. (Genesis 1:1)

Earth is easy to understand, but what does heavens mean? Elsewhere in Scripture, heaven signifies the unseen realm, but not in Genesis 1. God used the word heaven to name the firmament (1:8). He formed the sun, moon, and stars in the heavens (1:14). In this text, the word heavens describes the physical reality above the surface of the earth. It does not include the unseen realm.

Therefore, Genesis 1:1 completely describes physical creation—the earth and everything above it. God created the entire physical universe in the beginning. Verse 1 of Genesis 1 is the only reference. God reveals no description of what He made.

But we can guess. The quality of His original heavens and earth is clear; both the Bible and our experiences provide ample evidence of His imagination, ability, and character.

For sheer imagination, nobody has more. God can imagine and create anything. Fingerprints are a common example of the breadth of His creativity; we could choose DNA as well. Both are unique to every person.

We think there is one sunrise and one sunset per day. In terms of our current geophysical rotation, that is correct. But we don't look at sunrise and sunset with science. Through our eyes, their beauty penetrates our hearts.

Seven billion people live on earth; for each He imagines and coordinates a unique viewpoint. They see seven billion unique sunsets and sunrises. The color spectrum is one of His palettes; your feelings provide yet another array of colors.

For paint brushes, God uses the air around you and your position on the globe. The position of the sun is a brush of seasons; the humidity and weather around you add even more variety. Even where you stand is useful, as the surrounding landscape reflects certain wavelengths. Even jet contrails and the clarity of your eyesight are available to this Artist. For each of us, God imagines and executes a unique event—twice a day.

God's ability is unlimited as well. I attempted to play golf for a few years. I always wondered if He controlled the interaction of the golf ball dimples with the air as it flew. Did He fly my golf ball into that sand trap? On purpose? It certainly would not be beyond His ability.

Because of our materialistic naturalism, we think of God's ability in physical realities. But to me, His most impressive ability is self-restraint. If you or I were God, I daresay self-restraint would not be our strong suit. I believe our power usage would mirror Bruce Nolan, the newsman played by Jim Carrey in the movie *Bruce Almighty*.

The strongest basis for imagining the original creation is God's character. The Bible is replete with revelation about it. Such verses as the following suggest the qualities latent in that first world.

> But the fruit of the Spirit is love, joy, peace, longsuffering, kindness, goodness, faithfulness, gentleness, self-control. (Galatians 5:22–23)

> The kingdom of God is not eating and drinking, but righteousness and peace and joy in the Holy Spirit. (Romans 14:17)

God's character is also righteous and holy. He expresses his wrath every day (Psalm 7:11). But wrath is absent during step one; no sin has yet occurred, not even the rebellion in heaven.

God far prefers to relate with His love rather than His righteous anger. He declared His character to Moses on Mount Sinai; count the phrases of love to see His emphasis.

> And the Lord passed before him and proclaimed, "The Lord, the Lord God, merciful and gracious, longsuffering, and abounding in goodness and truth, keeping mercy for thousands, forgiving iniquity and transgression and sin, by no means clearing the guilty, visiting the iniquity of the fathers upon the children and the children's children to the third and the fourth generation." (Exodus 34:6–7)

God's imagination, ability and character assure us that His creation in Genesis 1:1 was far better than we can imagine. God had free rein, unopposed by any sin, unrighteousness, or wrongdoing.

STEP TWO: REBELLION IN HEAVEN

We've discovered step two in previous chapters: the rebellion in the unseen realm. After their effort to replace God Almighty, the devil and his angels now have His consuming fire as a permanent implant.

STEP THREE: AFTER THE REBELLION

Exiled to Earth, the rebels craved the coolness which its water provided.

Compared to their ultimate fate in the lake of fire, their exile on earth is a hotel pool vacation: not home, but better than the alternative.

> The earth was without form, and void; and darkness was on the face of the deep. And the Spirit of God was hovering over the face of the waters. (Genesis 1:2)

Whatever Earth looked like before they fell, its beauty was replaced by void. All the form created by God, satan and his angels destroyed. Lucifer and his rebels altered the earth to their liking. Every quality God originally installed in Earth was completely absent afterwards.

Whatever light existed in Genesis 1:1, it was nowhere to be found after Earth's demolition by darkness. Whoever and whatever God had placed on earth for a relationship, any interface with the Spirit of God was now prohibited. Earth was completely reversed from God's originally perfect creation. It was formless and void. Only the presence of their inward heat kept Earth's deeps liquid and misty.

This despoiling of God's Earth was the work of the exiled Lucifer. To despoil is synonymous with such words as strip, deprive, rob, pillage, and plunder. For Lucifer to despoil means that he robbed God of Earth's beauty, and ruined what God had made originally.

Our God has exhibited long-suffering with our fallen race. Previously, He had long suffered the despoiling of His original handiwork. Earth's ruination by satan and his angels took place right in front of Him.

The six days of Genesis 1 are like many Bible statements; they presume the reality we found in the three origin chapters. In a sentence, the war in the unseen realm spilled out into the physical creation. After their exile to earth, the kingdom of darkness spoiled what God had created. They emptied and darkened it to suit their need for cooling.

COOLING POOL

Most of us have seen nuclear power plants, recognizable by one distinct feature: cooling towers. The structures are giant and steam rises from their surface far above the ground. Within them is water, super-heated by nuclear radiation.

Imagine the massive amount of water required to cool extreme heat. You have just pictured the distinguishing feature of satan's demolition. Earth was nothing more than a giant cooling pool for him and his angels.

In the condition of Genesis 1:2, our knowledge of physical laws tells us the water should freeze, that mists should condense and dissipate. What would keep it liquid? Warmth was necessary, but from where? The internal heat of God's burning judgment in the devil and his angels was its only source. They would have left no other heat source remaining.

When they get to the hotel, children want to swim in the pool. When your day is hot and the bright sun warms the water, where do you go to cool off? You swim to the bottom of the deep end.

To cool themselves, the fallen Lucifer and his angels destroyed all dry land, light, and life out of the way. No form was found; no light was allowed; no life remained. They knew no days; no timekeeping was possible. They wanted the Earth covered with water.

The unholy angels inhabited the deep, for simple relief from the fire of God. Even His light aggravated their pain; for them, only total darkness would suffice. When the Holy Spirit inspected the results, He found no form, no thing, and no relationship—only deep, dark, faceless waters.

COUNTERFEIT

Genesis 1:2 was not the last time that Earth was covered with water. The deep that satan and his angels created was a counterfeit of something God Himself would do.

The Flood was a dramatic reshaping of Earth, to be studied in Book Four of the *Unseen* Series titled *Nobody Sees These Enemies: How to Discern and Disarm Unseen Tempters.*

God's flooding differs from satan's flooding. His holiness was the motive; His love left a remnant— Noah and his family.

STEP FOUR: EARTH RECLAIMED

In a rapid-fire reign of terror upon darkness, God undid the destruction that satan and his angels had wrought. How did each day's work affect their dominion?

Discussion and reflection questions for Chapter Ten can be found in the Reader Engagement Resources

---

PART THREE

THE CALAMITY
OF DARKNESS

CHAPTER ELEVEN

THE SEVENTY-TWO HOUR BLITZ

DAYS ONE, TWO, AND THREE

The kingdom of darkness had imposed formlessness on God's original Earth. In Days One through Three, a span of seventy-two hours, He restored form and imposed it on them. The subsequent days next fill the void which they had created by destroying everything.

WHY, GOD?

If the only decisive decree of God was the eternal punishment of the devil and his angels, it could have started immediately. He had prepared an eternal fire before even creating them; He could have sent them straight there. There would have been no need for this intermediate age.

But before the foundation of the world, God made two other decrees. Both of them required creatures made in God's image who could reproduce and be able to die. The enemies had an important part to play, but it was not dominion.

Our discoveries about the origin of the devil and his kingdom of darkness require an improved reading of the six days. How did each day integrate with God's three decrees? The kingdom of darkness had imposed formlessness on God's original Earth. In Days One through Three, a span of seventy-two hours, He restored form and imposed it on them. The subsequent days next fill the void which they had created by destroying everything.

DAY ONE

> Then God said, "Let there be light"; and there was light. And God saw the light, that it was good; and God divided the light from the darkness. God called the light Day, and the darkness He called Night. So the evening and the morning were the first day. (Genesis 1:3–5)

God's first reshaping action was to reintroduce light. We might have expected Him to eliminate darkness; He did not (and still does not). He limited it without destroying it, which only occurs in Revelation 21.

He established a boundary where light exists and darkness cannot penetrate. Already, with only one new shape, Earth was no longer formless. God's seventy-two hour assault on darkness had begun. After God spoke light, there was morning and evening, day and night.

He spoke light and day and they suddenly existed. This happened with no sun, moon, or other heavenly bodies, which come three days later on Day Four. How does this accord with the physical laws we know today?

Day One does not tell us the origin of the light. But other Scriptures describe the light source: God Himself. He is THE physical law. To describe Him, James used light that never dims.

THIS IS FOR US

James and John were disciples whom Jesus nicknamed Sons of Thunder. They wanted to call down judgment fire to destroy unreceptive people.

We think that way too, seeing that the devil and demons have caused so much misery.

Fire will come upon them—in God's time. Meanwhile, the kingdom of darkness is instrumental in fulfilling His original three decrees.

> Every good gift and every perfect gift is from above, and comes down from the Father of lights, with whom there is no variation or shadow of turning. (James 1:17)

The exalted Jesus is known by the blinding light of His person. John saw it twice: at the Transfiguration and on Patmos.

He was transfigured before them. His face shone like the sun, and His clothes became as white as the light. (Matthew 17:2)

His countenance was like the sun shining in its strength. (Revelation 1:16)

Combine these facts about the resurrected Jesus with God's decree before the foundation of the cosmos that the Lamb be slain. Jesus' nature as the Second Person of the Trinity put Him outside of time. It's plausible that the physical radiance witnessed at Transfiguration was the light source of Day One.

It's not surprising that John chose light to describe Jesus in the gospel he wrote. John's Revelation records another time of light without sun or moon because of God's person. Just like Day One, God's light will be pervasive; sun and moon will be superfluous. The physical laws we know will be governed by Physical Law Himself.

This is the message which we have heard from Him and declare to you, that God is light and in Him is no darkness at all. (1 John 1:5)

The light shines in the darkness, and the darkness did not comprehend it. (John 1:5)

The city had no need of the sun or of the moon to shine in it, for the glory of God illuminated it. The Lamb is its light. (Revelation 21:23)

TIMEKEEPING

In Day One, God's light introduced timekeeping. Whether time had already begun in the original creation is not clearly stated. But Genesis 1 is clear that God created the time markers of day and night, morning and evening, on Day One. That's why we can count the hours in God's seventy-two hour raid on His enemies.

We inhabit an age with two timekeepers. Our sun and moon are visible as Earth rotates. Sunlight touches only half at a time, but the sunlit portion is constantly moving.

As Earth rotates west to east, the mobile dividing line of night and day sweeps Earth's surface from east to west. The division of day and night is a mobile boundary called the terminator, visible to our astronauts and satellites. Like the movie series, this name accurately describes how light terminates darkness.

But the terminator boundary requires sunlight, unavailable until Day Four. No sun yet existed when God named Day and Night; no terminator swept across Earth's face. He invented morning and evening before heavenly bodies could impose them upon Earth's rotation.

God purposely created timekeeping for our age. When this age ends, the timekeepers of morning and evening will be no more.

> There shall be no night there: They need no lamp nor light of the sun, for the Lord God gives them light. (Revelation 22:5)

WORDS

Day One also introduced words. When God uttered, "*let there be light,*" He pronounced the very first recorded words. He used words both to create and to name. Each created thing was named with His words. On Day One, He called the separated lightscape Day and Night. He word-named these two elements of the time rhythm.

What He caused over the six days, He often named with words. We are the only race to use words intelligibly. God is why; we were made in the image of a word-user. Well before we were created in His image, He used words.

From His verbal power, we now have everything we identify in physical reality. Before God Himself was known by any name, His words created everything in our world.

AS SEEN TODAY

Our word use is exclusive to our species. That is unacceptable to evolutionary theory and its worldview of materialistic naturalism.

Religious faith in evolution blinds scientists. They foolishly endeavor to prove we are not the only race that uses words. Many gorillas and monkeys have been "edu-ma-cated" in the process, as Jethro Bodine would say.

END OF DAY ONE

The first twenty-four hours were demarcated and one cycle had elapsed. In the period of mere hours, His blitz of the kingdom of darkness had begun. Stripped of their exclusive domain of Earth, they would never destroy indiscriminately again. God's impenetrable light forever confined their free movement.

If earthly warfare is any guide, God's rapid-fire assault would leave the kingdom of darkness in the confusion of suddenness. We can easily picture the fearfulness of their uncertainty. "Why is God invading our dominion? Is this all He is doing? What will happen next? How can we prevent it? Should we fight, retreat, or surrender? We thought we were safe!"

DAY TWO

> Then God said, "Let there be a firmament in the midst of the waters, and let it divide the waters from the waters." Thus God made the firmament, and divided the waters which were under the firmament from the waters which were above the firmament; and it was so. And God called the firmament Heaven. So the evening and the morning were the second day. (Genesis 1:6–8)

The most frequent question I've heard: "what was the firmament?" We'll defer that query until Day Four, where its effects of the firmament suggest its composition.

The common word these first two days is *divide*. Dividing and limiting the kingdom of darkness resulted from Day Two, just like Day One. From the preceding study of Luke 11, we know that division will cause the kingdom of darkness to fall—such as the dividing that God performed in His seventy-two-hour onslaught.

When the Holy Spirit hovered over the deep, He received no response. His actions confirm His displeasure with that. On Day One, light imposed a boundary on darkness. Day Two introduced a new boundary on their cooling waters, nor was it the last. Their watery territory would suffer again on Day Three.

The firmament was not set on top of the waters, but *in the midst of them*. The firmament was not air, nor on top of air, because God's word choice matters.

Many translations use *firmament*; the second most used is *expanse*, and a few use *sky*. The closest thing we have above our heads is sky. We have no firmament above our heads. Rockets traverse our sky into space, where exploration has proven there is no moisture or water above our sky.

But it's a mistake to assume that our sky today was the firmament of Day Two. Structural changes occurred simultaneously with the Flood. That's one reason the word *sky* does not appear in the NKJV translation until Elijah and King Ahab (1 Kings 18:45). In contrast, the NIV uses *sky* extensively from Day Two onward. I regard that as mistaken, because of the following discoveries in the text.

This illustrates the error of assuming constancy in physical reality. Things change because God likes fruitfulness and multiplication. If something overhead changed before our recorded history, how would we know about its previous condition? No video exists in our newsrooms, no archival newspapers.

The eyewitness accounts handed down the generations are our only source—the Bible. God chose the languages and words for the Bible.

Day Two would not have a word suggesting firmness if the result was air, or clouds, or enveloping mist. These attempts at explanation presume that our sky was the original firmament. That is a heavy burden which requires contortions of thought. Such logic-pretzels dismiss our God's love of words.

But this interpretation explains why the firmament had waters above and below. It was a firm, dividing barrier.

THE DIVIDING BARRIER

Like Day One, form again replaced formlessness. A hard division subdivided the dark emptiness of pervasive cooling water in a new top-to-bottom layering. That dividing barrier was the firmament.

God named the firmament that was above Earth's surface with the word *heaven*. Naming Day and Night seems important; every language names them to this day. But why did He name the firmament? And why did He call it *heaven*? Our concept of pearly gates and streets of gold has to take a back seat, because the first heaven in the Bible is the hard barrier in the midst of waters above Earth's surface.

The purpose of Day Two was to subdivide the waters which cooled the devil and his angels. Just as Day One's light reduced the territory of their darkness, Day Two's firmament shrank the territory of their coolness.

Imagine your country getaway looks out on a beautiful farm, the biggest anywhere. Then surveyors come in and mark off property lines. You know the expansive acreage is being developed for subdivision. The nearby city is invading; your getaway will be crowded by many neighbors.

Let's expand the analogy. Suppose you owned that beautiful farm, yours to do as you please and go where you wish. You're the biggest landowner around, the King of the Hill.

How would the sudden surveyors affect you? Or hearing bulldozers on your farm? And no legal defense can prevent it because your title to the property is defective. I daresay you would find yourself disrupted, distressed, helpless, and humiliated.

WHERE'S THE FIRMAMENT NOW?

Where did the firmament go? There is nothing today that correlates to a firmament; what happened to it? And what about waters above the firmament? There is no water in space above the sky, so what is God revealing?

These are important questions on which the credibility of God's revelation hangs. We unwisely ignore such questions. We have learned by now that the difficulties of Scripture are our beacon for advancement. Acknowledging puzzles and mysteries is vital for our growth as living human spirits. By faith in Jesus, we are born again into a puzzling unseen realm. The Bible reveals that realm for our effectiveness on God's behalf.

Book Two of The *Unseen* Series, *Nobody Sees This Unseen Realm: How to Unlock Bible Mysteries*, explained the benefits of Bible puzzles. The God of revelation will explain what He wants us to know. He promised He would in John 16:12 and 1 John 2:27.

Raised within the materialistic grid, we focus on the objects that were made. People who do not want to believe the Bible sometimes use Day Two as a smokescreen. They use the firmament, which no longer exists, to discredit God's entire revelation.

Christians and translators want to eliminate offense. Since there's no firmament

AS SEEN IN 1976

One hostile Bible professor showed me a diagram he thought Day Two required. This supposed chart of the firmament required disbelief that outer space even existed. With that single opening, he ridiculed every insecure Christian until their faith was dead.

I kept my thoughts to myself: *Professing to be wise, they became fools* (Romans 1:22). Meanwhile, I trusted God that I would know what I needed when He wanted me to know it. After all, if I trusted Him to save my soul, I could trust Him to teach me.

now, they use *sky*. However, that prevents explanation of the separated waters. *Sky* also cannot explain how overhead water could flood the earth in Genesis 7:11.

Modernizing Bible vocabulary can obscure God's word choices. Here, *sky* may feel friendly but it hides the subdivision of darkness's cooling waters. God has a good vocabulary. His word implies a firm structure.

If there has never been such a barrier between the waters, then Genesis 1 demands to be interpreted poetically. Twenty-four-hour days is a side issue if we can't identify the firmament. If one statement is poetic, then all the Genesis 1 revelation could be as well.

Clearly, there is no firm barrier overhead today. But Genesis 1 only requires it to exist *then*; the text does not require a firmament to exist today. Some firm physical barrier must have existed after Day Two, but the text does not say it was permanent. Something happened to it, as we shall see.

END OF DAY TWO

Day Two left the enemy with a shrinking cooling pool. In forty-eight hours, God had subdivided both their darkness and their waters.

Think how we feel when our cozy nests are suddenly upturned. We can only imagine the fright of uncertainty that would plague the legions of satan after the preceding two subdivisions. But we know four days remained.

DAY THREE

> Then God said, "Let the waters under the heavens be gathered together into one place, and let the dry land appear"; and it was so. And God called the dry land Earth, and the gathering together of the waters He called Seas. And God saw that it was good. (Genesis 1:9–10)

Day Three imposed more containment upon darkness. When God raised dry land out of the water, He further reduced the watery territory of satan and his partners. This twenty-four hours stripped them in two ways; not only did they lose their giant cooling pool. Before the day ended, God also put reproducing physical life on the earth.

The dry land command came after another restraining order upon darkness. All their waters under the firmament had to recede and make way for land. Across the earth, shorelines confined the cooling pool everywhere.

God described to Job how He imposed limits upon the enemies' cooling hideout.

> Or who shut in the sea with doors,
> When it burst forth and issued from the womb;
> When I made the clouds its garment,
> And thick darkness its swaddling band;
> When I fixed My limit for it,
> And set bars and doors;
> When I said, 'This far you may come, but no farther,
> And here your proud waves must stop!' (Job 38:8–11)

Where previously no limits existed, the kingdom of darkness found themselves in a shrinking prison cell. In a 1960s Italian movie, Hercules was locked in a shrinking room. The walls and ceiling began coming inward, threatening to squash him. Similarly, in an episode of *Wild Wild West*, James Conrad found himself in a collapsing. Of course, they both escaped, but for satan the helplessness was total. Unlike fictional heroes, the kingdom of darkness had no escape. The devil was completely defenseless against his Enemy, our God.

Back to our hotel pool analogy: how did the children feel when you arrived at the hotel and the pool was only half full? Darkness watches their cooling pool shrink, day after day.

God formalized the division He had made with word-names. Once there was only one deep. Now there are two things, both named by Him: the land and the seas.

IN ONE PLACE: CONTINENTAL DRIFT

In what way were the waters gathered into one place? On our globe today, the seven continents divide the water into multiple bodies. Something must have changed because they are not in one place.

In 1596, a Flemish mapmaker named Ortelius could draw on the expanding global exploration. He observed the continental shapes fit together. Several scientific generations later, Alfred Wegener developed the first comprehensive theory in 1912, now called *continental drift.*

Distinct miles-thick portions of the earth's crust are in continual motion. Called plates, they roughly correspond to the continental shapes. Geological evidence shows that the continental plates drift, called tectonic shifts. This movement is observable, measured by instruments and satellites at the plate junctions.

These plates of enormous thickness cause cracks by their movement, both between and within each plate. The result is a patchwork pattern of faults and tectonic boundaries surrounding the globe.

Between the vast tectonic plates of thick rock, the tense junctions build up tremendous heat. The rock is melted into liquid magma, penetrating the surface as our volcanoes. The unimaginable pressure on cracks and boundaries can suddenly release. When shifts occur, they release the latent energy as spasms, *a.k.a.* earthquakes.

These movements in the earth's crust are ongoing, observable, and measurable. However, geological theoreticians have two unprovable beliefs in their presuppositions. With their grid of materialistic naturalism, they close the universe to God's influence on physical reality.

Second, they believe that the movement has always been a constant speed. Again, the error is assuming constancy, that what we experience has never changed.

For example, the Atlantic Ocean has a plate boundary running north-south in its middle; it spreads apart nearly two inches per year. That is proven. But the unprovable speed assumption leads to an unprovable conclusion: a jillion years was required for the continents to arrive at their present position.

The scientific method cannot be used to validate the two beliefs, so their conclusions require faith in a constant rate of spread. But this result only disqualifies their estimate of the time requirement.

Plate movement and its direction have been scientifically measured. By reverse engineering from each plate's present position and direction, scientists have theorized the original position of the plates: all in one land mass.

This matches the Day Three revelation. As for the rate of spread, we will review it with the firmament in chapter thirteen.

God named the gathered waters with a plural word: Seas. We use the plural seas for our largest oceans: *the high seas.* Plural is certainly their geographical placement now. He also named the land, which He described using the adjective *dry.*

DRYNESS

To call land *dry* cannot be accidental. That had to hurt the fallen rebels

166

with consuming fire in their nature.

Dryness is as much a theme in Scripture as water. We saw in Luke 11 that demons inhabit people to avoid dryness. In Ezekiel 32, Egypt's dryness is a punishment. Desiccation is death irreversible. In Ezekiel's vision of the valley of dry bones, the *very dry bones* represent abject hopelessness.

God made the land dry, and waters it lavishly. Springs and mists turned that dry land into a garden. Of the eleven verses in the Bible describing Eden, five are about its watery quality. Its single spring formed the headwaters of four rivers; three are historically the major ones in their regions. The Gihon of the time is the Nile of Egypt, and the Hiddekel is the Tigris. The Euphrates of today originated in those headwaters.

> Now a river went out of Eden to water the garden, and from there it parted and became four riverheads. The name of the first is Pishon; it is the one which skirts the whole land of Havilah, where there is gold. And the gold of that land is good. Bdellium and the onyx stone are there. The name of the second river is Gihon; it is the one which goes around the whole land of Cush. The name of the third river is Hiddekel; it is the one which goes toward the east of Assyria. The fourth river is the Euphrates. (Genesis 2:10–14)

Since Day Three, water follows the path of least resistance. Its erosive force forms channels and canyons. The arid lands of today's Middle East are desert, except for human irrigation. However, their wadi, gorges, and canyons show enormous water erosion, all in the past. These coincide with the nations judged in Ezekiel because God judges the waters of nations who reject Him.

Desertification expresses God's judgment. Why else would the destiny of His enemies be a lake of fire? The dryness provides them no rest from the fire within them. We saw earlier that demons need people for moisture. In their Pit, there is not even a drop of water for cooling.

Belief in climate change has become a religion for some. They attribute desertification to human causation. They are right, but wrong about how it happens. It is God's doing.

He uses water to shepherd mankind to righteousness. When people choose an enemy status, He withholds the water. God imposes dryness on His enemies and all who follow them. Related calamities multiply: mudslides, destructive fires, famine, and extreme weather patterns.

SHRINKING STOPS ON DAY THREE

The image of a shrinking prison cell summons the terror satan and his partners might have felt. They didn't know when the shrinking would end, if ever.

In fact, God finished the boundaries on Day Three. On the first day, He limited darkness with the creation of light. The second and third days divided their watery domain. The giant cooling pool was no more, now twice subdivided by firmament and by land. It must have felt like a swimming pool half full, with no deep end for cooling off.

In a staccato seventy-two hour blitz, God completed the forming of the formless. All that remained was to fill the void, which began on this Day Three after He raised the Land.

EARTH BRINGS FORTH

Then God said, "Let the earth bring forth grass, the herb that yields seed, and the fruit tree that yields fruit according to its kind, whose seed is in itself, on the earth"; and it was so. And the earth brought forth grass, the herb that yields seed according to its kind, and the tree that yields fruit, whose seed is in itself according to its kind. And God saw that it was good. So the evening and the morning were the third day. (Genesis 1:11–13)

The second event on Day Three began filling the void. An additional pattern occurred when God used starting material. The light of Day One required no original material; the firmament of Day Two had no identified source.

Earth itself cooperated on Day Three, for the first time. The waters obeyed His command to gather into one place, causing dry land to appear. Earth next brought forth the vegetation at His command.

Brought forth is used of birth in the Bible. Even Jesus is brought forth. "*And she brought forth her firstborn Son, and wrapped Him in swaddling cloths*" (Luke 2:7).

Paganism, both ancient and modern, deifies Earth as a mother. They detect a true thing, that the earth brings forth, but interpret it apart from God's revelation. What God created in physical reality bears witness to Him, but the fallen human race interprets it to reject Him. Apostle Paul described in his letter to the Roman churches how Earth shows true things.

What may be known of God is manifest in them, for God has shown it to them. For since the creation of the world His invisible attributes are clearly seen, being understood by the things that are made, even His eternal power and Godhead, so that they are without excuse. (Romans 1:19–20)

THE EAR OF EARTH

Earth brought forth because of a verbal command. Genesis 1 reveals that Earth can respond.

No scientist relies on speaking to physical matter—but we can. The many healings by Christians are just one example, which is rapidly multiplying around the world. Among our tools for healing, we have scientific research and medical development, but there is another. We can command verbally, and Earth responds cooperatively.

People who love and follow Jesus Christ are the living human spirits Earth wants to serve. We have a unique kinship with Earth because God made us from its raw material of dirt. He made no other creature from Earth material.

God made Earth with responsiveness to us; our faith in Him includes this recognition. He authorized us to conduct His affairs, and Earth wants to cooperate. In his letter to the Roman Christians, Paul also wrote that it groans, frustrated as it awaits the sons of God. He says, *until now*—the time since Pentecost.

The Holy Spirit had originally hovered over the face of the Earth, unwelcomed by the kingdom of darkness. Now He walks around on it, in us. The Earth wants to bring forth for Him. The sons of God now walk the Earth; it is no longer frustrated.

For the earnest expectation of the creation eagerly waits for the revealing of the sons of God…. because the creation itself also will be delivered from the bondage of corruption into the glorious liberty of the children of God. For we know that the whole creation groans and labors with birth pangs together until now. (Romans 8:19, 21–22)

On Day Three, God said, "*Let the earth bring forth.*" Centuries later, Jesus said to the winds and waves of Galilee, "*Peace! Be still!*" They are the same action with equal power. God's command in the mouth of an authoritative person entices Earth to respond. This is a necessary conclusion from Jesus' miracles and teachings. Likewise, His words in our mouths permit physical reality to satisfy its craving to serve its intended rulers.

Jesus calmed the storms; Peter walked on water upon hearing Jesus' *Come.* Five loaves of bread and two fish responded to the Son of Man, as did the fig tree which obediently withered. Jesus affirmed even mountains would uproot and move for miles at our word, in respect of God's words in our spoken faith.

> Have faith in God. For assuredly, I say to you, whoever says to this mountain, "Be removed and be cast into the sea," and does not doubt in his heart, but believes that those things he says will be done, he will have whatever he says. (Mark 11:23)

Earth and all its physical laws now submit to the will and words of God which we speak. Earth respects our position as its rulers. We are made of its dirt, and we rule on behalf of God. With Him in us and His words in our mouths, we are the superior physical law.

> If you abide in Me, and My words abide in you, you will ask what you desire, and it shall be done for you. (John 15:7)

Earth may not respond to our comfort, ambitions, or urgencies. The cross didn't disappear under Jesus; His body was not spared from death. Apostle Paul was whipped five times; the cat-o'-nine-tails did not vanish. Christians by the millions have been martyred and continue to be. Troublesome physical realities irk Christians at all times.

But Earth never declines the commands of its Master Creator. Jesus' statements train us how to speak for the Father to anything and anyone in all creation.

THIS IS FOR US

The question for us is clear. When we command Earth, do we speak what He says? The alternative is our own words of self-interest, clothed in religious expectations.

> He who speaks from himself seeks his own glory; but He who seeks the glory of the One who sent Him is true, and no unrighteousness is in Him. (John 7:18)

> As My Father taught Me, I speak these things. (John 8:28)

> For I have not spoken on My own authority; but the Father who sent Me gave Me

170

a command, what I should say and what I should speak. And I know that His command is everlasting life. Therefore, whatever I speak, just as the Father has told Me, so I speak. (John 12:49–50)

THE VEGETATION

Before sun and moon existed, Earth brought forth vegetation for God. His light alone produced photosynthesis, growth, and reproduction. Into the greenery, He installs a reproductive pattern, *according to their kind*. Each type of plant will only reproduce itself.

In evolutionary theory, mutations cause entirely new organisms. God's Day Three disallows this unprovable belief. Three times, God said, *according to their kind*. From their first creation, each type of plant reproduced only its own kind.

This event is the first reproduction in the Bible. How foreign it must have been to the heavenly host, holy and evil alike. But it would soon be excelled, on Day Four, with yet another escalation on Day Six.

AFTER DAY THREE

Day Three completed God's physical restrictions on the kingdom of darkness. The light hemmed in the darkness. The firmament and the land shrank the territory of satan's dominion. Now Earth obeyed the voice of a new Master. Darkness no longer dictated the shape of Earth.

The devil cannot prevent Earth from responding to God. When God commanded with His words, Earth obeyed. Whether satan likes it does not matter.

The calamity of darkness worsens daily.

---

*Discussion and reflection questions for Chapter Eleven
can be found in the Reader Engagement Resources*

CHAPTER TWELVE

RULING LIGHTS IN THE FIRMAMENT

DAY FOUR

In chapter seven, *Fire and Water*, we saw the changes of heaven's structure after Lucifer's sin and casting down. God's throne, where once was fire, is now surrounded by the sapphire ice. It's possible that you, dear reader, have considered heaven and earth to be static, constant, and unchanging. Our preceding discoveries in the Bible have shown that is not the case.

The unseen realm and earth are both dynamic, subject to change permitted or executed by God's omnipotent hand. Whether it is Earth's continental drift, or heaven's new pavement, change is a force God uses.

Our forebears debated only two choices, between slowly mutating evolution and God's final, fixed creation. This book honors that hard-won legacy. I agree that Genesis 1:3ff occurred in six twenty-four-hour days. However, this book argues biblically that Genesis 1:1 and 1:2 represent two epochal changes preceding those six days. Using other passages, we've seen the six days were creation from something.

Such an unaccustomed interpretation can activate knee-jerk defense against any threat to our God's engagement, sovereignty, and omnipotence. But as the sovereign God, He can make changes. His sovereignty also permits change through destruction, as we saw with Earth's ruination by the fallen Lucifer.

After all, we are counting on a much bigger event than Genesis 1. Apostle John saw the new heavens and the new Earth, described in Revelation 21; the ones we know, completely gone.

We can penetrate the Bible's mysteries by accepting God's sovereign use of change. He manages the chaos and change within His cosmos, even changes caused by the kingdom of darkness. As Hebrews 1:3 says, He *"upholds the universe by His word of power."* If we believe that, chaos poses no threat to our faith nor to Him. None of the six days benefits more from accepting this than Day Four.

DAY FOUR

> Then God said, "Let there be lights in the firmament of the heavens to divide the day from the night; and let them be for signs and seasons, and for days and years; and let them be for lights in the firmament of the heavens to give light on the earth"; and it was so. Then God made two great lights: the greater light to rule the day, and the lesser light to rule the night. He made the stars also. God set them in the firmament of the heavens to give light on the earth, and to rule over the day and over the night, and to divide the light from the darkness. And God saw that it was good. So the evening and the morning were the fourth day. (Genesis 1:14–19)

Day Four begins like Days One through Three: God is dividing. The boundary between day and night had already occurred on Day One. Days Two and Three divided the waters. Now, on Day Four, He created the bodies of our solar system to mark and officiate Day One's division of day and night, light and darkness. God's command repeats that dividing assignment twice.

God also intended the new heavenly lights to benefit activities on the surface of Earth. They would be timekeepers for seasons, days, and years, signaling the times for planting and harvesting. Such activities assume people—not yet created but on the drawing board, so to speak.

In contrast to bringing forth Day Three's vegetation, Day Four's heavenly lights came about without Earth's involvement. It provided no raw material; God said, "Let there be the dividing lights," and there were. What we know as the sun ruled the day and the moon ruled the night.

His word choice has significance. He used the word *rule* three times, and *divide* twice. Seven times we see the word *light*. Several words are repetitive. But not once did He use the words we might expect: *sun* and *moon*.

Lucifer and his angels were exiled to God's original earth. Had they also eradicated the heavenly bodies of the original creation? Was the absence of lights in the heavens the work of darkness? The Bible does not provide an answer, to my knowledge.

All we are told is that Day Four began with no lights in the heavens, and ended with a greater light, a lesser light, and stars. The void satan and his angels had preferred, God filled.

IN THE FIRMAMENT

God's order for Day Four uses *in the firmament* three times. That firm structure between the waters was as significant on Day Four as on Day Two, when He first made it. God's decree places all three physical light sources *in the firmament*.

We don't have a firm barrier over our heads now, and our understanding of space is the most advanced in human history. There is no water above the sky; we've been there. There is no roof on the waters below, which would obstruct our rockets. With these present physical realities, Day Two and Day Four seem nonsensical.

The firmament was between waters above and waters below (1:7). The present layers are the earth with dry lands and seas, under sky, under space. Should we assume the layers we know now are what God formed on those two days? Then we (and our Bible translators) also must assume that the firmament is sky. But that requires us to think space is water.

THIS IS FOR US

The puzzle leads us deeper into the Word of God, exactly as He intends. Every Bible study isn't to this depth, of course. Most times in the Bible, we are communing with God.

Many puzzles we humbly defer, patient until the right time. Reading this book may be such a time for you.

This is a common result of assuming God meant what we experience today. The implications of equating the Day Two firmament with our sky make it an unsatisfying explanation.

Before addressing this, we have another difficulty: the night-ruling moon.

THE MOON PUZZLE

I described these Bible discovery techniques in Book Two of the *Unseen Series*, titled *Nobody Sees This Unseen Realm: How to Unlock Bible Mysteries*. When we test our answers to its puzzles, more puzzles often result. The moon is one such problem.

God revealed His command to the moon in 1:16, *to rule the night*. If God had said to rule the tides, we would have no problem, because whether it is visible, its gravity pulls our oceans one way and another. But His actual words represent a problem for us because the moon does not always appear at night. Often it is visible in the daytime. And through the lunar month, the moon's appearance cycles.

A full moon sheds much light. I've been on high mountain tops under a full moon, and it is as bright as day. With snow on the ground, a full moon can have a blinding effect. I have hiked miles under its bright rule. But when the moon is a sliver of a crescent or completely waned, it does not rule. Venus or Jupiter are the brightest to see, but neither illuminate nor rule anything. The moon we have today is not constant and does not rule the night—another disparity with the text of Genesis 1.

STANDARDS FOR RULING THE NIGHT

We can improve our understanding of the lights set in the firmament by solving the moon puzzle. Two discoveries result; the first is a change in the speed of earth's rotation. The second is the nature of the firmament.

God created people on Day Six. Our first parents passed what they knew, through Noah, down the generations to Moses, whose written record includes Genesis 1. Our ancient forebears learned and followed the agricultural seasons which the ruling lights governed. From generation to generation, they handed down a story about the moon using the words *rule the night*.

For them to formalize that phraseology, the lesser light had to be their brightest source of light on *every* night. It also had to be directly over the one land mass on which everyone lived. By the end of Day Four, God's word choices require this circumstance. Anything less would not be ruling the night.

Continental drift explains that the lesser light could *rule the night* for all land in one mass. All people lived on it, seeing the lesser light at the same time. We might say they were all in the same time zone, unlike today's population globally dispersed into twenty-four time zones.

Since the land mass has subdivided and circumnavigated the globe, the moon can't rule the night for everyone everywhere. But at the end of Day Four, that would have been the condition.

But things have changed so dramatically since Day Four that the moon isn't over *anybody* every night. It waxes and wanes, and often appears in the daytime.

Some dramatic change replaced the rule of the moon with today's night-and-day behavior.

DRAMATIC SPEED CHANGE

To rule the night for all people on the one continent, the lesser light would have to appear every night. Our own satellites can stay over the same spot of land using an orbital pattern called geostationary orbit. Could God have done that with the moon when all land was one continent?

I first explored this by diagramming the orbits. We know the moon doesn't vanish and reappear every night; it is always revolving around Earth. In our time, it's visible in the daytime, illuminated by the greater light. But with a firmament between people and the heavenly bodies, the moon would be overhead but indiscernible while the greater light ruled the day.

Could there be an orbital circumstance of any kind, where the lesser light was over everyone alive on one land mass, ruling their night every night? Yes, my diagram showed this was definitely a possibility. I also identified what had to change between Day Four and today if that were true.

Earth rotates on its axis, like a line through the center between the North and South poles. Overhead, the moon revolves around Earth. To rule the night, the lesser light would have to be in a geostationary position over the one land mass, just like our satellites.

But the moon no longer rules the night for anybody anywhere because Earth's rotating speed is not in sync with the lesser light's orbital speed. For the lesser light to be over one Day Three land mass all the time, a certain speed of rotation is required.

The moon has no friction acting upon it in the vacuum of space, and no event here would change the speed of the moon's travel through space. Only a change from the original rotational speed of Earth could cause today's moon behavior.

A difference from today's Earth's rotation speed is the only way that the moon could be geostationary on Day Four. I sought out a physics professor, who kindly responded to my query.

He wrote the speed of the moon in its revolution around Earth is 2,228 miles per hour ("mph"). Earth today rotates at 1,040 mph.

For the moon to be constantly over one land mass, Earth must rotate at only 35.2 mph. The present 1,040 mph is thirty times too fast for that. This tremendous difference between the slow and the present rotation speed tells us why the moon does not rule our night now, as it did after Day Four.

So what happened? The only possible reason is that something must have changed the rotational speed of Earth. But is there anything in the Bible that could have caused such a changed speed? Does anything in the Bible even talk about that? Yes.

HOW GOD CHANGED EARTH'S SPEED

To produce such a physical speed change in Earth's rotation, unimaginable power and energy are required. The physics professor volunteered the amount of energy required to produce that rotational acceleration from 35.2 to 1,040 mph.

The largest nuclear bomb ever detonated by the Soviet Union, the Tsar Bomba, had an energy output of around 100 Megatons. This blast destroyed buildings over 30 miles away, an area of around 3,000 square miles or about 1/65,000 of the Earth's surface. In other words, 65,000 such bombs could destroy the surface of the earth.

The necessary change in rotational energy of the Earth would be the equivalent of 500 billion Tsar Bombas. Dividing that by the 65,000 Tsar Bombas could pretty well destroy the surface of the Earth. The energy required to get the Earth spinning at its current rate [1,040 mph from 35.2 mph] would be enough energy to destroy the entire surface of the Earth about 7.7 million times.

That is unimaginable energy required for an unimaginable speed change in Earth's rotation. Any such cause must come after a period of human existence when it rotated the 35.2 mph for the lesser light to rule the night. Has any event ever produced that much energy?

Imagine a spinning top, or its later form, a Beyblade. You can turn it with your fingers and have a slow speed. But when you pull the string, it rotates much faster. This depicts the dramatic difference in the rotation of Earth. What size string would be needed if Earth was the top?

The entire surface of Earth would have to be destroyed by such immense force. As movie fiction says, it has to be an extinction-level event.

In fact, Genesis records that event: the Flood.

> In the six hundredth year of Noah's life, in the second month, the seventeenth day of the month, on that day all the fountains of the great deep were broken up, and the windows of heaven were opened. And the rain was on the earth forty days and forty nights. (Genesis 7:11–12)

The Flood is reviewed extensively in the next book of the nine-book *Unseen* Series. Here we simply assess its significance for Day Four and the firmament.

THE WATERS UNDER THE LAND

We cited Eden's description earlier. Genesis 2 records the gushing nature of earth's surface after God rested on the seventh day.

In many places today, our water comes from underground. Rainwater filters through soil and percolates down to an impermeable layer of rock below. There it accumulates, called the water table. This can be hundreds or thousands of feet below our feet.

The heavy ground above the water table exerts great downward force. Wherever water has a path back to surface, that pressure squeezes it out. This occurs when we dig a well. Water forces its way up, using geysers, springs, and rivers both above and beneath the surface.

Everywhere the pressurized waters go, the earth's surface erodes to accommodate them. From caves to river channels, the force of water produces erosion.

This was true in Eden's garden as well. There, one gigantic geyser filled four channels with the headwaters of the then-world's four largest rivers (Genesis 2:10–14). There was no rain, so how was the garden watered? Underground water misted up and kept all land surface moist.

THE FOUNTAINS OPENED

Today's theorists assume continental drift has always been the same rate, requiring millions of years. But imagine if all that change was squeezed into the forty days which Genesis 7 reports about the Flood. The ground beneath our feet would suddenly crack and split hundreds of miles apart in a matter of mere days or hours.

What would someone in an airplane see? The movie *2012* visually portrayed such cataclysmic results. The water of the sea gushed into the rapidly expanding cracks. Crashing tons of water wracked and scoured the land. All vegetation, animals, people, and structures were swept from the face of the ground. The immense friction of immense weights released immense volcanic explosions. And the movie's characters called it an extinction-level event. Great geysers of water punctured and scoured the surface violently. These joined the scouring splash and the volcanic destruction.

Like land today, the single land mass of Day Three would have a water table. The cracking of the surface in a sudden continental spasm would squeeze out that pressurized water. Every hole, fissure, and crack opened by the instant continental drift would become an orifice for the explosive force of a million fire hoses. The great geysers would scour the entire surface land.

But what words would be available to you, to describe such a never-before event? How would an ancient observer on the original continent describe that? This statement would do it: "*All the fountains of the great deep were broken up.*"

We know from the end result that all dry land suffered total destruction. Just as God had found it in Genesis 1:2, the earth was again covered by a great deep—one of His own making. The account preserved and handed down to Moses' pen describes the cataclysmic scouring.

> Now the flood was on the earth forty days. The waters increased and lifted up the ark, and it rose high above the earth. The waters prevailed and greatly increased on the earth, and the ark moved about on the surface of the waters. And the waters prevailed exceedingly on the earth, and all the high hills under the whole heaven were covered. The waters prevailed fifteen cubits upward, and the mountains were covered. And all flesh died that moved on the earth: birds and cattle and beasts and every creeping thing that creeps on the earth, and every man. All in whose nostrils was the breath of the spirit of life, all that was on the dry land, died. So He destroyed all living things which were on the face of the ground: both man and cattle, creeping thing and bird of the air. They were destroyed from the earth. (Genesis 7:17–23)

THE WINDOWS OF HEAVEN

The fountains of the deep were not the only source of water. *The windows of heaven were opened.* (Recall that heaven was the word-name God had given the firmament.)

We read it as a poetic metaphor because we are used to poetic writing. The phrase *"windows of heaven"* appears in 2 Kings and Malachi metaphorically. We use the saying today because of the Bible's influence.

But it is a mistake to assume that Moses simply used a poetic image of windows to describe a deluge of rain. Just as *the face of the deep* was a purposeful choice of words in Genesis 1:2, I believe God's revelation purposely names the *windows* of Genesis 7:11.

Somehow, Noah and his family looked up and saw windows overhead. The word *window* is next used when Rahab lets down Israel's spies from her window in Jericho's wall. Just like we use it, it is an opening in a structure.

The structure overhead suddenly developed windows. What was the immediate result? Forty days of water covering the entire land mass.

We are very familiar with rain, as was Moses in compiling the account handed down. But what could the word *rain* have meant to Noah? Rain had not yet fallen upon the earth (Genesis 2:5).

As the cataclysm began, the people then alive saw windows over their heads. Through the open, new windows, something began falling to the surface. The waters once held above the firmament could now pour down upon earth's surface.

Gushing from below and falling from above, the waters covered every mountain on that single land mass by fifteen cubits (23 feet). If that were to happen with today's mountain heights, what total volume of water would be required? Skeptics have posted the calculation online: 813 million *cubic miles* of water.

That volume erroneously assumes the fixed constancy of today's land masses in today's positions with today's mountain heights. In the time of the single land mass after the six days, the volume would be less. In addition, the seas would not require flooding.

Whatever the volume, just one cubic mile of water weighs 9.2 *trillion* pounds. The total weight of the floodwaters would be incalculable, known only to God. Imagine the deformation of Earth that such sudden, enormous weight would cause. The forces would easily produce the energy for changed rotational speed.

Our vantage point in this study is the kingdom of darkness and the impact of God's six days on them. Any reader is welcome to improve this understanding and explanation.

THE FIRMAMENT IDENTIFIED

What firm structure would elicit the idea of windows? Let's test the explanatory power of solid, translucent ice. When God signaled the firmament of ice to melt, what would that look like? As windows opening.

A firmament of solid ice explains why the sun and moon are named the greater and lesser lights. Identifying the firmament as ice organizes a fresh new grid. It will help interpret many Scriptures including Genesis 1.

FOUNTAINS + WATERS + SHIFTS = ROTATIONAL ACCELERATION

We can reverse engineer from the changes wrought by the Flood. It shows why the lesser light was ruling the night after Day Four, and why it does not do so now.

To accelerate the rotational speed of Earth from 35.2 mph to 1,040 mph required lots of power. The calculation above said it would require five hundred billion of mankind's most explosive weapon ever, the Tsar Bomba.

We don't have the necessary details to calculate the force of the Genesis 7 flood. It is certainly plausible that the force would be adequate with these three contributors:
1. the explosive movement of one land mass into seven continents,
2. the violent thrust of the disrupted waters of earth, and
3. the collapse of a global firmament of ice onto Earth's surface.

THE EXPLANATORY POWER OF ICE

A solid firmament of translucent ice has tremendous explanatory power for many Bible mysteries. Other proposals for the firmament include sky, cloud cover, or extreme humidity. By comparison, solid ice far exceeds them in explaining Bible revelations.

To begin with, why didn't God call the lights of Day Four *sun* and *moon*? Why refer to them as greater and lesser lights? The ice overhead explains it. Today we know the sun and moon are bodies in space, like the planets and the stars. But if a sheet of ice was over our heads, we could not see them. Looking up, we like the ancients would see the sun as a greater brightness during daytime, and the moon as a lesser brightness.

The spot of the sun would be discernible in the ice, but its shimmer and spread would affect the entire structure like a prism—a brightness we have never experienced. We would see the beam of moonlight as a single spot of light as well, yet even its lesser brightness would fall upon the entire firmament.

In chapter eleven, I wrote its effects would identify the firmament. The immediate effect was to hide the bodies of outer space from view. No one living under the firmament would identify a source for their daytime light. The record handed down through Noah to Moses simply describes the original perception: a brighter, greater light that always ruled the day.

An ice firmament solves the moon problem in two ways. First, when the ice collapsed onto Earth and joined the force of the instant continental split, it plausibly caused rotational acceleration. Prior to it, Earth could have rotated at the 35.2 mph speed that kept the lesser light overhead at all times—geostationary.

Second, with everyone on one land mass, the ever-present moonlight always ruled the night as a less bright luminescence in the ice firmament. Although the moon would be overhead during the day as well, the sun's greater brightness illuminating the ice firmament would drown out the lesser light.

Genesis 2:5 says that rain had not begun. The first mention of rain is God's bulletin to Noah about His intentions to cause rain for forty days and forty nights. The ice firmament explains why there was no rain. Sample the temperature with today's clear skies at 50,000 feet and it's cold: minus 65 degrees Fahrenheit (minus 54 Celsius). Block the sunlight with a dome of ice and it's even colder. If we assume that water froze at 32 degrees F then as now, the firmament of ice would easily stay frozen until God initiated its melting.

God talked to Noah as if clouds and rainbows were brand new after the Flood. Have you ever wondered why? The firmament of ice prevented both. God causes rainbows when sunlight hits raindrops from clouds. They are water vapor lifted into the atmosphere by warm upward drafts of air.

Prior to the Flood, the intervening ice prevented rainbows. There were no sun-warmed air pockets to lift water vapor into clouds. Forty days after the windows opened and melting began, the firmament of ice was gone.

Sunlight could evaporate surface water for the first time, and warm the air wherever its rays passed. Updrafts of the warm air could carry humidity into clouds, where condensation would produce rain. Rain and sunlight could meet for the first time to make a rainbow.

This is the sign of the covenant which I make between Me and you, and every living creature that is with you, for perpetual generations: I set My rainbow in the cloud, and it shall be for the sign of the covenant between Me and the earth. It shall be, when I bring a cloud over the earth, that the rainbow shall be seen in the cloud. (Genesis 9:12–14)

Another change after the Flood was the rapidly shortening lifespan. People lived for centuries because the firmament of ice had protected their bodies and DNA from deterioration. But God had decided in Genesis 6:3 that He would reduce our lives to one hundred and twenty years. When He removed the ice, Noah and his descendants were fully exposed to the UV rays our dermatologists warn us about today. Thus the human lifespan was gradually shortened as the sun-effected DNA was reproduced over generations.

In chapter seven, *Fire and Water*, we learned that the pavement surrounding God's throne changed from fire before Lucifer's rebellion, to a crystal ice like a skating rink. Realities on earth are often copies of heavenly realities (Hebrews 8:5, 9:23). A firmament of ice would signify to the heavenly hosts that earth was His footstool.

Heaven is My throne, and earth is My footstool. (Isaiah 66:1)

Do not swear at all: neither by heaven, for it is God's throne; nor by the earth, for it is His footstool. (Matthew 5:34–35)

THE FOOTSTOOL

How were Lucifer and his angels affected on Day Four? Their dislocation continues apace. Days One through Three confined them. With Day Four's greater and lesser lights in the firmament, their darkness of Genesis 1:2 was all gone.

Day One had left a cycle of Day and Night. For darkness, that represented a 50% reduction in their preferred light intensity of 0%. The new measurement was God 50%, darkness 50%.

Because of Day Four, illumination was constant, thanks to the spots of light in the firmament. They illuminated its entire breadth to some degree, twenty-four hours a day, seven days a week. The constant illumination reduced darkness' proportion to 0% around the clock.

Nor was it accidental that God's Day Four used the word *rule* three times. Prior to God's seventy-two hour blitz, Lucifer and the other fallen angels ruled Earth. They destroyed all that God had made, killing all life, demolishing all structures, extinguishing all light, and eliminating all form. They did as they pleased.

Now the rebels' dominion over Earth was being stripped, to their humiliation. Even the heavenly lights ruled over them and denied them the preferred darkness.

They were well on their way to becoming Jesus' footstool.

The Lord said to my Lord, "Sit at My right hand, Till I make Your enemies Your footstool." (Psalm 110:1)

Then comes the end, when He delivers the kingdom to God the Father, when He puts an end to all rule and all authority and power. For He must reign till He has put all enemies under His feet. (1 Corinthians 15:24–25)

But this Man, after He had offered one sacrifice for sins forever, sat down at the right hand of God, from that time waiting till His enemies are made His footstool. (Hebrews 10:12–13)

WHAT'S NEXT?

The Scripture reveals no response by the rebel spirits. The events of Days One through Four had been unpredictable for them, and they did not know what lay ahead.

Discussion and reflection questions for Chapter Twelve
can be found in the Reader Engagement Resources

CHAPTER THIRTEEN

UNIMAGINABLY BAD

DAYS FIVE AND SIX

Day Four ended with the full restriction upon the former domain of the exiled Lucifer and his angels. Their darkness was now limited, and what little remained, the lesser light penetrated. Their deep cooling pool was now bound by dry land, now filled with reproducing greenery.

We read Genesis 1 with familiar hindsight; we see no surprise in these events. This was not the case for the kingdom of darkness. They did not know when God would stop restricting them. Whether they would have any room left at all was uncertain.

Lucifer's empire of IOU trading had seduced a third of heaven's angels to join his ill-advised rebellion. Imagine the humiliation as they all watched his helplessness. Whatever promises he had made to win their allegiance, they were all proven bankrupt—again. The satan whom Jesus described as a liar was completely defenseless, unable to hold any IOU over God.

NEW PLANS?

Upon satan and his partners, God had now imposed a cyclical twenty-four-hour schedule. Would every cycle contain these staccato terrors? How long would God continue? What else could go wrong?

The habitual theft, murder, and destruction of satan had already ruined earth once. As God performed his rhythmic rearrangements, did satan start planning to reverse them? He might have a justifiable confidence, from his point of view. Of course, this is speculation; Scripture reveals only its plausibility.

Did the devil believe he could ruin it again? That fits the devil we know, certainly. "Been there, done that."

NO

What God did on Days Five and Six ruled out any repeat destruction by satan. On these two days, He completed filling the void. Only one Person could ever ruin Earth again: God Himself.

Genesis 1 reveals no response from darkness, partly because God left them no room to respond. In the fog of war from His six-day assault, the kingdom of darkness lay passive under His restricting hand.

BRAND NEW

They could only guess what lay ahead. Nothing the arch-planner enemy could expect would include what God next filled the earth with. It was brand new, never done before, and unimaginably bad.

Lucifer and his partners had never reproduced. No holy angel reproduced. None of them died. The population of living beings was unchanging. They never knew a growing population.

The next two days may have been God's most shocking attack for the kingdom of darkness. The entire world of spirit, holy and evil alike, suddenly faced an entirely new reality. In the next forty-eight hours, God made creatures that reproduce.

Day Five turned unimaginably bad for the kingdom of darkness. On Day Six: even more unimaginably bad.

DAY FIVE

Then God said, "Let the waters abound with an abundance of living creatures, and let birds fly above the earth across the face of the firmament of the heavens." So God created great sea creatures and every living thing that moves, with which the waters abounded, according to their kind, and every winged bird according to its kind. And God saw that it was good. And God blessed them, saying, "Be fruitful and multiply,

and fill the waters in the seas, and let birds multiply on the earth." So
the evening and the morning were the fifth day. (Genesis 1:20–23)

To the devil and his angels, the 24/7 light of the heavenly bodies invaded
their preferred darkness. Now Day Five invades their water. Living things
suddenly fill their giant cooling pool. Imagine craving a cool drink and
opening your refrigerator for relief from heat, only to find the drink has
something growing in it.

After Day One, they might have thought, "at least we have Night." After
Day Four's lights, their consolation would be only the Seas left to them.
Now even that remnant is denied them. There is reproducing physical
life throughout the Seas satan had thought his to rule.

OTHER CREATURES

Although God had terrorized, tightened, and reduced the domain of
darkness, at least their kingdom still had Earth to themselves. Day Five
put an end to that.

God's command gives His name for these new beings, *living creatures.*
The phrase *every living thing* also appears. Other creatures now occupied
and crowded the exilic home of satan and his angels.

The rigid, destructive satan could never have foreseen this development.
Once previously, there had been light; he ruined it into total darkness.
Original creation had beauty, which the rebels had destroyed. The rebels
could imagine God restoring those because they had seen them before.
When Days One through Four restored both light and loveliness, the
angelic rebels could interpret it as a restoration, rather than a creation.

The kingdom of darkness may have consoled themselves by planning
to ruin Earth a second time. After all, they had already emptied and
de-formed it to their liking between Genesis 1:1 and 1:2. As in war, the
battle line can ebb and flow in the course of events. Perhaps the kingdom
of darkness thought they could bide their time. Later they could repeat
it. This fits with the arrogance shown in their first revolt against God.

But the introduction of other creatures? Darkness could not have imagined that. There had never been other creatures.

DISTINCT FROM SPIRITS

The creatures created on Day Five are distinct from the spirits of the unseen realm. The fallen Lucifer was not a native of Earth nor were his partners. Prior to Day Five, no living being was an Earth-native. Now in their seas and in the air above, are the first native Earth creatures, integrally connected to it.

The spirits of the unseen realm, both holy and unholy, are spirits with bodies. They can use their bodies on Earth, but are not bound to it. Instead, they are bound to their spirit identity, which is constant. Every existing being had been spirit until Day Five.

Now that changed. There are creatures which are physical first, and not spirit at all. This had never happened. Nothing ever existed that wasn't spirit; now it did. Distinct, new beings filled the sea and covered the earth: sea creatures and birds.

TAUNTING

Maybe if it had been us, we would have made people, and then the animals. Why did God do it in the order He chose? At least one reason: to taunt the kingdom of darkness.

The devil and his angels craved palliative relief for their inward burning heat. The water was a necessity to soothe the penalizing transformation of their original natures.

But God's sea creatures love the waters. They are natives there; it is their native habitat. In their own refuge, the burning rebels suddenly are outsiders. First God had squeezed their watery coolant into a smaller space. Now He crowded them further. All around them were now beings at home in the Seas, much more than the rebels.

The birds are a similar taunt. Physical dimensions do not limit the bodies of angelic spirits, nor do our laws of gravity. They are often depicted with wings, which are not needed because they are spirits. Angelic bodies do not need aerodynamic lift like birds and airplanes in order to ascend the air.

The birds were another class of natives, another reminder that Earth was not satan's property. They filled the new air between the ground and the firmament. God made birds at home in the air. He physically designed them to use air; He integrated their bodies with it. Even the bones of birds interact with air as they flap their wings; thus doves whistle as they ascend from their perches.

Knowing the pride of satan and his partners, this could only sting.

DISTINCT FROM EACH OTHER

The new Earth natives are also distinct from each other. Day Five names two classes, sea creatures and birds. But within them, God's command creates a wide variety of unique species.

We might read, "let there be a lot of creatures." What God actually creates by His speech is *"an abundance of living creatures."* This is no ordinary abundance, as in a lot, or many, or a gigantic amount. He says, *"let the waters abound."* An internet search puts the number on today's abundance: 240,000 distinct species of aquatic animals.

And each reproduced according to its kind. With the lavishness of God, it's implausible that He only created one mating pair in each species. If each aquatic pair reproduced an average of 100 per year, the number would soon be in the trillions. The kingdom of darkness would feel like their cooling pool was growing moldy and infested.

The birds also have many species; God made *"every winged bird according to its kind."* A similar search says there are 10,000 species. The birds aren't in the water that satan called home, but fly across the face of the firmament, between the dome of ice and the ground. They epitomize freedom of movement to the kingdom whose rulers would not let his prisoners go (Isaiah 14:17).

So much variety, all in one day, the very emblems of freedom and frolic—this is spitting in the destroyer's face.

BLESSING

As if more living creatures weren't bad enough for darkness, they hear God bless the creatures. God blesses people and things many times in Scripture; this was the first. It would certainly be the first blessing that the angelic host ever heard; the Bible gives no suggestion that God ever blessed the spirits of the unseen realm.

How would God's blessing manifest? None of them would know. It would be like hearing a foreign word for the first time. For the angels, holy and unholy alike, only the results would define blessing for them. No definition existed, but it soon would.

REPRODUCTION

And God blessed them, saying, "Be fruitful and multiply, and fill the waters in the seas, and let birds multiply on the earth." (Genesis 1:22)

The foreign word was soon defined by one result: reproduction. No spirit had ever seen it before.

This reproduction was sexual. It was not spawning like in video games, nor the division that causes cell multiplication. God created each species, birds and sea creatures alike, with a male and a female. All the mating instincts were implanted in these pairs.

The mating birds manifest a vast array of mating rituals. Before they existed, God imagined their color, sounds, and flight patterns. Each species has implanted instincts to attract a mate. God's blessing contained all their unique mating behaviors. Fruitfulness to multiply is the first definition of God's blessing.

CONSISTENCY

Each distinct creature had unique and specific traits, all passed down *according to their kind*. This had also been the pattern of the grass, herbs, and trees. Threaded throughout the multiplying abundance and lavish variety was order.

Evolutionary theory correlates with distrust of the Bible because the theory assumes that reproduction according to their kind is not true. For natural selection to operate, mutations are required. Organisms of one kind reproduce a brand new kind.

But God's revelation says, not true. Each species reproduces consistently—like father, like son.

ABUNDANCE

When we memorize each Day's result, we use the actual stuff, so Day Five was the day of fish and birds.

The abundance of their species and numbers isn't our go-to definition for that Day; it certainly would have been for the devil and his angels. In contests of force, we use the phrase *overwhelming numbers* and it applies to Day Five.

The sea creatures and birds were abundance, fruitful and multiplying. Their number was large and would grow with every birth. In baseball there's a squeeze play where a runner is caught between two defenders; they close in on him while passing the ball back and forth, eventually tagging him out with the ball in their glove. God's Day Five put a squeeze play on the kingdom of darkness. It would have felt like squeeze, squeeze, squeeze.

The devil, in contrast, hates abundance. He uses power to oppress others by imposing scarcity. He has a prison for spirits and won't open the door (Isaiah 14:17). Earth was formless and void after Genesis 1:1, because satan and his angels destroyed its original form and fullness. Jesus summed up their ways by saying, *the devil does not come except to steal, kill, and destroy* (John 10:10).

But in the next breath, Jesus said, "*I have come that they may have life and have it more abundantly.*" "More abundantly" is a double-modifier adverbial phrase, as in "abundantly abundant." God is not stingy. What He does is lavish. Solomon saw this principle installed throughout life.

The generous soul will be made rich, and he who waters will also be watered himself. (Proverbs 11:25)

The principle of abundance is a governing principle for our choices. Its opposite is the scarcity, which we indulge out of fear. Apostle Paul wrote the Corinthian Christians about their giving habits. He used a scarcity word, *sparingly*.

God revealed His operating system of life with this issue; abundance governs our giving today. We don't give because we have abundant supply; we give because we trust that our Father God loves abundance. He is the cheerfully abundant God who wants His children to have hearts like His. He lives in us; His abundance is within us. By our own abundant actions, we abundantly portray our abundant Father to everyone beset by scarcity.

But this I say: He who sows sparingly will also reap sparingly, and he who sows bountifully will also reap bountifully. So let each one give as he purposes in his heart, not grudgingly or of necessity; for God loves a cheerful giver. And God is able to make all grace abound toward you, that you, always having all sufficiency in all things, may have an abundance for every good work. (2 Corinthians 9:6–8)

DAY SIX

Now the denouement begins. The word refers to a dramatic tale or presentation. A moment arrives when all the plot lines are drawn together, when the mysteries are solved, when the inevitable conclusion is apparent. Day Six is the denouement of God's six-day reclamation project.

Like the third day, Day Six has two components, beginning with the first land-based creatures. They move about on Earth's face, rather than live in its Seas or fly in its Skies.

> Then God said, "Let the earth bring forth the living creature according to its kind: cattle and creeping thing and beast of the earth, each according to its kind"; and it was so. And God made the beast of the earth according to its kind, cattle according to its kind, and everything that creeps on the earth according to its kind. And God saw that it was good. (Genesis 1:24–25)

Beasts, cattle, and creeping thing: these words encompass all the land-based creatures He created at that point. Day Five's same patterns of abundance and multiplication by their kinds apply to the land animals. The focal point for the kingdom of darkness: Earth natives suddenly populated all the dry land which hemmed them. Dry Land, Seas, and Sky, all full of multiplying life.

The land creatures are another taunt for the burning rebels. Life requires water. Moving about on the dry land are beings composed of water. How jealous would satan be? The fallen angels have no water, no moisture, within them. Jesus' parable about the rich man and beggar portrays how water is the scarcest element in hell.

> Father Abraham, have mercy on me, and send Lazarus that he may dip the tip of his finger in water and cool my tongue; for I am tormented in this flame. (Luke 16:24)

Prideful jealousy of God infected Lucifer before his fall. In a continuing humiliation, he and his partners now witness creatures of moisture, which they once were but can never be again. Moving about on dry land are animals containing their own moisture.

GOODNESS

Each twenty-four hours, God evaluates the results. *"And God saw that it was good."* Like blessing, good may have been a foreign word to the angelic host. Scripture gives no indication that He ever used the word concerning the spirits of the unseen realm.

Suppose you did something and others heard you say, "it is good." What would they mean? "He liked it and was glad He did it. He didn't need to amend anything after finishing." Certainly, the evidence shows God's evaluation included these. Imagine the angels' reaction upon hearing Him say, "It is good."

Compared to ours, God's good is much broader. The word appears 743 times in the NKJV. The tree of the knowledge of good and evil is the first use after the six days of goodness. That tree and the good it offered is a significant topic of Book Four of the *Unseen* Series, titled *Nobody Sees These Enemies: How to Discern and Disarm Unseen Tempters.*

When God uses the word *good*, He is evaluating, i.e., determining a value. In contrast to the devil who destroys, God values. God preserves value; satan steals and destroys it. Animals are valuable, He says—and something even more valuable is next on the Day Six agenda, its second component.

THE IMAGE-CREATURE

Then God said, "Let Us make man in Our image, according to Our likeness; let them have dominion over the fish of the sea, over the birds of the air, and over the cattle, over all the earth and over every creeping thing that creeps on the earth." So God created man in His own image; in the image of God He created him; male and female He created them. Then God blessed them, and God said to them, "Be fruitful and multiply; fill the earth and subdue it; have dominion over the fish of the sea, over the birds of the air, and over every living thing that moves on the earth."

And God said, "See, I have given you every herb that yields seed which is on the face of all the earth, and every tree whose fruit yields seed; to you it shall be for food. Also, to every beast of the earth, to every bird of the air, and to everything that creeps on the earth, in which there is life, I have given every green herb for food"; and it was so. Then God saw everything that He had made, and indeed it was very good. So the evening and the morning were the sixth day. (Genesis 1:26–31)

Undoubtedly, of all the Scripture passages in this Book Three, the creation of man is most frequently preached. There is a lifetime of study available in it, with well-known elements of great significance. But our attention is not on those; others have explained them well. We are asking, how does the creation of man affect the devil and his kingdom?

We are God's replacements for satan.

We've listed the many distinctions of Day Five and Six's previous natives. Like the creatures upon dry land, we are land-based creatures composed of water and elements. The blessing of God is on us, as it was for the previous creatures. For the onlooking angelic host, Day Five had defined blessing as the ability to reproduce and multiply according to our kind.

But people have a brand new quality. No other being ever created has it. We are in God's image.

For the kingdom of darkness, for God to create an image-creature was even more unimaginably bad. We represent God on Earth. In cooperation with Him, we replace satan. With God Almighty, we will run a squeeze play on satan, right into the lake of waterless fire.

MULTIPERSONAL LOVE

Angels do not marry each other or reproduce—but we do. A Triune God created us in His image, which is multi-personal unity. Genesis 1 tells our creation in a Hebrew rhyme. In contrast to English-language rhyming with similar sounds, Hebrew rhymes two or three parallel ideas. Verse 27 is a three-part parallel rhyme:

So God created man in His own image; in the image of God He created him; male and female He created them. (1:27)

In His image, we are multi-personal. Built into us is His own capacity for intimate love and shared identity, using our two genders. What a contrast to the destructive division, hateful isolation, and self-centered manipulation of satan.

His self-portrait on Earth is the marriage of one man and one woman. He made us male and female to represent His Triune nature. Our truthful oneness as husband and wife is an image of the Triune God of love.

Sadly, our deviations are numerous. Homosexuality is abominable, counterfeiting the image of God. People can be bigamists, whether all at once or in a sequence of mates. Animal mating does not portray God; we do. God intended us as replicas of His multi-personal oneness.

Jesus asked the woman at the Samaritan well about her five marriages. He later told her that God seeks worshipers to worship Him in spirit and in truth (John 4:24).

Our oneness in marriage is part of worshiping God that way. This explains Jesus' stringent limits on divorce in all but one condition. The highest priority for marriage is not our happiness, comfort, and welfare. The priority is to display God's nature of love throughout the seen and unseen worlds.

LIVING SPIRITS

Unlike the previous reproducing creatures, people in God's image were spirit, soul, and body. God intended that they reproduce according to their kind; all we, their descendants, might have been born as spirits without having to be born again.

Sin prevented that, and our spirits died. This was dictated by God's original decree: "*the Lamb that was slain before the foundation of the world*" (Revelation 13:8).

Adam and Eve had both spirits and souls. Their spirits could be intimate with God Almighty, a spirit. Their fellowship was unbroken and pure—spirit to spirit.

In their bodies, they walked with God in His body. Which Person of the Trinity has one? The resurrected Jesus walked with them physically in Eden. It was He who brought the animals to Adam for naming. Aware that no animal would be the right mate, Jesus gently helped Adam learn it as well.

The physical Son of God put Adam to sleep. The words of Apostle John included Eve's formation from Adam's rib: "*All things were made through Him, and without Him nothing was made that was made*" (John 1:3). Adam's relief upon seeing Eve was possible because of Jesus' gentle leadership.

Genesis 1 gives no evidence that the other reproducing creatures had souls. God cares for them, He said in Jonah 4:11, and measures people by their treatment as Solomon observed (Proverbs 12:10). When Jesus brought the many animals to Adam for naming, doubtless He was kind to them, and connected in His way. Pet owners like myself can certainly hope, but the Bible lends no credence that animals have individual souls.

Would the angels have had a story about their creation? No angel had seen God create them, any more than we can see our own birth. But now the angels beheld what it was like. They watched the creation of new spirits, and not just any spirits. Ours were spirits like God's. No wonder the holy angels expressed such great joy and amazement when they sang at Jesus' birth.

> And suddenly there was with the angel a multitude of the heavenly host praising God and saying:
> "Glory to God in the highest,
> And on earth peace, goodwill toward men!" (Luke 2:13–14)

DOMINION

God blessed the birds and sea creatures with fruitful reproduction, unimaginable and bad for the fallen angels. His blessing on Adam and Eve was a far greater threat to darkness—even more unimaginably bad.

> Fill the earth and subdue it; have dominion over the fish of the sea, over the birds of the air, and over every living thing that moves on the earth. (1:28)

Just six days ago, satan and the rebel partners had free rein upon the earth; they did whatever they wished. Their dominion was uncontested and total ever since their fall from heaven.

But with the creation of mankind, God commands a brand new creature to fill and subdue that same Earth. The do-as-we-please liberties of darkness ended at that moment. We can only imagine the shudder of dread upon hearing God speak that blessing to the new image-creature.

The blessing contained a command: fill the Earth and exercise dominion over it and all within it. God anointed human beings to rule every living thing He had created.

The exiled enemies had extinguished whatever life existed after the original creation in Genesis 1:1. Day Five reversed that; the sea creatures now invaded the waters and the birds enjoyed the wide-ranging freedom. The self-contained moisture of land-creatures teased the fiery rebels. Yet satan could entertain a plan to ruin it all over again.

Our creation in God's image introduces a creature to oppose and replace the dominion of darkness. God told us to fill, subdue, and have dominion over it.

His words confirm His awareness it would be a gradual process. Nothing in the Bible shows our growing dominion is completed until the end of time. But the force is unstoppable. God's new image-creature would definitely supplant the dominion of darkness.

In heaven before his fall, Lucifer could move about freely, set up sanctuaries, and engage in trading with other angels. That was gone. In exile after his fall, he had the same freedom of movement on Earth, but now it was gone as well.

And even more unimaginably bad, God set up a dominating force that would replace the kingdom of darkness entirely. Jesus described that force to His disciples this way.

I will build My church, and the gates of Hades shall not prevail against it. (Matthew 16:18)

DEATH

Genesis chapters two and three expand upon the early stages of people's creation. Eden is described, as well as interaction between God and our first parents. Adam and Eve didn't know they were naked. No comparative evaluation existed within them; no shame had entered the world. God told them about the one forbidden tree. He said, *in the day that you eat of it, you shall surely die* (Genesis 2:17).

We saw that *day* is a well-defined word in the total creation account. Adam and Eve would not have a long-accustomed definition for the word, but we do. The people who handed this down to Moses' pen knew what day meant. If God meant twenty-four-hour days for the staccato reclaiming, is it reasonable He would mean something different by using day here?

They did die that day. Yet they lived 900 more years. Their bodies lived, and their souls lived. They had babies and began filling Earth with children.

What died were their spirits. It's easy to imagine the losses they suffered felt deathful. We certainly know it from long human experience, the way of all the earth. Apostle Paul explained how we died because Adam and Eve died.

Through one man sin entered the world, and death through sin, and thus death spread to all men. (Romans 5:12)

Jesus identified the only remedy to Nicodemus in John 3:5–6. A person has to be born again with a living spirit.

Unless one is born of water and the Spirit, he cannot enter the kingdom of God. That which is born of the flesh is flesh, and that which is born of the Spirit is spirit.

In Book Four of the *Unseen* Series, we begin our review of nineteen repetitive strategies for mass influence which the kingdom of darkness has used against people. The first is satan's inducement to Adam and Eve. We will explore why God left them unwarned and unarmed to resist the father of lies.

CHOICE

The creatures made in God's image had the power to choose. We could even commit spirit-suicide by disobeying God.

God Almighty made us able to argue, disobey, forsake, and insult Him. It's easy to imagine satan's sinister smile upon learning that. He would have delighted upon learning that God's image-creature could choose death.

But our power of choice does not require us to reject or disobey God. The satan had only his own experience to go by; one wrong choice and it was over for him. In contrast, repentance is available for every human being until death.

Repentance and forgiveness would be two more foreign words the devil didn't know. He would not have had the foggiest concept of them. The angelic host, whether loyal or rebel had never seen the privilege of a choice to repent.

RESTORATION

Jesus' mission was to activate repentance in people. The filling of the Holy Spirit was the outcome of His death and resurrection. Everyone who follows Jesus can have the complete image of God restored in them; we become living human spirits.

Understanding darkness's instinctive dread of us, we see the restorative breadth of Jesus' salvation. He came to restore that which was lost (Luke 19:10).

Because Jesus substituted Himself for our consequences, human beings can now become living, maturing spirits. God's original image-creature was lost but now is found. His dominion is restored because God the Spirit is again on Earth, in us. He described such spirit-born people to Nicodemus; it's worth a second look.

> Jesus answered, "Most assuredly, I say to you, unless one is born of water and the Spirit, he cannot enter the kingdom of God. That which is born of the flesh is flesh, and that which is born of the Spirit is spirit. Do not marvel that I said to you, 'You must be born again.' The wind blows where it wishes, and you hear the sound of it, but cannot tell where it comes from and where it goes. So is everyone who is born of the Spirit." (John 3:5–8)

The breadth of Jesus' restorative work is the subject of Book Six in the *Unseen* Series, *Nobody Sees This Warrior: God's Secret Ambush*.

Dear reader, your faith in Jesus elevates you to a new identity with new senses. You are a living human spirit like Adam and Eve were. With your spirit, you are capable for interaction and effectiveness in the spirit world. This functionality is open to you because you have a reconciled, living relationship with God.

If you have not realized this new identity in your life, be sure to see the appendix, About the *Unseen* Series, for further guidance. The subject of your living spirit comprises the entire topic of Book One in the *Unseen* Series, titled *Nobody Sees This You: How to Live as a Spirit in the Unseen Realm*.

THE DEVIL'S REPLACEMENTS

One purpose for the race of men is to replace Earth's previous dominators. What they ruined, we are to rebuild. All the life and beauty that they stole, we are to restore. The dominion they enjoyed, we take from them. The boundless territory they enjoyed in the formless void, we bind, limit, and restrict.

Our creation is God's pre-planned response to the war in heaven. We were the pinnacle of God's six-day reshaping. He reclaimed Earth and created us as His stewards for it.

With the Holy Spirit, the Church of the spirit-born continues the squeeze play on the kingdom of darkness. Its gates are in continual retreat before us, whatever the deceptive news headlines might suggest to the contrary.

WHY THE DRAMA?

After our review of Genesis 1, we can look back and take in the whole picture with wisdom. The rebels of the unseen realm ruined what God had made, and He took it back in one hundred forty-four hours.

It's a natural question to wonder why the omnipotent and loving God took that long. In our practical day, one of us might have done the whole thing in about a split second. "I want My earth back." Boom, instantly. So why did God take an entire six days for something He could have done instantly?

I don't know all His reasons yet, but at least one is clear: for us to know Him and His ways. Obviously, God revealed to someone the events preceding our creation. Whether to Noah or his ancestors, or first to Moses, our Father wanted us to know His ways. What do we see in Genesis 1 about Him?

He is deliberate and methodical. This is the opposite of impulsive, capricious, and trigger-happy. Simultaneously, we see how creative and imaginative He is. Everything He did in those rapid-fire days were beyond imagination for the destroyers and liars of darkness. They could not have prepared for His never-seen-before inventions. He made brand new creations and used new words—about us, words He never used for them.

We also see how He imposes His will upon His enemies. People take God's power lightly, until He exercises it. Then we find out just how irresistible it is.

King Nebuchadnezzar of Babylon is a prime example. After God made him insane for seven years, the king repented with these words. We too must live in such a repentance, or the foolishness of invincibility can infect us as it did Lucifer.

And at the end of the time I, Nebuchadnezzar, lifted my eyes to heaven, and my understanding returned to me; and I blessed the Most High and praised and honored Him who lives forever:
For His dominion is an everlasting dominion,
And His kingdom is from generation to generation.
All the inhabitants of the earth are reputed as nothing;
He does according to His will in the army of heaven
And among the inhabitants of the earth.
No one can restrain His hand
Or say to Him, "What have You done?"
At the same time my reason returned to me, and for the glory of my kingdom, my honor and splendor returned to me. My counselors and nobles resorted to me, I was restored to my kingdom, and excellent majesty was added to me. Now I, Nebuchadnezzar, praise and extol and honor the King of heaven, all of whose works are truth, and His ways justice. And those who walk in pride He is able to put down. (Daniel 4:34–37)

God's actions over the six days reveal His complete understanding of satan. He corralled darkness into seas penetrated by light and invaded by living creatures.

And the light shines in the darkness, and the darkness did not comprehend it. (John 1:5)

This review of the six days strengthens our trust in God. Like a cat toying with a mouse, God toys with darkness and they are completely helpless. They cannot escape. They cannot rebut. And they cannot lessen the burning installed within them.

WHY ANY OF THIS AT ALL?

These discoveries still leave us with many questions. Here's a good idea: "Let there be no more devil," and boom, gone! Just like that. Why didn't God blink satan out of existence?

If we are in God's image, why don't we have God's immunity to the kingdom of darkness? "Let us make man in our image, including that devil can't beat them." That single statement would provide us so much relief.

Why make us in His image but vulnerable to temptation? Why put a brand-new creature on the same Earth with the long-experienced chief of evil? Why install any risk of death into His image-bearer? And why not warn Adam and Eve about satan?

How about us: why not just tell us plainly, instead of waiting two thousand years for us to dig it out of multiple scriptures? Why let incomplete explanations consume so much of the Church's energy?

Why let darkness hide, sneak, kill, and destroy for all this time? Why are the devil and his angels permitted to relate, communicate, and coordinate? Why let satan have any kingdom at all?

The Bible demands these questions of any student. For their answers we hearken back to God's three original decrees. Our why questions all find their home there; every vexing query above originated in His three decisive actions.

BEFORE THE FOUNDATION OF THE WORLD

Before the foundation of the cosmos, God's Word decided what the end result would be. Everything between the original creation and the final outcome is driven to fulfill His three decisive decrees.

First, an eternal fire was prepared for the devil and his angels. For this decision to be fulfilled, there had to be rebels. They had to elect their enemy status, repeatedly for a long time, confirming God's wrath.

We saw in Exodus 34:6–7 that God far prefers to exhibit covenant love. The wrath of His holiness is neither instant nor arbitrary. Continued existence is allowed the rebels because His wrath is not capricious. At every opportunity, these enemies rebelled electively.

If that was the only decree, it could have started the moment they rebelled, straight to the lake of fire. The intermediate period we occupy would not have been required. But we are here, because of the other two decrees.

With our creation, God committed Himself to a long span of centuries. The gospel truth wasn't even revealed fully for thousands of years. Yet no matter how long it took, our creation is part and parcel of God's decrees before the foundation of the cosmos.

The second decree: his eternal human partners were chosen. This decree required our race to be created with a free will. We could agree with God or His enemies, both individually and corporately.

And for our entire lives, we confirm our choices. Because of His grace, one sincere repentance wipes out all previous choices of rebellion. But this is only possible if His holy wrath is satisfied—the subject of decree number three.

Third, the Lamb was slain before the foundation of the world. His voluntary, substitutionary atonement would provide that satisfaction. Because of this decree, God made Himself subject to death in His Second Person.

Only a penalty of infinite consequence could satisfy His limitless wrath against all my unholiness. Only repayment by an infinite being could make up for the infinite loss caused by my sin.

The death of the Second Person of the Trinity was the satisfaction that God decreed. For Jesus to die, He had to be incarnated in a mortal body, subject to death. God made us able to die so that the Lamb could be slain—*before the foundation of the world.*

Discussion and reflection questions for Chapter Thirteen can be found in the Reader Engagement Resources

---

CHAPTER FOURTEEN

THE ENEMIES OF THE ENEMIES

Spiritual events are afoot in the twenty-first century. People are becoming Christians at a greatly accelerated pace. The unseen realm is pressing into our visible world. Calamity is breaking out at every turn. The structures of social trust are in danger of collapse. Darkness is putting on quite a show; it may be their last gasp.

We have an ordination and anointing to push back the gates of darkness' domain. To arise into that influence, Christians must become wise to God's enemies.

Lest Satan should take advantage of us; for we are not ignorant of his devices. (2 Corinthians 2:11)

WHAT WE'VE DONE

The reader of this Book Three in the nine-book *Unseen* Series has welcomed new questions and puzzles as shoehorns into the Bible's mysteries of reality. We have taken a deep dive into obscure Scriptures not commonly preached. Several methods have been employed: historico-grammatical, inductive, and typological.

From the Bible, we have explained the origin of the devil and his replacements. The Bible reveals much more about the kingdom of darkness which occupies the bulk of the remaining six books. Their titles can be seen in the front of this book.

Throughout the series, we test our discoveries by their explanatory power and consistency with the entire Word of God.

ENEMY TEMPTING

The rebellious spirits in the unseen must protect themselves from us. Think about it. Our enemies are spirits, and so are we. Our enemies are bereft of life, but we are filled with the Author of Life.

We are living human spirits restored to God's image, in whom He makes His home. The Spirit of God still searches Earth, from His home in the bodies of Jesus' followers.

> If anyone loves Me, he will keep My word; and My Father will love him, and We will come to him and make Our home with him. (John 14:23)

Living human spirits are multiplying daily; an increasing number of people are saved globally. These are reinforcements for our kingdom. In stark contrast, the kingdom of darkness has no means of reinforcement. They cannot create new spirits. Any advancement they may achieve is completely dependent on cooperative people.

The evil crime family has no hope against us, and they know it. They know what God ordained before the foundation of the world. We will dislocate satan and his partners. We living spirits are their dread. The enemies of God have become our enemies.

> I have pursued my enemies and overtaken them;
> Neither did I turn back again till they were destroyed.
> I have wounded them,
> So that they could not rise;
> They have fallen under my feet.
> For You have armed me with strength for the battle;
> You have subdued under me those who rose up against me.
> You have also given me the necks of my enemies,
> So that I destroyed those who hated me.
> They cried out, but there was none to save;
> Even to the Lord, but He did not answer them.
> Then I beat them as fine as the dust before the wind;
> I cast them out like dirt in the streets. (Psalm 18:37–42)

Oh, that You would slay the wicked, O God!
Depart from me, therefore, you bloodthirsty men.
For they speak against You wickedly;
Your enemies take Your name in vain.
Do I not hate them, O Lord, who hate You?
And do I not loathe those who rise up against You?
I hate them with perfect hatred;
I count them my enemies. (Psalm 139:19–22)

BASICS ON FIGHTING UNSEEN ENEMIES

In the last twenty years, many good Christian books have become available regarding spiritual warfare. There is no need to duplicate their insights here. The standard methods are well known.

First, spend time with God. He wants to be known, but like any friend at any level, it requires time together. He is worth the time, as much as He might request.

Next, be a lifelong student of God's Word. Whenever you hear your thoughts say, "It can't mean that," look again. Let every puzzle, every difference of interpretation drive you into what He says in Scripture.

Third is what we often call prayer, but the meaning of the word has seen more meaningful days. Alternative words today are intimacy, communion, and agreement.

Of equal importance to each of these is regular worship with other Christians. Your local fellowship may be people just like you. Periodic fellowship with the many age groups, situations, cultures, and ethnicities draws us closer to the Lord Jesus. He was the One who invited us all, and He redeems the good in each to benefit the other.

> For as the body is one and has many members, but all the members of that one body, being many, are one body, so also is Christ. For by one Spirit we were all baptized into one body—whether Jews or Greeks, whether slaves or free—and have all been made to drink into one Spirit. For in fact the body is not one member but many. (1 Corinthians 12:12–14)

MATURE FIGHTING

God justifiably expects us to grow. Our warfare against unseen spirits of evil cannot remain at the basic level. Paul wrote that we wrestle against these principalities and forces of wickedness in the unseen realm. How can we possibly succeed? By maturing as a spirit, we gain the necessary capabilities.

As we grow, we can discern enemies and allies in the unseen. Our communion with God becomes less thought-based, less feeling-dependent, and less habit-limited. The Divine Person within us is available constantly; His presence never leaves; our Father is right at hand. But He will not force Himself upon us. God will not make you mature. You must choose Him; He wants to be pursued.

> Yet indeed I also count all things loss for the excellence of the knowledge of Christ Jesus my Lord, for whom I have suffered the loss of all things, and count them as rubbish, that I may gain Christ. (Philippians 3:8)

As we mature into the living human spirits God originally wanted, we speak in languages from the Holy Spirit. We continually expose any remaining grip of darkness on our lives, using deliverance ministry and occasional retreats. Angels and demons alike become discernible to us. Our meekness navigates the dangers of exposure to the mighty unseen participants. The entirety of Scripture's tapestry backing melds with our entire worldview.

Book One of the *Unseen* Series is *Nobody Sees This You: How to Live as a Spirit in the Unseen Realm.* I was beginning a two-thousand mile Interstate 10 motorcycle ride when the Holy Spirit within me said, "Exit here." Immediately there was an Office Depot and He next said, "Get a handheld recorder." The book was dictated on that ride.

> Your ears shall hear a word behind you, saying,
> "This is the way, walk in it,"
> Whenever you turn to the right hand
> Or whenever you turn to the left. (Isaiah 30:21)

Such instructions are not common, but neither was it common for Jesus to spit on a man's eyes (John 9), or Elisha to lay himself face-to-face on a dead body two times (2 Kings 4:34–35). We don't measure whether to obey God's voice within. We don't wait for God to lead others the same way, as if it provides extra security. Instead of comparing His in-the-moment directions to norms among people, it's better to obey. Obedience to Him is its own reward, but He adds many more on top of that.

Therefore let us, as many as are mature, have this mind; and if in anything you think otherwise, God will reveal even this to you. Nevertheless, to the degree that we have already attained, let us walk by the same rule, let us be of the same mind. (Philippians 3:15–16)

If a Christian is to exercise the authority that Jesus promised, for Jesus' purposes, such mature fighting is necessary. It's simple: God leads the fight. Listen to Him and do what He says. When He wants your advice, He can ask for it and you will know.

GOD'S TARGET

The rebels were not annihilated, their spirits were not shredded, and darkness was not cast out of Earth. His eternal decree requires that enemies be kept alive in eternal suffering of His wrath.

What if God, wanting to show His wrath and to make His power known, endured with much longsuffering the vessels of wrath prepared for destruction? (Romans 9:22)

His original decree about us who are chosen requires agents of our testing. One such agent is the kingdom of darkness. The devil, his angels and his demons all serve God's purposes.

That He might make known the riches of His glory on the vessels of mercy, which He had prepared beforehand for glory. (Romans 9:23)

Lucifer's experience demonstrates, even being made as the seal of perfection does not prevent eternal alienation from God. That's why Adam and Eve were not made perfect. By testing in the process of life, we prove our love and faith in Him. The enemies help purify us into the overcomers that will be safe in eternal salvation.

In this you greatly rejoice, though now for a little while, if need be, you have been grieved by various trials, that the genuineness of your faith, being much more precious than gold that perishes, though it is tested by fire, may be found to praise, honor, and glory at the revelation of Jesus Christ. (1 Peter 1:6–7)

ENEMY TARGET

The kingdom of darkness is more helpless than ever. That's why they sneak beneath sight to trick us. Their goal is to bring us under the wrath of God. It's how they tricked Israel also, and the Old Testament is full of the evidence. The difference with us is that He lives in us.

God in fact cultivates our maturity as spirits. If He did not, we certainly could not do it. He patiently recognizes that we mature gradually. He doesn't ask us to go by *shoulds* and *shouldn'ts*, as Jesus' persecutors did. He wants our obedience as we take each step toward him. He cultivates, and we cooperate.

The enemies of God interpose themselves if we let them, using several tricks common today.

THREATEN YOUR HAPPINESS

Most people want a happy life. Afterward we want to avoid hell, go to heaven, and live forever. That certainly describes me. The kingdom of darkness threatens our happy lives, recognizing that we love this world. They encourage fear in us by threatening our priority. Jesus fingered the problem in Matthew 6:24.

> No one can serve two masters; for either he will hate the one and love the other, or else he will be loyal to the one and despise the other. You cannot serve God and mammon.

Priority on our happy life tempts us to ignore the unseen realm. We postpone our readiness for eternity when we prioritize our happy life in this world of men. Jesus described that temptation with these words: *"the cares of this world, the deceitfulness of riches, and the desires for other things"* (Mark 4:19).

This enemy tactic is exposed by a study of Job's complaints. When the court of heaven convened in Job chapters 1–3, satan accused Job of loving God only because God gave him a good life. In his first effort, satan stripped Job of that wealth and family. In the second round, even Job's health and reputation were stripped. And the heart of Job's vulnerability was exposed:

> For the thing I greatly feared has come upon me,
> And what I dreaded has happened to me. (Job 3:25)

Our desire to be safe and happy is not ungodly. God Himself wants us to be prosperous; as we saw, He loves abundance. But to fear the loss of happiness tricks us into loving it more than Him. It's evident in how we pray; we use God so we can be prosperous. That was Job's weakness. As righteous as he was, he was using God to maintain his happy life.

Even Christians can enter an agreement with the kingdom of satan: "you leave my life alone, and I will leave you alone." However, there is always fine print. Evil spirits are thieves without honor or mercy.

How do we become the enemies of these evil tempters? When we forswear the priority of a happy life, the tempters are completely disarmed. When we trust our Father to give us all that's needed, we defeat these evil enemies.

> The Lord God has given Me
> The tongue of the learned,
> That I should know how to speak
> A word in season to him who is weary.
> He awakens Me morning by morning,
> He awakens My ear
> To hear as the learned.
>
> The Lord God has opened My ear;
> And I was not rebellious,
> Nor did I turn away.
> I gave My back to those who struck Me,
> And My cheeks to those who plucked out the beard;
> I did not hide My face from shame and spitting.
>
> For the Lord God will help Me;
> Therefore I will not be disgraced;
> Therefore I have set My face like a flint,
> And I know that I will not be ashamed.
> He is near who justifies Me;
> Who will contend with Me?
> Let us stand together.
> Who is My adversary?
> Let him come near Me.
> Surely the Lord God will help Me;
> Who is he who will condemn Me?
> Indeed they will all grow old like a garment;

The moth will eat them up.
(Isaiah 50:4–9)

OFFER YOU IDOLATRY

The kingdom of satan seeks leverage over human beings. People can become the IOU trading partners of darkness, which uses our fears to keep us under control. The idol of a happy life turns us into cowards easily threatened and leveraged by darkness.

Those who regard worthless idols
Forsake their own Mercy. (Jonah 2:8)

For My people have committed two evils:
They have forsaken Me, the fountain of living waters,
And hewn themselves cisterns—broken cisterns that can hold no water. (Jeremiah 2:13)

A worse consequence is our offense against God. Given the choice between fearing loss and fearing Him, it is offensive to fear Him less. That is the definition of an idol. God's first commandment on Mt. Sinai was about this. He will not be subordinate to other worships.

You shall have no other gods before Me. (Exodus 20:3)

For rebellion is as the sin of witchcraft, and stubbornness is as iniquity and idolatry. (1 Samuel 15:23)

Jesus spoke the Beatitudes in Matthew 5:1–13. The second one shows us the way out of our idolatry: "*Blessed are those who mourn, for they shall be comforted.*" This mourning opens the door for the subsequent Beatitude qualities. Our Father greatly desires to reward each one with its promise.

God's hatred of idolaters showed the enemies how to make God hate us. They trick us into having greater priorities than our relationship with God. Look around, or look in the mirror: darkness easily succeeds. The kingdom of darkness has done this habitually for thousands of years.

Our enemies are very skillful. People in contrast are poor in spirit and are easy prey for these spirits of evil. We fall victim as individuals, as societies, as cultures, and as regions. Their principalities blackmail entire nations with the loss of secure happiness.

Israel fell for it, the subject of Book Four in the *Unseen* Series. The kingdom of darkness only had to make Israel odious to God. Despite Israel's great status before God, their fears were leveraged by darkness. God fingered their idolatry in many places, such as Isaiah 57:11.

And of whom have you been afraid, or feared,
That you have lied
And not remembered Me,
Nor taken it to your heart?

Their efforts could even appear to be righteous, yet God saw through them. Israel was using Him to ensure the safe happiness they loved more.

I will declare your righteousness
And your works,
For they will not profit you. (57:12)

Revealing the futility of our idols is one element of God's judgment.

When you cry out,
Let your collection of idols deliver you.
But the wind will carry them all away,
A breath will take them. (57:13a)

Individuals and nations cycle through these times of idolatry. People easily fall prey to the tricks of darkness because we are all poor in spirit. That's why judgment is a blessing, because we can repent and put our trust in God Himself.

But he who puts his trust in Me shall possess the land,
And shall inherit My holy mountain. (57:13b)

That's what we Christians do. We are born again as living human spirits, seated in heaven with Jesus.

They are God's enemies. We are their enemies.

THE END OF CREATION

After Genesis 1, the kingdom of darkness had been terrorized. Their territory now shrunken and their isolation now populated, God had only one thing left to do: rest.

He did not need rest. Jesus said that the Father was always at His work (John 5:17). Jesus Himself holds everything in existence by speaking it continually (Hebrews 1:3). But as great as the warfare is, He commands that we rest as well.

Let's take stock of our situation as we close this Book Three and pave the way for Book Four of the *Unseen* Series. Imagine the opening lines of your evening Heaven News.

> *Welcome to Heaven News Today, Yesterday, and Tomorrow. Breaking news: God created a race of spirit beings with mortal bodies to dominate Earth for Him and replace the exiled Lucifer. God has placed His image on Earth in these mortal men and women. In their relationships, His Triune nature of love is now expressed continually there.*
>
> *And this race is multiplying daily. They reproduce new images of God by their sexual actions. More spirits are being born daily through faith in The Son of God. The Earth is fuller every day with the image-creatures of God. The Church of living spirits is pushing back hell's gates.*
>
> *Next up: what does this mean for the rebel kingdom of darkness? Where can they hide now that their watery refuge is shrunken and populated? How can the devil and his partners ever recover from the six-day assault of God? The new spirit beings in mortal bodies will replace satan—but how? What will God do to help them?*
>
> *Stay tuned to Book Four of Heaven News Today, Yesterday, and Tomorrow!*

Discussion and reflection questions for Chapter Fourteen can be found in the Reader Engagement Resources

---

READER
ENGAGEMENT
RESOURCES

ABOUT THE
UNSEEN SERIES

PARADIGM LIGHTHOUSE

The *Unseen* Series comes to you through the ministry of Paul and Diane Renfroe, named Paradigm Lighthouse. Their calling is to help you mature as a living human spirit—but what does that look like?

The undeniable fact is this: between you and God is an inexpressibly enormous difference in scale, being, and quality. He is an eternal Spirit who is both perfect love and perfect rightness—a severe contrast to us.

Yet for all this gap, He can adopt you as His intimate child, born as a spirit. The Lighthouse name expresses the explosion of lighthearted safety that His peace implants into every such person. He fills you with His Holy Spirit, repeatedly, more and more.

This event and process pulls your thinking and beliefs into agreement with Him. The Paradigm name identifies this process as profound, life-changing paradigm shifts. One perception of reality supersedes another, as He blows your mind with the unseen things He reveals.

Further in and further up to our Father God is a lifelong process, and well worth every sacrifice known to mankind. This experience of large-scale paradigm shifts has also characterized the history of His Church, a core observation of the Present Truth movement.

The nine numbered books in this series are sequential. However, each contains the following series orientation and a summary of the preceding books, so any book is a beneficial starting point. For your full benefit, read each book for its unique contribution to your paradigm of reality.

Each book of the series is available where you purchased this one, and if not, you may visit ParadigmLighthouse.com. There you can also contact us to receive ministry directly, both public and private.

YOU

A burgeoning number of people worldwide are perceiving unseen realities today. The gap between seen and unseen, between natural and spirit, is narrowing. You were magnetized to this book and the *Unseen* series, and you are not alone. I wrote this series to equip you and your friends for holy perception of the *Unseen* Realm.

Questions are normal:
- How can you interpret what you are faintly perceiving? Are there rules or guidelines?
- What's causing your growing awareness of the hidden world? Why you?
- Where do the Bible and your church fit in? Why isn't everyone receptive?
- Can you make your perception clearer? Can you make it stop?

The words *dread* and *terror* are often used because the unseen threatens us with loss of control. Its spirits which are holy can, if fully unveiled, intimidate, and reduce us to quivering. Those which are unholy can trick us and take advantage of us.

We know ourselves terribly ill-equipped for the invisible world of spirit, and gravely unprepared for the accountability of perceiving it. As mere human beings, we are poor in spirit. We can go through our entire lives without noticing they are pulling our string and jerking our chain. But we came by that ignorance honestly: mankind's default is to control that perception—or prevent it altogether.

The unseen world is now rapping harder and faster on the windows of our souls.

RESPONDING TO THE SPIRIT WORLD

There are two extremes we use to control our interface with the invisible world of spirit. The low intensity method is to control the unseen by ignoring it. The high intensity method is to manipulate the unseen and its spirits, long named sorcery.

Between these two extremes, people use the spirit world for gain. Religion, for instance, is a tit-for-tat effort to secure favor from God and obligate Him to us. When we complain about God's unfairness, we reveal the religion in us.

People use the unseen for gain in the seen world, and not just with religion. The list includes business, family, education, and government. Deeds can be beneficial and character admirable, all the while treating the unseen as a mere tool for the natural world.

Today, the spirit world is becoming harder to ignore, manipulate, and use. There are many ways we try to limit it. All of them express our default reaction: "Stay in the place we assign you!"

But in our days, the unseen is refusing to stay there.

THE BEST RESPONSE

You can receive a welcome into the spirit world. God, a Spirit, revealed a specific protocol. No one can be a spirit without following it. The results are very desirable.

It begins simply but its results defy imagination: you admit to God your poverty for His world of spirit. This admission brings an inward mourning over your poverty as a spirit. You recognize how distant you are from the true God, a Spirit. Drastically lower expectations follow as meekness arises within you. You mercifully respond to others after facing your own poverty.

Simultaneously, you have a growing hunger and thirst for the good that God intends. As you mature, old values become replaced with what God wants, and you are purified. You gain new abilities to create peace in relationships, both with God and among people. And you become loyal to God at any cost.

This summarizes nine qualities God likes to bless, which Jesus of Nazareth listed in the first book of the Bible's New Testament, Matthew chapters 5 through 7, together with the specific blessings God places on each quality. Their lasting name is the Beatitudes.

So how do you gain these desirable qualities? You become a living spirit with the following protocol.

THE PROTOCOL TO BECOME A SPIRIT

For anyone poor in spirit to become a spirit requires help—the help of the Head Spirit, God. He wants you to become a living spirit with Him! He has revealed the protocol so you can.

1. Admit that you are spiritually poor. You do not have what it takes to relate to God, who is a spirit, and holy. The lasting word for this situation is sin.

2. Admit the dire consequences of that spiritual poverty. These are distance between you and the God who would be your Father, slowness to honor and obey Him, damage to yourself and those around you, and hindrance to His good desires for mankind. The lasting word for this step is confession.

3. Admit that He solved this spirit gap. Jesus proclaimed that His death on the cross fully satisfied God in the spirit world, where we are so poverty-stricken. When you believe this and follow Jesus, God the Father gives you birth as a spirit. Immediately, God adopts you as His own child, just as Jesus was. The lasting word is faith, because your adoption is unsee-able, and is perceived by trusting the truthfulness of what God's revealing.

4. Admit those three things directly to Him. Here's one way to express it to Him.

God, I admit You deserve much, yet I can only give so little. I want to follow Jesus so His death solves the spirit gap I have with You. So I ask you to forgive me. I put my trust in Jesus, that His death enables You to adopt me as your child. I don't know what to expect, but when You show me and help me, I will respond to You as my Father, with the best of my ability.

THE PROTOCOL TO STAY A SPIRIT

After you admit these facts, the spirit world tests your genuine intent. Did you mean it? Will you really maintain your new relationship with God?

The host of heaven observes your persistent commitments in this seen world. This includes angels who serve us, sent by God. Also included: spirits who hate people, including you. These evil spirits try to imprison your spirit. If they cannot, then these destroyers try to disrupt, discourage, dissuade, or deceive you.

Jesus knew this would happen and provided in the Bible a protocol for you to stay a living spirit.

1. Jesus started a protective group for people born as spirits after these admissions. Its lasting name is The Church, uppercase. Now it is globally huge, full of many churches, lowercase, in different forms. Not everyone in a church is the same. One quality is common: poverty of spirit and dependence upon God. In church, God trains and tests everyone born in spirit to grow our ability to love others graciously.

2. There is a book He provided to everyone born as spirits; that book is the Bible, the subject of Book Two. Jesus rose from the dead and could still be here, but He did not remain physically in the seen world. His preferred method was to fill us with His Spirit and give us a Bible.

   To see and hear Him with our spirit's "eyes" and "ears," He endorsed an authoritative collection of writings—our Bible. It holds many yesterdays, written over 1,500 years and compiled in 397 AD. There are many translations available from its original, well-known languages. In it, you will find God and He will reveal the invisible to you. The Bible is an ancient book written by forty people distant in time and culture, both from each other and from us. That's why effort is required to understand it.

   This book, *Nobody Sees This Unseen Realm: How to Unlock Bible Mysteries*, describes that effort in detail. The effort is amply rewarded because the Bible is a proven book which also trains and proves your spirit. God uses His Word to grow your spirit for effective activity in both the seen and the unseen worlds.

3. Other commitments—not mere behaviors—help us grow as spirits. One example is self-sacrificing thoughts and deeds, such as service to others. Another is giving money as tithes to our particular church group and offerings to others. Obedience to God's explicit commands governs all our commitments. Submission to the leaders He provides us trains us to lead others as well.

THE EVENT OF YOUR SPIRIT'S BIRTH

The above admissions cause an unseeable event: you are born as a spirit into the unseen world. Anyone who sincerely follows the above protocol becomes a newborn spirit. Jesus described it to someone in the fourth book of the New Testament, John chapter 3 verse 6: "*That which is born of the flesh is flesh, and that which is born of the Spirit is spirit.*"

When we are born in this seen world, that's the limit of our being; we cannot participate in the spirit world. The Bible's word for this is the flesh. Every person is born in the flesh. But when we believe Jesus and follow Him, we are born into the unseen world. The Bible's word for that is the spirit. Only followers of Jesus are born in spirit.

THE MATURING

Your spirit begins as an immature spirit, just as your body was born immature. Likewise, either you feed it or it withers unnourished. Either you mature as a spirit, or you atrophy.

Church, the Bible, prayer, and obedience are good ways to nourish your spirit. Denying the cravings of the flesh strengthens your spirit, just as weight training strengthens your muscles. As your spirit matures, your spirit asserts its dominion over your natural self, as it should.

This Book Three of the *Unseen* Series is foundational because it equips you to study God's Bible for yourself. Maturity means that you are not dependent on others for your study of the Bible.

Maturing as a spirit is impossible without God's Spirit within, and we ask God's Spirit to fill us more every day. Holy is the adjective used to describe Him, so His lasting name is the Holy Spirit.

Some ask insincerely or without holiness. Some try to limit the spirit and control the unseen. As your spirit matures, you may feel the pain and desperation in their futile effort. Yet upon them we always have mercy and desire their best; God is patient with us all.

YOUR UNSEEN SPIRIT

As a newborn spirit, the world of spirits immediately recognizes you as an active participant. They see you as a spirit born of God's own doing. The unseen spirits who are holy are angels who rejoice as God assigns them to help you mature. Unholy spirits, including demons, are assigned to deter you by their chief, the devil.

The *Unseen* Series is a guide for every born as a spirit by following Jesus Christ. You have entered this very active but unseeable world. Being a spirit being raises many questions we'll investigate in this series. How do you act? What actually are you capable of, as a spirit? As a spirit, do you hear, like you do in your body? See? Feel? Smell? Taste? Do you talk as a spirit?

How do you distinguish between your unseen spirit and the more immediate parts of yourself? How do you identify and respond to the spirits you encounter?

If you are adopted by God as your Father, how does that interaction occur? Surely you talk together—but how? How does He speak in the Bible? In your prayers? In your dreams? What does He do, and what's your part? Do you have to forget old things? What new do you need to learn?

Take heart: Your Father will not leave you hanging. He may test your persistence. He may prove your sincerity by requiring patience—but you can count on Him.

THE FORGETTING

Even as a living spirit, everyone has some baggage from the old days. Parents and predecessors hand it down to us. Some baggage is from living by our own wits without full access to God's help and protection. There is also baggage that evil spirits tricked us into carrying. A constant experience of maturing spirits is shedding such baggage. Forgetting these hindrances is a welcome process.

That baggage includes our definition of impossible. When your spirit grows, you constantly see the falsity of limits which you once accepted without question. Forgetting these limits signals your growing intimacy with your Father.

A regular habit is to break agreements with old beliefs and habits in favor of what God reveals to us. Bible study is one cause of this action: His Word performs its discovery process in our hearts. Our area of agreement with God expands when we relinquish our newly discovered agreements with the kingdom of darkness, while the dominance of the seen world wanes.

THE LEARNING

The Father of your spirit, God Himself, desires intimacy with you. It is a process over time; there is much to learn about one another. He packaged His revelation in a book for us, and it simply takes effort and time to find Him in it. This is one reason He puts His Spirit into us, so we can understand His thoughts. Apostle John, one of Jesus' first four followers, described it in his first letter, chapter 2 verse 27: "*The anointing which you have received from Him abides in you [and] teaches you concerning all things.*"

THE PAYOFF

This forgetting and learning process requires outside help. The guidance of mentors and leaders is indispensable; God will lead you to the right ones.

Most important is God's active, vocal presence within your skin. This occurs by the repeated filling of the Holy Spirit, more and more very time. Reliance upon His Word is a constant need—as it should be for a meek, poor in spirit person.

God is a Spirit, and He will teach you to use your spirit senses. With His life inside you, you will be alive beyond imagination. You will surpass the discoveries of the *Unseen* Series. Your participation in the unseen world of spirit can only become more effective.

Welcome to the world of the spirit-born.

ADDITIONAL RESOURCES FOR THE *UNSEEN* SERIES

OBTAINING CREDENTIALS FOR THE ONLINE DISCUSSION GROUP

As an owner of a book in the *Unseen* Series, you can request login credentials for a secure online discussion group at ParadigmLighthouse.com, to share your meditations and your progress. The group is limited to readers of the *Unseen* Series. There, you can share your reflections and discoveries. I am growing also and treasure your discoveries as you walk through this book and meditate on the scriptural principles.

With the correspondence and reflections our readers share there, we can all see how God is speaking to us, His body, about our spirits. I'm sure we will find patterns in God's speech to us. Doubtless we can use this book from our discoveries together.

To obtain your log-in username and password, please visit Paradigm-Lighthouse.com and follow the instructions you see after clicking *Request Log-in Credentials*.

REVIEWS ON AMAZON

Please visit Amazon.com and Goodreads.com to leave your review for *Nobody Sees This Creation: The Origin of the Devil and His Replacements*.

Every reader review helps someone else feel safe to purchase and benefit from this Book Three of the *Unseen* Series. Your review can help others enjoy release from spiritual victimization. As you know from your own online shopping, the number of reviews for a book matters—whether the reviewer agrees or not. Short or long, general or specific, your review will make a positive impact.

SOCIAL MEDIA

Neither the author nor publisher utilize social media. If you do, please mention the book by its title, *Nobody Sees This Creation: The Origin of the Devil and His Replacements*. Our ranking on Amazon is affected by people searching for the book by name.

You may also like to share the ParadigmLighthouse.com link, where people can purchase the books as well.

BIBLE STUDY
DISCUSSION QUESTIONS

[for Nobody Sees This Creation: The Origin of the Devil and His Replacements]

FOREWORD, PREFACE, AND INTRODUCTION

1. In the foreword, Dr. Hamon describes a frightening evil spirit and an infection of fear. Has such a thing happened to you? If so, how did you deal with it? How did it affect you?
2. Up until now, how would you describe your familiarity with the unseen realm? What has helped you? If you are a Christian, is there a Bible verse you have relied upon? If you haven't committed yourself to Jesus and His provision, how have you dealt with the unseen beings?
3. What did you think about the Bible being love or hate, life or death? Does it affect you that way?
4. The introduction ends with a synopsis of the book. Were these concepts new to you?

CHAPTER ONE: OUR ENEMIES INTRODUCED

1. In what you read, were any questions answered? Puzzles solved? Or did you have more questions after chapter one? Let's open the discussion for these.
2. The chapter included angels because our enemies are angelic in their original nature. Was something about them new to you? It talked about Jesus as the Angel of the LORD in the Old Testament. Let's look at Judges 6 about Gideon and see how Jesus was in it.
3. Let's read Ephesians 6:10–12 together about the collective ruler-ship of darkness. If you had Apostle Paul's life, what wrestling would you be thinking about writing these sentences? If you were

him, how would meekness and poverty of spirit fit with wrestling unseen rulers?

4. How do you feel about having plural enemies to wrestle? How can you place stronger trust in your divine authorization? Would one of you like to volunteer your experience after receiving deliverance ministry?

5. The chapter talked about a contrast between cowardice and exaltation. After reading the chapter, how do you see yourself seated in the heavenly realms (Ephesians 2:6)? The enemies' jealousy is active against us for replacing them. How do you see their jealousy manifesting in your life?

PART ONE: THE CALAMITY OF HEAVEN

CHAPTER TWO: TYRE, SYMBOL FOR LUCIFER

1. Ezekiel had a journal. If one of you keeps a journal of your times with God, let us know why. What benefit is it?

2. Let's read 2 Peter 2:10–11 and Jude 8–10 together. The basis of fair judgment is honor for God and His choice. Throughout the book, the author emphasizes meekness and respect. How do you feel about this, in relation to the kingdom of darkness?

3. In our Bible study group, who has had experience with typology? It is important as the source of revelation about satan's origins. Has anyone received training in typology? What are your thoughts about typological and symbolic interpretations?

4. Tyre is prominent in chapter two because the author says it is God's symbol for Lucifer. What did you think about that? Patterns of trade hold significance for the coming chapters in the book; what were your questions about trading?

5. There was a sidebar about our creation mandate to dominate the earth. What was your response to that? What does it mean to do that?

6. At the end of chapter two, the author introduces the time trombone. Since it matters for the rest of the book, does one of you feel comfortable summarizing the idea for us?

CHAPTER THREE: LAMENTING LUCIFER

1. Had you ever thought God might lament Lucifer's fall? What was meaningful to you in the sections describing Lucifer?
2. Lucifer's trading was a focal point in the chapter. How would you summarize the way it affected him? How did Lucifer's trading affect God? Do you agree it showed disdain? How are we tempted to exhibit disdain toward God?
3. What were your responses to the IOUs discussed in the chapter? How do IOUs manifest in our lives? How do we recognize ones that are godly, and one that are not?
4. The dramatic alterations in Lucifer's nature have significant implications for the balance of the book. Let's read Ezekiel 28:11–19 together and see what we find about Lucifer's before and after.

CHAPTER FOUR: THE SIN OF LUCIFER

1. Let's begin our study with Isaiah 14:12–17, if someone would read it aloud for us. While you are listening, pick out what tells you about Lucifer.
2. The chapter contrasts the fallen angels of darkness with the holy angels. Which ones do you identify with? Could you relate to the movie angels, or Zechariah, or the angels worshiping in Revelation?
3. Chapter four includes several consequences for Lucifer and his defiance. It listed the penalties awaiting him, as well as God's topsy-turvy actions, reversing the devil's pattern of power. Yet we are commanded not to gloat disrespectfully. How do we pray against the work of darkness in keeping with these things?
4. How did the section *Deep Contrast* affect you?
5. Do you agree that the insights so far have significant explanatory power for things in the Bible? What puzzles are you solving so far?

CHAPTER FIVE: REBEL PARTNERS

1. Early in the chapter are two sections about reading the book of Revelation. Would one of you summarize the comments about meekness, and encryption? How do we all feel about that guidance for reading Revelation?
2. Had you ever thought of the devil being limited to a body? If that's true, what changes in your reaction to temptation and troubles?

3. Would someone read Revelation 12:1–9 aloud for us? As you listen, we want to track IOUs and the new things in Lucifer's existence. Let's discuss them.

4. The chapter talked about Lucifer's recruitment methods. Where do we see parallels in our society today? The disciples thought in IOU terms; how can we recognize when we are making the same mistake and falling into Lucifer's patterns?

5. Jesus' parable about swapping places: as you see it, how did that relate to Lucifer's fall? What does it mean if you took his place? And what about the crime family image? How have their mafioso tactics affected your life?

6. As this chapter ends, there's more description of the time trombone. Since we first discussed it, how has that idea been helpful in our Bible study?

CHAPTER SIX: DIVIDED PARTNERS

1. Let's begin with the two passages in the chapter, Isaiah 14:18–21 and Luke 11:14–26. Would two people volunteer to read those aloud? As they are reading, let's watch for the evidence of division in the kingdom of darkness, and then we'll discuss what we hear.

2. How did you feel about satan's tempting Jesus to accept the place of his partner kings? What outcomes could Jesus have found tempting on the one hand, or disgusting on the other?

3. Our own maturity requires us to understand the principles of Luke 11 in our dealings with darkness. What does Jesus' rebuttal tell us about being Christians? How is our oneness a rebuttal of darkness? How do they benefit from our division?

CHAPTER SEVEN: FIRE AND WATER

1. The author says that fallen angels crave moisture for relief from their inner burning. Has anyone heard that before?

2. Let's read several passages about the fire and dryness of hell, if someone will volunteer for each one. After we read them, let's see if we agree about dryness and the evil spirits of darkness. Ezekiel 28:16–18, Luke 8:26–33 and 11:24, Luke 16:22–26, and Revelation 20:10–15.

3. The chapter had many Scriptures about water and watery structures. Would someone read Exodus 24:12, Ezekiel 1:22–28, and

Revelation 4:3, 6? How do we feel about the section *Summary of Fire, Dryness, and Water?*

4. Can anyone relate personally to the Scriptures that demonic forces fear dryness and crave moisture? Let's discuss how these things relate to our daily lives.

CHAPTER EIGHT: BEFORE THE FOUNDATION OF THE WORLD

1. The chapter is brief enough for us to discuss page by page together. Our living human spirits are the opening topic. Would someone read John 3:6–8, 4:23–24, and 7:38–39? If you are a spirit, how does that affect your outlook on life?
2. There's a lengthy discussion of word choices: the two words for foundation, and the words for earth and world. What was your feeling about that topic?
3. How did you feel about God's decrees before creating anything, when He existed alone? What did it say to you about God, for Him to delay completion of His revelation until the last 100 of 1,500 years?
4. What did it mean to you that Jesus was the primary teacher of hell?

PART TWO: THE CALAMITY OF EARTH

CHAPTER NINE: THE TEST ABOUT ORIGINS

1. This chapter is in our faces, you might say, because it's saying that darkness set the terms of debate about creation and evolution. The author talks about the pressure to be right, and receptivity to God. Let's be sure we understand the issue and how to recognize them.
2. Would someone review the three shells for us in the shell game? How do you see today's origins debate supporting satan's desires? If you were God, with the desires listed in the chapter, what would you enjoy seeing in each Christian?
3. Has any of us given lengthy study to our worldviews? How does materialistic naturalism manifest itself in our daily lives? Let's check ourselves: how open am I to unseen reality? How closed are we to non-natural, non-physical causes? What would maturing in this area look like for each of us?

4. If one of us has studied the philosophy of science, would you tell us about it? How did you feel about the section *The Religion of Science*? Have any of had to deal with religious faith in scientific theories?

5. Let's talk about testing. How is it related to explanatory power? The author talks about rigidity; have we known rigid or inflexible Christians? Some react on the other end, as if nothing is knowable. Both extremes have used the Bible. Have any of us seen someone go to great lengths to protect their existing explanations? How did their behaviors compare with the meekness of a maturing Christian?

CHAPTER TEN: CREATION IN FOUR STEPS

1. Again, the author takes on things we have always assumed. On a scale of 1 to 10, ten being totally convincing, how do you rate his argument for creation in four steps?

2. In this chapter, he makes a comparison of the traditional creation interpretation, and what he calls the new template: that the six days of Genesis 1 were God reclaiming dominion of Earth from darkness. How does each of us rank the explanatory power of this template?

3. Let's review the four steps of creation. The author uses several analogies; did you have one that related the most to you? What did you think when you read about the watery deep being the giant cooling pool of darkness?

4. What does it say about our God that He let the exiled rebels ruin what He made, and then later recovered it from them? What is the impact of this on your faith in Him?

PART THREE: THE CALAMITY OF DARKNESS

CHAPTER ELEVEN: THE SEVENTY-TWO HOUR BLITZ

1. The author integrates God's reclamation of Earth with the things created on the first three days. Has anyone in our group thought of that prior to reading this?

2. Could I have three volunteer readers—one for each of the first three days in Genesis 1? While each reads, let's notice the effect on the kingdom of darkness. Did you agree they would feel like subdivision was imposed on them, in a shrinking room, and be afflicted

with uncertainty and fear? If they are uncertain and fearful after these events, what realities today would afflict them in similar ways?

3. How is the formlessness reduced each day? Why does the author say that God's new boundaries introduce form?

4. Was continental drift a new idea to any of us? The author distinguishes between the observable fact of it and the theories about the speed. What responses did we have?

5. Would someone read Romans 8:19–22? Had you ever thought the sons of God are revealed now? Have you ever thought we were those sons of God?

6. If you have witnessed or experienced a physical miracle, would you volunteer that to us? How is Earth and physical reality responsive to us? How is our daily life impacted when we believe Earth wants to respond to us?

CHAPTER TWELVE: RULING LIGHTS IN THE FIRMAMENT

1. Would someone read Revelation 21:1 and 21:22-27? How does that compare with what we have read in Genesis 1 so far?

2. This entire chapter is about Day Four, so let's read that. The author reverse engineers from the Flood to the choice of terms, *greater light* and *lesser light*. He concludes the firmament must have been ice. First, let's lay out his rationale together, and then we'll review how the moon figures into his conclusion.

3. Had you ever thought of our physical world being subject to such dramatic changes? How does this affect our expectations in daily life? How do you feel about being filled with this God the Spirit after seeing what He can do? Does this make it easier to expect the impossible when God tells us to command it?

4. Let's evaluate the explanatory power if the firmament is ice. What other Scriptures are better explained by this? There were quite a few in chapter seven, *Fire and Water*.

CHAPTER THIRTEEN: UNIMAGINABLY BAD

1. Let's begin as the chapter begins, considering the response of satan and his partners to the four days so far.

2. Would someone read Days Five and Six in Genesis 1? While they read it, let's notice God's inventiveness., and list all the distinctions

that darkness would have seen. What did you think of God taunting darkness?

3. Had you ever thought of God's blessing being an unknown to the holy and the fallen angels? Let's discuss the brand new evidence of blessing that the chapter lists.

4. Day Six finds land creatures on the dry land, culminating with our race as the image-creatures. How did the chapter's list of our qualities affect you? Name one or two you like to see manifested more greatly as you mature in your Christian life as a spirit.

5. Beginning with the section *Restoration*, the last pages in the chapter talk about God's reasons for the drama, and about what He revealed about Himself in it. The author uses His decrees before the foundation of the world as the reason for His time and effort. How did this reinforce your relationship with God? What was new to you?

6. The last page justifies all the drama of creation with God's decree about the Lamb slain before the foundation of the world. Let's list adjectives about that, and we'll use them in tonight's prayer time to express our worship to Him.

CHAPTER FOURTEEN: THE ENEMIES OF THE ENEMIES

1. How do you feel, being an enemy of God's enemies? Has your relationship with God been worth having fallen angels as your enemies? Why?

2. The author lists four basics of fighting these unseen enemies. Let's list them and give ourselves a grade on each one. We'll let A stand for regularity and consistency, B for acceptable but needs improvement, C for mediocre, and D for danger.

3. Mature fighting involves growing as a spirit. If any of you speak in tongues, how does that help your spirit? How does God make Himself known to each of us when we are in communion with Him?

4. Would five of you volunteer to read ten verses each from Psalm 18? It's David's psalm about enemies who were both seen and unseen. Do you believe God gets angry when His enemies corner you? What victories and capabilities could you relate to?

5. David relates how God helped him to run against a troop, bend a bow of bronze, and leap a wall. Would someone volunteer a time when God showed you how to fight an unseen enemy?

6. This is the last chapter. After reading this book, how have you and your life been affected?
7. Let's close with a volunteer to do your best newscaster imitation and read us *Heaven News Today, Yesterday, and Tomorrow.*

ABOUT THE AUTHOR

Paul Renfroe is a Memphis native and Florida resident, with his wife Diane Renfroe of four decades. They have two sons and one grandson.

Through their businesses, they help people who want to preserve their savings and have their legal control documents up to date. Their ministry and publisher is Paradigm Lighthouse, created to implement the mind of Christ in people born as spirits.

Paul & Diane are members of Vision Church at Christian International, in Santa Rosa Beach FL, and are graduates of The Ministry Training College. In their church journey they have served at every level of leadership and service except pastor. They are ordained to minister through Vision Church, under the leadership of Apostles Tom and Jane Hamon.

Paul's academic endeavors include a Bachelor of Arts with Distinction from Rhodes College (Memphis, TN), where he majored in Bible, Church History while minoring in Philosophy. After graduating, he and his wife served twelve years as campus staff and state directors for InterVarsity Christian Fellowship (Madison, WI).

He has also served as board chairman for several nonprofits and participated in the founding of one school and two churches. With his ability to see what others do not, Paul has been instrumental in several turn-arounds with nonprofits and ministries that were in decline.

His life includes many more encounters with death than is common. Eight times including his birth with a defect, doctors have diagnosed Paul with a fatal condition. He has received many healings, both with doctors and without them. Not surprisingly, Paul has also participated in healing many people from physical ailments—including death.

Paul's vision for the *Unseen* Series developed over five decades of following Jesus sacrificially. His reputation for knowledge of the Bible is rarely exceeded. With practice he has an acute ear for God's voice, and a sharp discernment of the topics people wrestle with.

In the *Unseen* series, this depth and breadth has been condensed for you to go even further. May God bless you as He has Paul—with lifelong hunger for intimacy with Him.